# RED DAWN

# RED DAWN

## The Ballad of Tom Watson and Liverpool FC's First Champions

Jeff Goulding
& Kieran Smith

First published by Pitch Publishing, 2025
1

Pitch Publishing
9 Donnington Park,
85 Birdham Road,
Chichester, West Sussex,
PO20 7AJ

www.pitchpublishing.co.uk
info@pitchpublishing.co.uk



A CIP catalogue record is available for this book
from the British Library.

ISBN 978 1 80150 707 3

Typesetting and origination by Pitch Publishing

Printed and bound in the UK on FSC® certified paper in line with our continuing commitment to ethical business practices, sustainability and the environment.

Printed and bound by CPI Group (UK) Ltd, Croydon, CR0 4YY

# Contents

# Contents

For Tom Watson. Liverpool Football Club is what it is today because you laboured and sweated to lay the foundations of our first and future glories. Rest in eternal peace 'Owd Tom'.

And, for our forever 20. As we dreamed in song, he took us to victory. Oh, his name is Diogo.

*'Dear Old Tom! Who can ever forget that cheery, chubby face, the series of dimpling ovals radiating goodwill and happiness to all and sundry? Who can forget the strange pawky accent, so reminiscent of his favourite Tyneside, that grating at first on our Lancashire ears, by and by sounded so natural, and became with familiarity warm and happy in its intimacy?'*

– Victor Hall, *Liverpool Echo*, 1924

# Acknowledgements

LIKE *UNTOUCHABLES: Anfield's Band of Brothers* before it, this book represents our quest to reveal long-forgotten stories, and to illuminate the lives of those who built and sustained our club in the early years of its rise. We would never have been able to get this volume over the line without the support of many individuals and organisations. Bringing these stories to light is a passion we share with many and, when we have needed it most, several key people came to the fore to help us out. To Mark Platt, author and museum curator at Liverpool FC, George Chilvers – co-author – with Mark – of *Old Liverpool FC In Colour*, thank you for your support and advice, and for your generosity in sharing some wonderful images of Tom and the teams who delivered our first two First Division titles, and for allowing us to photograph some of the club's incredible collection for this book. To Jonny Stokkeland, Liverpool FC's official archivist, we are very grateful to you for acting as a sounding board on key dates and statistics as we navigated the vast wealth of information that's out there, some of which is less than reliable, and for those old boardroom papers. Thanks also to Chet Murarji for providing important clarity on people, data and statistics.

To Kjell Hanssen from PlayUpLiverpool, Arngrimur Baldursson and Gudmundur Magnusson from lfchistory.net, Partick Thistle's thethistlearchive.net, Everton's evertoncollection.org.uk, David Speed (club historian) and David Allan (Museum and Collections

Manager) at Heart of Midlothian FC, thank you for your publicly available physical and online records, which have been an invaluable source of information, providing us with important background and many leads as we researched this book. And, to Billy Smith from bluecorrespondent.co.uk, we owe you a debt of gratitude for your meticulous transcription of many old newspaper reports. And to Gavin Abrams, great nephew of Johnny Walker, thanks for sharing your precious family heirloom with us.

We must also extend our appreciation to Liverpool Football Club for their generous cooperation, and for making the telling of this incredible story possible, as well as generously donating photographs from their archive. Thanks also to Rob Mason, official historian at Sunderland FC, and Paul Joannou, official historian at Newcastle United FC, who were both so generous with their time, for their willingness to share their own research with us, and for helping us to avoid many errors in retelling the early history of their great clubs. Rob – we will forever be grateful to you for allowing us to use the iconic Thomas Hemy painting in this book. To Mike Gibson, thanks so much for sharing the wonderful clipping of an 1892 interview with Tom Watson during his Sunderland days.

In addition, the work of the incredible archivist Adrian Killen, and match programme collectors Andy Marsden, Rob Gowers and Andrew Weir continues to contribute to and inspire our work. We couldn't be more thankful for their help and support. Please do check out the incredible *Liverpool Football Programmes: The Definitive Collector's Guide* by Andy Marsden and Michael Adams.

In addition, we are grateful to Mark Platt, and Stephen Done, authors and the current and former museum curators at Liverpool Football Club, Rob Mason and Paul Joannou, official historians at Sunderland and Newcastle United, and Professor Stephen F. Kelly, author and historian, for their reflections of Tom Watson's legacy.

Finally, we extend our appreciation to Pitch Publishing for their belief in the project and for their generous patience and support throughout the process of producing this book. We hope we have done justice to Tom's story.

# Foreword

## *'The greatest Liverpool manager you've never heard of'*

BACK IN spring 2024, we were on a call with Phil Reade and Mark Platt. Phil is the son of lifelong Red, author and columnist Brian Reade. He's also a creator at Liverpool Football Club. Phil is responsible for some of the club's best documentary and short film content. Mark, a historian and author, was once a producer at LFCTV, Liverpool FC's in-house television channel. He's now its museum curator.

Mark has been a great help to us, and in particular, on behalf of the club, he provided us with a great deal of photographic content dating back to Anfield's early years, which we used in *Untouchables: Anfield's Band of Brothers*. He also acted as a sounding board and even as a 'critical friend' when it came to the editing and review process. Needless to say, we were keen to seek out his support for the book you're currently reading, *Red Dawn: The Ballad of Tom Watson and Liverpool FC's First Champions.*

We had asked Phil to join the call, as we had stumbled upon the idea of producing a short film to both promote the book and raise awareness of Tom's story and his contribution to the club's incredible history. With no film evidence related to Watson, in terms of matches or interviews, all we had to tell his story were archive photographs and print material from newspapers, books and journals. We were unable to track down surviving descendants who were able to recall stories or share any meaningful insights with us. Those still with us had seemed to know little of their illustrious family history. Indeed, if anyone reading this does have any information, please contact us. We would love to talk to you and update the story in due course.

Our thinking was that a film montage, maybe set to music evocative of the era, would be an excellent way to bring the story to life, and, let's be honest, promote the book. But what would be the hook for the modern generation of football fans? How would we connect Tom's tale across so many generations to the experiences of those who travel home and away today? Why would he matter to them now?

It was probably Phil – but it might have been Mark, we're not sure – who, after listening intently to our babble, coined the phrase that entirely sums up what Tom is to us and our football club. He is, quite simply, the greatest Liverpool manager most of you have never heard of, and we're going to put that right in this book.

Achieving this has been a labour of love – to use a tired old cliché, but frankly neither of us can think of a better way to put it – but a labour nonetheless. We're attempting the equivalent of football archaeology, delving as far back as the club goes, and beyond in some cases.

The people we're writing about are long since passed, even their nearest and dearest are no longer with us in some cases, and many of the Liverpool's own archives, which would shed a ray of light on their lives and daily dealings, have been destroyed. After speaking to Jonny Stokkeland, Liverpool FC's official archivist, we came to realise that so many important documents had simply been 'binned' before his time as an archivist; an act of cultural vandalism on the part of his long-departed predecessors equivalent to demolishing the original Cavern Club on Matthew Street, in our view.

Though it made the task facing us more challenging, neither of us was willing to shrink from it. But, to continue the Beatles-related metaphor, as John Lennon once said, 'Life is what happens while you're busy making other plans.'

Needless to say, we have both had our share of health, family and work-related things happening to us while putting together this book. So, our sincere apologies to those who have waited patiently and with some frustration for us to get it done. We're both delighted to finally be in a position to share our work with you.

If you didn't skip the acknowledgements, you'll have already seen that we couldn't have got the job done without the help and support of a lot of people. Most notably, and very early on in the process, we were delighted to enlist the help of author, and Sunderland FC's official club historian, Rob Mason. It was, of course, at Sunderland that Tom Watson established himself as one of English football's greatest and most successful managers. We're mentioning Rob again because, well, to be honest, we owe him an apology.

In a video call to Rob, one of us – okay, it was me (Jeff), I am the guilty one – suffered a slip of the tongue that might easily have ended the conversation before it had really got started. In attempting to ask why, in his view, Tom left such a successful and prominent club like Sunderland to join the newly promoted Liverpool FC – minnows by comparison – I inadvertently blundered my words, asking, 'I mean, Sunderland *were* a massive club, so why …' To which Rob, with a twinkle in his eye, immediately, and with much justification, interjected, 'Excuse me, Sunderland are *still* a massive club.'

He was, of course, absolutely spot on. My words were borne out of subconscious bias. I am a Liverpool fan, and I admit I see the world of football through red-tinted spectacles and with a Liverbird's-eye view. So I owe an apology to Rob and Sunderland for my faux pas. By way of recompense, I can now confidently say that, after researching and writing this book, I am utterly convinced that Sunderland are a huge club, which has made a significant contribution to the history of the English game. Everyone at Liverpool FC owes them a debt of gratitude for giving us Tom Watson. Kieran already knew that.

To fans of North East football, Tom is already a legend. He had a hand in establishing the club that now plays at St James' Park, being secretary for both the East and West End Clubs. It would be Newcastle East End who would later change their name to Newcastle United. He would then go on to create the fabled 'Team of All the Talents' at Sunderland FC, winning three First Division championships and finishing runners-up once between 1889 and 1896.

Sadly, to all but a dedicated band of North East and Merseyside football historians, the name Tom Watson probably means little. He is the greatest manager most of you have never heard of. It's our hope that this book will help at least some of you understand what a pivotal figure he is in our club's history, and indeed the history of football.

He led the Reds – yes, by the time he arrived, we had ditched the blue-and-white quarters and were now wearing red shirts and white shorts – to their first two top-flight league titles, and to our first-ever FA Cup Final. He was also a key figure in the administration of the local and national game. He's also our longest-serving manager, only leaving the club when he tragically died at the age of 56 in 1915.

Long before the greatness of Shankly, Paisley, Fagan and Dalglish, and generations ahead of Houllier, Benítez, Klopp and Slot, Tom Watson was tearing up trees and winning championships at Anfield, revolutionising training, the players' diets and imposing his personality on the whole club. As you will discover, the Watson way is eerily familiar in many respects, and hilariously unique in others.

We have loved learning more about the man, his exploits and his personality, and it has been our intention to provide you, the reader, with the most accurate account of Tom, his life and the players he worked with. This has not been easy. We've drawn upon countless newspaper articles, census records, births, deaths and marriages records, and meticulously compiled online archives in assembling this book. However, even these contain errors, flaws and contradictions.

We hope we've managed to navigate this 'minefield' and wherever possible cut through the fog of time to present the truth, as far as that's possible. The people highlighted in our acknowledgements have been a huge help in that respect. However, if we've unwittingly made an error or two of our own, we assure you it will not be for the want of effort and dedication to the cause of creating the most comprehensive account possible. We're always open to being corrected and we acknowledge that our journey of understanding will continue long after this book is published.

We hope we now have a more rounded view of who Tom was as a human being, as well as a manager of great repute. Of course, we use the term manager deliberately, knowing full well his title at Sunderland and Anfield was that of club secretary, at least for a time. But, he was the closest thing to a football manager as we understand that term today. And, as such, he transformed the role as it was carried out by the likes of McKenna and Barclay before him.

We sincerely hope that you find the same joy of discovery as we did as you peruse the pages of this book. It's a truly remarkable story of a larger-than-life figure who changed the course of the club we love forever. Enjoy.

You'll Never Walk Alone.

**Jeff and Kieran**

# Introduction

*'On the prowl as thieves and robbers of the night'*

COME WITH us to Ayrshire, to a time unknown in the latter years of the 19th century or maybe the early ones of the 20th. We're amidst hills of sand piled up outside the mysterious 'Nobel's Works, on the outskirts of a small town'. A furtive group of four men in heavy overcoats, and sporting flat caps and bowler hats lurk among the dunes, studying the gates of the factory intently. One of them, a large rotund individual, struggling to appear inconspicuous as an adipose 20-stone, middle-aged man, dispatches a scout to seek out their quarry working in the yard behind the building's perimeter wall.

These men are agents of an English football club, and their leader is Tom Watson, an extraordinary visionary and highly regarded secretary/manager. Their target is a Scottish footballer by the name of Simpson, who the men want to sign from under the noses of his current club. Only a matter of hours earlier they had arrived at the home of the player, and the man's wife had told them their target – being a part-time footballer – was at work in his day job.

Now, in secrecy, they plan to ambush their man, bamboozling him into moving south of the border, promising riches his hometown club could scarcely afford. However, this is dangerous work. Should they be discovered by the supporters or officials of their target's current team, then their lives would be in peril. This was football in the late 19th century, and this was the life of a club secretary, out on manoeuvres, scouting for men.

Out of nowhere, there's a huge commotion. Tom's scout is charging towards him, eyes wide and screaming for the men to abandon the mission and to 'run for their lives!' As Watson would later write while reflecting on the incident, 'Ours not to reason why, ours but to fly or die!'

The scouting party had not realised that 'Nobel's Works' specialised in the manufacture of dynamite, and its employees were determined to blow up Tom and his agents rather than lose their star player.

The above is adapted from a story Tom Watson told in the *Football Gazette* (South Shields), published on 9 March 1907. It's one of many anecdotes Tom shared under the headline 'Humours of Football', and it describes a scouting mission for future Sunderland player J. Simpson, originally from Kilbirnie. He played 41 non-competitive matches and one FA Cup tie for Watson's side, before breaking a collarbone in a practice match in August 1890. He would go on to work in a linen mill. We hope Tom felt his purchase was worth risking life and limb for. These stories certainly reveal much of the period, the state of the game and the man Tom Watson was.

Though the famous Bill Shankly would happily deploy the full range of his persuasive oratorical skills to convince players that their future lay with him, and that all their dreams could be realised if only they surrendered to his honeyed words, it's hard to imagine the great Scot having to risk life and limb to prise a player from their club. The story related above goes back to the very foundations of the game we love today, and it speaks to the pioneering spirit of men like Watson who were prepared to do whatever it takes to achieve success for their football club.

While the game in Scotland was seen to be at the vanguard, with its players highly prized for their skill at the combination arts by clubs south of the border, there was, as today, more money in the English game. Teams in England could exploit this fact, and were often able to steal away the flower of Scotland's football talent. In the 19th century, Sunderland and Newcastle were famed for this, as we will learn.

However, this story, a mere snippet in a full life devoted to the advancement of the sport, speaks also to Tom's physicality, his personality, sense of humour and self-deprecation. It is Tom himself, who describes his size and weight in the article he writes, revelling in the absurdity of a man with such a large frame trying to 'secrete himself in the sand'. That he recalls such a perilous event with such hilarity also tells us something of the man.

Tom was a larger-than-life character in every sense of that expression. He was a pioneer with an adventurous spirit, a great communicator, and hugely respected in the game throughout his career. He's often spoken of as being charming, jovial and as having a twinkle in his eye. He's described as silver-tongued, smart, business-minded and a great organiser, with many friends and admirers.

However, he could earn the ire of referees, officials, journalists and supporters alike. This is a man who spoke his mind, who was passionate in the service of his cause and single-minded when it came to his work. That will have undoubtedly upset some, and, like all of us, he will have possessed his fair share of human frailty. That we found it so hard to find evidence of this being committed to print surely suggests that, in terms of his character, the good far outweighed the bad.

Like many of the men who came after Tom, his working-class roots will have shown him the value of labour and collective effort. By the time he reached adulthood, he will have been well versed in the importance of being organised and the value of money, after watching his father struggle to eke out a living for his family as an iron moulder. And seeing how his mother made those meagre earnings stretch far enough to sustain their family.

However, it was his desire to explore a life outside of the drudgery of the daily battle for subsistence that led him to football, and catapulted him to stardom and a life his parents could never have dreamed of. Tom, after initially following his father into the iron industry, would later enjoy global travel, and would grow to hold great influence over others. Yet, despite his relative wealth and the esteem in which he was held, Tom seems to have maintained an even temperament, an innate modesty and a reputation for being assertive with others, but ultimately treating everyone with a sense of fair play and respect.

That he should earn legendary status in two regions and with two footballing institutions speaks volumes about the man. It is our belief that Tom deserves greater recognition for his feats as manager of Liverpool Football Club, that modern supporters should know of his achievements and his importance in our history. He remains, to this day, our club's longest-serving manager, racking up an astonishing 742 games in charge between 1896 and his untimely death in 1915.

This book is therefore dedicated to his memory. It explores his early life, his career in the North East and his many achievements on Merseyside. We hope that we have presented a fully rounded image of Tom, the football man and the person, and set him in a context that brings his story to life. He remains one of the true greats of the English game, and he has earned his place among the pantheon of Anfield's great managers. Indeed, in many respects, he could be seen as the earliest exponent of what we now call 'the Liverpool way'. This is his story, and we commend it to you.

## Chapter One

# Once upon a time in the North East: Becoming Tom Watson

OUR STORY begins in 1859, in the industrial heart of England, Newcastle upon Tyne. Queen Victoria was on the throne, and Lord Palmerston became the UK Prime Minister. This is the year Charles Darwin would publish his *Origin of Species*, Charles Dickens published *A Tale of Two Cities*, and, in Westminster, 'Big Ben' chimed for the first time. However, we're more concerned with events at 4 Heaton Street in the Byker area of the North East, where, on 8 April, iron moulder Ralph Watson and his wife, Mary Ann, are about to welcome into the world their second child, their first son, Thomas.

Life would have been difficult for the family, with the average wage for an iron moulder around 36 shillings per week, about £1.80 in today's money, and no doubt things became harder with the arrival of Tom's younger brother, John, born in February 1861.

By 1871, the family had moved to the village of Heworth, County Durham, and Tom's father had become a carter, or cartman, an unskilled job that included a significant pay cut. Young Tom developed a passion for sports in early life, which included cricket and football, before following in the footsteps of Ralph and becoming an iron moulder.

The main industries in the area during this period were shipbuilding and heavy industry, in addition to the production and export of coal. This was a strongly working-class community, and Tom's personality would have been forged in an ethos of hard work and collective effort. It was an environment that fostered innovation, organisation and a sense of local pride. Little wonder this was the birthplace of the Davy lamp, which allowed miners to crawl to ever-greater depths beneath the earth, extracting yet more coal.

George and his son Robert Stephenson were sons of the area and grew to be key players in the development of the early railways, which spread across the country. Another of the region's pioneers, Joseph Swan, independently invented the lightbulb, which Thomas Edison made famous in the United States.

Tom's younger days seem to have been split between school and a growing interest in sport. He would go on to develop an interest in cricket and football. After leaving school, he became an iron moulder like his father, and eventually married Catherine Lucas in 1878. The couple had a son, Ralph Lucas, and were now living at 281 Rosehill Terrace, Willington, Wallsend, not far from his birthplace in Byker.

According to research carried out by Paul Joannou, the official club historian at Newcastle United FC, Tom became so impressed with a fixture, having watched a game between St Bernard's and Rangers while on a visit to Scotland, that he established the Rosehill Football Club on his return home, and they became the first club in the mid-Tyne district.

Tom also represented the club on the Northumberland Football Association. After leaving them, he was elected secretary to Newcastle West End in 1886, at the age of 27. He then moved to Heaton in the east end of the city, where he became secretary of the West End's rivals in 1888. The East End club would later change its name to Newcastle United.

An interview with Tom, conducted by *The Clarion*, dated 17 September 1892, reveals that he quickly secured the signatures of several Scotsmen to play as amateurs, but with paid employment in local industry. At least one of them, Jock Smith, followed him to Sunderland and then Liverpool. Watson's ties to the Magpies remained loosely in the family as his sister, Elizabeth, married future Newcastle United director John Peel Oliver in 1887.

*Athletic News*, dated Monday, 29 September 1902, contains a retrospective report suggesting that a young Tom Watson was involved in lobbying Sir B.C. Browne, the mayor of Newcastle, to award a lease on the land to the East End club, upon which Newcastle United would eventually play. Tom's efforts were supported by Sir C.F. Hammond, an MP for Newcastle.

With the lease in place, the funds to enclose 'the meadow' at St James' Field were obtained, in large part thanks to financial support from local businessmen, simply named as Messrs Stanger and Robinson. The first game to be played by the East End club, at St James' Field, was a friendly match against Glasgow Celtic in 1892, which the North East club lost 1-0, after the demise of Newcastle West End. It's claimed that Tom's wife was the first lady to attend a match at the ground. This is a lovely story, albeit impossible to confirm.

Clearly, Tom Watson did much to bring about first-class football on Tyneside by developing both clubs. He would, of course, go on to play a pivotal role with the city's North East rivals, Sunderland.

Paul Joannou describes Tom as 'a cheery character with a Geordie twang, and sporting a large well-trimmed moustache in the fashion of the day'. He was known to be silver-tongued, and, a shrewd organiser and administrator, he was instrumental in founding the Northern League in 1889. His growing reputation would soon attract the interest of nearby Sunderland Football Club, who at the time were far more developed than both Newcastle clubs. The Wearside club reportedly forked out £150 per year to secure his services, a considerable uplift in his income.

This figure is attributed to John Grayston, the first secretary of the Sunderland Teachers' Association Football Club, in an article he wrote for the *Sunderland Weekly News* in 1931. However, according to Paul Days, writing for the Bleacher Report, World Football, in June 2018, Watson's brother disputes this, claiming the figure was actually two guineas per week, or 35 shillings (£2.10 in today's money).

It's claimed that Grayston met a 'down-at-heel' Tom Watson in a pub in Newcastle and persuaded him to join Sunderland. This is unlikely to have been happenstance. Watson's reputation at the Newcastle clubs was by now well established. He was also a keen advocate of Scottish players, a factor that would align him with Sunderland directors Robert Thompson, a prominent shipbuilder, and Samuel Tyzack, the owner of a coal mine who had helped to ensure that the club was one of the wealthiest in the country.

Their willingness to spend good money on the best talent from north of the border would have been very alluring to the ambitious young Tom Watson and, according to reports, his departure from the East End club was, at least initially, on good terms. Two separate articles in *Athletic News*, published on 26 and 27 September 1889 respectively, point to him joining Sunderland with the best wishes of many at his former club. There's even talk of a gala dinner being arranged in his honour.

However, he would soon earn the ire of his former employers. As reported in *Athletic News*, Tom had allegedly promised to bring back two players for Newcastle East End, while on a scouting trip for his new club. However, he promptly took them to Sunderland instead.

Watson was an influential and respected man in the North East. Known as forward thinking, he would go on to build the famed 'Team of All the Talents' at Sunderland. He was a key player in the FA, Football League and in local football associations, and also something of a pioneer in football communication. Tom would be instrumental in arranging for match progress to be transmitted every 15 minutes by the Post Office.

In Chapter Five, we'll learn how his Sunderland team became league champions in 1892, 1893 and 1895, as well as finishing runners-up during the 1894 season. But Watson was also gaining notoriety when he was appointed to the League's influential management committee, and a piece in the *Buckingham Advertiser and Free Press*, dated 25 April 1896, suggests he was racking up 12,000 miles per year as a result of his dealings in football.

His managerial style was described by John Grayston with these words: '[Watson] could rule his team with kindness and firmness, and always made himself the chum of the rank and file, who looked upon him as his brother.' While it's foolish to make comparisons with modern managers, Liverpool supporters might say there's more of a Jürgen Klopp to this description than, say, Bill Shankly, who, while certainly hard but fair, rarely allowed himself to become 'chums' with his players.

Other reports suggest that Watson even encouraged players to drink beer and red wine as part of his 'master plan'. *Athletic News* declared Tom as 'a Secretary who had few equals, and no superior'.

The 1891 census shows him living at 17 Warwick Street, just round the corner from the Newcastle Road football ground, and having footballers John Campbell and John Harvie as lodgers, along with trainer Robert Campbell (the footballer's step-brother).

By 1894, Tom was firmly ensconced within the hierarchy of Sunderland Football Club, his views on all matters respected. However, his plan to take the team to Philadelphia on a spring tour of the United States in 1895 drew much criticism. It seems some of his critics feared that the players would suffer injury or even death while on the trip.

An article in the *Edinburgh Evening News* dated 20 September 1894 details the whole story, including correspondence between

Watson and his counterpart in Philadelphia, a Mr Arthur Irwin. Needless to say, the necessary assurances were received as to the team's safety and the potential for financial reward. However, according to historian Rob Mason and to Mike Gibson, financial assurances of £2,000 were not received and the tour didn't go ahead.

*Lloyd's Weekly Newspaper*, 23 September 1894, describes the three areas in which Watson excelled as manager: identifying good players, knowing where to look for them and managing the business side of the club. In the article, Tom is referred to as urbane, being courteous and refined in manner.

Now a man of means, Tom was engaging, confident in his own skin and curious about the world. There are many tales of his travels, including more than a few amusing ones. Aside from his frequent sojourns to Scotland on the lookout for players, Tom would use his newfound wealth and contacts to explore Western Europe and much further afield.

One story, published in the *Liverpool Daily Post*, 8 August 1901, has the then Liverpool manager in Tsarist Russia and refusing to let the language barrier get in his way, to hilarious effect. This is how the paper tells the story, which Watson had relayed to one of its reporters:

> I ran across Tom Watson, the popular Liverpool secretary, the other day, and he was filled with the rosiest anticipations. He had just returned from a cruise in the Baltic, and a little story. One of the ports called at was Riga, and Tom, with characteristic promptitude, set out to see the sights. He very properly decided that the best way to accomplish this was to be driven through the town, and to this end he hailed a drosky. Now Tom's many accomplishments do not include a knowledge of Russian; but he didn't let that worry him. 'Cabman,' he said, in plain English, 'drive

> me round the town.' The Russian stared dully at Tom, and the latter repeated the order, this time indicating his purpose by swinging his arms in a series of circles. A light of comprehension dawned in the Russian's eyes, and shaking up his wiry little Finnish pony he drove the smiling secretary off at a rapid rate. They had, however, only traversed three short streets when the man pulled up short in front of a large circular building, and motioned to his fare to alight. Tom did so, and found himself at – the circus.

Though there's ample evidence that Tom was able to ruffle the feathers of local journalists, he certainly knew how to cultivate good relations with them, and clearly understood the value of communication and how to use it to his advantage. Reporters in both the North East and in Liverpool describe him as cheery, delightful and above all fair-minded. We've seen evidence of the esteem in which he was held by pressmen in Newcastle, who lavished him with gifts upon his departure from the East End club. And it seems he was no less respected in Liverpool. This report, published much later, in 1925, in the *Liverpool Echo*, tells us something of his character: 'Tom Watson was beloved by Liverpool Pressmen, for he was the soul of courtesy to them and treated all of them as men of honour until he discovered them otherwise. Then he shut up like an oyster. And quite right too.'

Another report, in the *Reading Observer*, dated 12 October 1899, by a journalist who knew Tom in his Sunderland days, gives an interesting insight into Tom's health and temperament. Describing him as a 'gentleman of medium height, inclining to the robust physique, with a fresh, healthy, rosy complexion that would do credit to any shepherd who ever tended flocks in Arcadia', the reporter goes on:

> Time was when he looked one in the face with a pair of laughing grey eyes that won one's confidence and esteem at a glance, but I suppose the ravages of time or physical weakness has impaired his sight, for he has had to call the optician to his aid. I have observed. But he is still the same smiling, genial, level-headed worker as in the days of yore, when Roker possessed charms not to be found elsewhere in the United Kingdom.

These comments and similar are plenty in the press clippings of the time, and although it's inconceivable that Tom, a mere human after all, didn't have his moments or get on the wrong side of players, officials and journalists alike, it seems for the most part that he was genuinely held in high esteem by most. Perhaps another reason for this was his even temper and ability to absorb defeat and victory as if they were the same, a characteristic shared by many successful managers today.

The *Liverpool Echo* journalist continues, observing: 'Win or lose, one seldom finds much difference in Tom Watson. He is one of the somewhat select few of club officials who know how to bear themselves in the hour of victory as well as in the hour of defeat.'

Tom had experienced ups and downs while at Sunderland, and he had learned to handle setbacks and would never get too carried away by success, a trait he clearly carried with him throughout his career. Watson is credited with creating the fabled 'Team of All the Talents' and had led the Wearsiders to three First Division championships, in 1892, 1893 and 1895, while in 1894 they had finished runners-up to Aston Villa. He managed all of this in just eight years.

In 1896, Tom was 37 years old and becoming one of the most decorated and experienced secretaries in football. That year, events at Sunderland FC meant that, for the first time, he would consider leaving his beloved North East and moving his family across the country.

Liverpool FC as an organisation was just four years old, but possessed an ambition to match the most well-established clubs in the game. Thanks to their charismatic owner, they possessed the resources necessary to turn the head of this working-class football genius. At Anfield, he would be destined to become the club's longest-serving manager, and lead them to their first two First Division championships.

We will discuss the circumstance of his departure from Sunderland in more detail in due course. First, let's explore his chosen destination, the city of Liverpool, and the people whose persuasive powers and ambition convinced him to set up home on the banks of the Mersey for the rest of his life.

## Chapter Two

# Once upon a time on the Mersey: Tom's next adventure is born

IN THE 1890s, on the banks of the River Mersey, the city of Liverpool, located some 168 miles from Sunderland, was reaching the peak of its economic powers. Visitors from all over the country and indeed the world would marvel at its spectacular dock system and huge brick warehouses. The river itself was an awesome sight, as waves of seafaring vessels made their way in and out of the port.

The docks were a hive of activity as thousands of workers loaded and unloaded ships. It was hazardous work and shifts were long. This was a place of vast wealth and extreme poverty, civic opulence and unrelenting toil. The trade in slaves from Africa had ended decades earlier and now Liverpool's economic might was largely predicated on trade in cotton and tobacco and to a lesser extent other commodities.

Nevertheless, it was a city known throughout the Empire and beyond. As early as 1791, Thomas Erskine, the 1st Baron Erskine, had written:

> That immense City which stands like another Venice upon the water ... where there are riches overflowing and everything which can delight a man who wishes to see the prosperity of a great community and a great empire ... This

> quondam village, now fit to be the proud capital of any empire in the world, has started up like an enchanted palace even in the memory of living men.

However, as we wrote in *The Untouchables: Anfield's Band of Brothers*, Liverpool was a city that showed two faces to the world:

> [...] a city that had come to dominate world trade, making great strides in public health and the arts, but which was also a place of staggering contrasts. A time traveller visiting Liverpool during this period would marvel at the immense wealth and Victorian splendour of the city centre and port, while being staggered by unrelenting poverty and disease of its court housing.

Conditions in the tightly packed streets around the waterfront and further inland would doubtless worsen with an influx of Irish refugees fleeing famine in 1846. In the years that followed, some half a million Irish people passed through the city, many of them settling in the Scotland Road area.

Liverpool had now increased dramatically in size from barely 2,000 acres in 1830 to more than 13,000 in 1890. Many of its 600,000 citizens were crammed into tightly packed terraces and 'court housing', essentially hovels that existed in dark narrow alleyways. The city's leaders would respond to the growing social crisis with further expansion, this time outwards.

By 1850, around 30 per cent of Liverpool's inhabitants were immigrants, predominantly from Ireland, but also Scotland, Wales, the surrounding areas of Lancashire, China, Scandinavia and Africa. This cultural melting pot contributed greatly to the city's economic success and the formation of its famous accent, known as Liverpool English or Scouse. Linguists and sociologists argue that by 1890 the accent had settled into a stable and distinct dialect, different to the one spoken elsewhere, in Lancashire. Therefore, we can say that those attending games at Anfield and Goodison would have spoken with accents recognisable to those who grace those stadiums today.

Prior to 1890, the suburbs of Anfield and Everton had been largely rural areas populated by wealthy families seeking escape from the squalor and disease of the centre by building the large villas we see on Anfield Road now. At the midpoint of the decade, the suburb would also experience an explosion of dense terraced housing, giving it a character that would be recognisable to visitors to Anfield today.

Several large parks providing recreation spaces and fresh air for Liverpool's inhabitants had been constructed decades earlier. Stanley Park opened in the Anfield area in 1870, following nearby Newsham Park, located in the Tuebrook area of the city, which had opened two years earlier. Sefton Park in the south end would be added in 1872. However, Everton Park is a much more recent addition to the city's green belt, having been built between 1984 and 1989. When Tom Watson arrived in the city, the area that now looks out on Liverpool's grand waterfront was host to densely packed housing.

The growing movement of Liverpool's merchant class led to the creation of the townships of West Derby, Walton and Fazakerley, Bootle, Toxteth and Garston. However, this would present the city's councilmen with the problem of ensuring these 'émigrés' didn't escape paying their fair share of taxes. They would overcome this by effectively annexing these areas.

There was, of course, significant resistance to this, and in 1903 the vigorous opposition of Bootle prevented a bill being passed in Parliament that would have seen that area incorporated into the city of Liverpool. Nevertheless, by 1907 most of these townships were brought into the fold. And with that, the city's overall size increased to almost 17,000 acres.

On the international stage, just as it would years later in 1914, Liverpool would give the flower of its youth to Empire, with many from the city serving in the Boer Wars (1899–1902). Most notably, the Liverpool King's Regiment was involved in one of the most notorious battles of the conflict, as they fought to relieve the siege of Ladysmith, receiving a battle honour in the process. The ensuing battle over a hill named Spion Kop led to a significant defeat and huge casualties for the British. We'll learn later how, a decade after the arrival of Tom Watson in 1896, a vast mound of earth on Walton Breck Road – home to thousands of Liverpool supporters – would come to bear the name of that ferocious battle. In total, 179 men from Liverpool died while serving in the Boer War.

When it came to football, the city's dominant team was, of course, Everton. Formed in 1878, they had played their football first on the nearby Stanley Park, before moving to a field just off Anfield Road owned by John Houlding, a Conservative mayor of Liverpool and wealthy brewer. Their nearest local rivals were Bootle FC, who played at Hawthorne Road. Throughout Tom Watson's North East rise, he would have doubtless been aware of the growing strength of football on Merseyside.

Houlding's team, having been founder members of the Football League in 1888, had put the city of Liverpool on the sporting map when they were crowned champions of England in 1891. Sunderland had joined in 1890 and, just two years later, under the guidance of Tom Watson, they took the league title from Everton. He then led the North East side to glory again in 1893 and 1895, gaining the admiration of Merseyside's footballing elite in the process.

However, simmering tensions within the board of Everton Football Club would soon reach boiling point, and the club president, John Houlding, was ousted in 1892. The schism would lead to the creation of a new football club – Liverpool AFC – and, with it, a footballing rivalry that has endured ever since.

For his part, Watson was all too aware of the machinations of Liverpool's two clubs. He had been present as an observer at the meeting of the Football League when the newly formed Liverpool AFC's application to join the Second Division had been denied in 1892, forcing them to compete in the Lancashire League.

The events that directly led to the fracturing of the Everton Football Club are chronicled in an innocuous column, situated in the top left-hand corner of the now defunct *Liverpool Mercury*, dated 16 March 1892. This most portentous tale is told under the rather perfunctory headline:

THE FUTURE OF EVERTON FOOTBALL CLUB
LIVELY MEETING
MR HOULDING REMOVED FROM THE PRESIDENCY

The article describes, in somewhat reserved tones, stunning details and reads like a fly-on-the-wall account of the fracturing in two of one of England's top teams. Despite the low-key headline, this was a hugely contentious and, at times, incendiary meeting.

The *Mercury*'s reporter on the scene reveals how, in a packed committee room in the Presbyterian School on Royal Street, Everton Valley, an extraordinary battle was being waged that would ultimately lead to the city's only top-flight team tearing itself apart.

Before the assembled shareholders and members at the meeting was a motion to remove the club's president, John Houlding, a brewer and politician, from the board. Houlding, a wealthy local Conservative politician and mayor of the city, had set up a new company, the Everton Football and Athletic Grounds Company Limited. However, he had been unable to get it registered, as two companies with such similar sounding names couldn't exist.

The move had no doubt been part of Houlding's plans to strengthen his position at the club and ensure a return on loans he had made to Everton. His plans were discovered by rival members and, suspicious of his motives, they were outraged. Factions within the club's hierarchy had been at war for months now. The row stemmed from the fact that Houlding, whose family owned the ground at Anfield, wanted to raise the rent.

In perusing the report of the meeting – and to some extent reading between the lines – we're left with the impression that Houlding may have known what was coming and had already worked out his response. Rather than feeling the heat, it almost feels like he was enjoying himself.

The board had called this 'Extraordinary General Meeting', ostensibly to carry out a coup, removing their president in the full glare of the local press. In the chair for the night was George Mahon, a Liberal politician and Christian Methodist and, as Houlding entered the room, Mahon offered to give way to Houlding, the then president. Tensions appeared to be high as one half of the meeting cried 'hear, hear', while the rest roared 'no, no'. The reporting certainly gives the impression of a hostile gathering, though the headline of the article that describes it as merely 'lively' and the tone of the reporting suggest that such behaviour was not too surprising. It's also possible that some of the participants were playing to the gallery to some extent. Nevertheless, this represented a pivotal moment in Merseyside football history, scores were being settled and no prisoners taken.

Perhaps sensing the drama of the occasion, Houlding rose to the challenge. 'I am here to reply,' he's reported to have said, and then with a twinkle in his eye, he added, 'and a criminal never takes the chair, he steps into the dock.' This remark appears to have brought the house down. Laughter and applause mixed with cries of 'shame!' are said to have rung out, creating an almost pantomime-like feel to the occasion.

A seemingly furious debate raged, with claim and counterclaim flying in all directions. The committee accused their president of 'underhanded deeds'. He had, they said, sought to set up his own company and register it with the Football Association (FA). He steadfastly denied any wrongdoing, but it could not have been clearer that a historic split was on the cards.

The meeting ended with a motion being carried to remove Houlding from the presidency. Just three days later, on 15 March 1892, Liverpool FC and Athletic Grounds Limited was formed. Houlding had simply changed the name of the company he had unsuccessfully attempted to register earlier, and the FA granted it official recognition three months later, on 3 June.

Everton FC then moved to Mere Field Green (later Goodison Park), located on Goodison Road, a short walk from the now vacant Anfield, which was, of course, owned by their former president, John Houlding. It has been home to Houlding's newest creation ever since.

While disagreements over finance undoubtedly played a significant role in the eventual removal of Houlding and the decision by the remaining board members to vacate Anfield and move across Stanley Park, as we reveal in *The Untouchables: Anfield's Band of Brothers*, the story is far more complicated and is as much about religion, politics and a clash of cultures as it was about finance.

Houlding and his allies were Unionists, members of the Orange Order and Freemasons. This would have put them at odds with his main rival, the non-conformist Christian and Methodist, George Mahon. Perhaps chief among Mahon's and his acolyte's gripes with Houlding was his association with the brewing of alcohol and the nearby Sandon Pub.

Rather than simply being an argument over rent, it seems likely to us that a combination of factors contributed to the eventual breakdown in relations between factions on the board and the subsequent vote in 1892 to remove Houlding as president. Indeed, the dispute over finance feels more like a pretext for the split, rather than the primary cause of it. In any case, this failure by the board to hold itself together would unwittingly set in motion one of the most enduring rivalries in English football.

Houlding had now been left with a football ground – and it seemed a box full of blue-and-white kits – but no team. Not to be outdone, together with John McKenna and William Edward Barclay, who had remained by his side after the split, he went on to establish the city's second great football team and turned to Scotland to fill its ranks. In doing so, he would cement his reputation as a dominant figure in the early development of the game on Merseyside.

Houlding's close alliance with Barclay and McKenna had developed over several years. Barclay was born into a middle-class family in Dublin in 1857. His father, David, was the governor of the Malone Reformatory, an institution that provided an alternative to prison for young offenders, a position that would have ensured the family was comfortably off.

William took full advantage of his good start in life, achieving two university degrees – a Bachelor of Arts and one in science – and his addresses show that he travelled extensively during his young life, making homes in Belfast, Aberdeen, Lancashire – where he married in 1878 – and eventually in Liverpool.

He married Emily King, a Yorkshire woman, around the same time that St Domingo FC (who later became Everton FC) were being formed and started playing their inaugural games on Stanley Park. By now Barclay was following in his father's footsteps and was employed as the governor of an industrial school in Everton, a position he held until 1898.

His work saw him providing education, board and lodgings to poor and neglected children of the borough. He was now established in the city and clearly a man of some means, a factor that would have placed him in the same circle as other influential men such as Houlding and John McKenna. The three are most likely to have connected through their involvement in both the Orange Order and Freemasonry.

The influence of Ireland and Irish culture and politics on the character of the city of Liverpool is well known, and it's not surprising that this stretched to the development of the city's football clubs too. Upwards of 200,000 Irish families lived in the crammed streets in the city's Scotland Road area. The thoroughfare had previously been a stagecoach route taking passengers from Lancashire to Scotland but was now home to descendants of the great famine in the mid-19th century.

This concentration of people, who came from both Unionist and Republican traditions, in such cramped conditions, created a volatile atmosphere and contributed greatly to the area's culture, influencing the accent of Liverpool's people, and no doubt helped create the city's radical spirit. However, the tensions between those communities led to sporadic outbreaks of sectarian violence and played a role in Republican campaigns on the British mainland.

Nonetheless, it was Liverpool's proximity to, and the cultural impact of immigration from, Ireland that placed the likes of Barclay and McKenna in the orbit of Houlding. The men would become firm allies on the board of Everton Football Club.

McKenna, born in County Monaghan in 1855, had travelled to Liverpool on business sometime around 1880. After meeting Houlding, he was soon invited to Anfield to watch an Everton game.

McKenna found work as a vaccination officer at the West Derby Poor Law Union and was also an enthusiastic rugby player. He had helped form a regimental rugby club before joining the West Lancashire County Rugby Football Union as a professional. No doubt this experience had caught the eye of Houlding, who may well have thought McKenna's administrative skills would serve Everton well, and he soon became a fixture on the board, where he assisted with the expansion of the club.

Following the split in 1892, Houlding asked McKenna and Barclay to become joint secretaries of his newly formed club. It's said that Barclay took on the role of secretary-manager, while McKenna focused on team affairs and on-the-pitch matters. However, it was John who telegraphed the FA, asking them to admit the club to the Football League, a request that was promptly turned down.

In any event, claims that the board of the newly formed club blundered in not simultaneously applying to join the Second Division, an error often laid at the door of John McKenna, may be wide of the mark. As we reveal in *The Untouchables: Anfield's Band of Brothers*, a letter written by Barclay to *Field Sport* magazine in June 1892, and describing himself as honorary secretary of the Liverpool Association Football Club, tells a different story, and seems to have also been Barclay's way of announcing the new club to the football world:

> Sir, [...] we have joined the Lancashire League, and have thus provided a very interesting series of fixtures for our first team. We regret that we could not see our way to make application to enter the Second Division of the league, as we felt, after very careful deliberation, that the gates would be no better than the gates drawn with Lancashire clubs, whilst the traveling expenses would have been very high.

It seems clear from the following passage that the newly formed board of Liverpool AFC meant business, and had lofty aspirations for the future:

> We hope to meet some of the league clubs during the season, and already engagements have been made with some of the leading Scottish clubs for odd dates. Cup ties – English, Lancashire and Liverpool – will fill vacant spots,

> and altogether I think the 'bill of fare' at Anfield will not disgrace the past.

Working alongside McKenna, who is credited as having recruited the much-vaunted 'Team of Macs' – players drafted from Scottish football to make up Liverpool's first team – Barclay as honorary secretary would have certainly approved the signings of these men. In his letter to *Field Sport*, he boasts:

> As to players, the following have signed: Andrew Hannah, Renton, back; Sydney Ross, goal, Scottish League vs. Scottish Alliance; half-backs James Kelso, John Cameron and James McBride (Renton), and F. Rogers (Liverpool); forwards, Jock Smith (Sunderland), Thomas Wyllie (Everton), John Miller (Dumbarton), Andrew Kelvin (Kilmarnock), and one or two men of less repute. In addition, we shall have at least four of the best players in Scotland, with whom we are now negotiating. Our supporters may rely on it that we shall take the field with men who can and will play football and good exhibitions of the dribbling code will be seen at Anfield.

In his letter, Barclay is announcing the creation of Liverpool's famed 'Team of Macs', a squad of players recruited mainly from Scotland, where it was common for surnames to contain the 'Mc' prefix. While some of the men named above went on to great success in Liverpool's inaugural season in the Lancashire League – most notably Andrew Hannah, Thomas Wyllie and Jock Smith – others played only minor roles, or, as in the case of F. Rogers from Liverpool, played no role at all.

The men who made up the board of the newly formed Liverpool Football Club possessed great ambition. By assembling a team made up of Scotsmen – known for being pioneers of combination football and for their toughness and skill – they were signalling their intent not just to rival their city neighbours, but to become a force throughout the country.

## Chapter Three

# The adventures of the 'Team of Macs': Liverpool FC before Tom Watson

JUST SIX months after John Houlding had been ousted from the presidency of Everton Football Club, Liverpool were lining up at Anfield for their first competitive game in the Lancashire League. Their opponents were a team called Higher Walton, and the game would be played at Anfield on 3 September 1892.

A team consisting of Sydney Ross in goal, Andrew Hannah, Duncan McLean, Joe Pearson, Joe McQue, Jim McBride, Tom Wyllie, Jock Smith, Malcolm McVean, Jonathan Cameron and Andrew Kelvin had been assembled, and these players – the first-ever men to represent Liverpool Football Club – would leave their changing facilities in a nearby house and go on to rout their opponents 8-0. However, the mostly empty terraces meant they would receive little fanfare.

Sixty miles away, in Accrington, the reigning English champions – Sunderland – were beginning the defence of their crown with a 6-0 victory. It was an ominous victory as far as the rest of the league was concerned, as the North East club, under the guidance of Watson, would romp to their second league title, unbeaten at home and becoming the first team to score 100 goals in a single season.

Across Stanley Park, Everton were held to a 2-2 draw by Nottingham Forest in front of a crowd of 14,000 at the newly opened

Goodison Park. They would end the campaign a full 12 points behind the eventual winners, in third place, with defensive frailties proving costly.

However, this was not Liverpool's first official game. That was a friendly rout of Rotherham Town just two day earlier. The match was well documented in *Field sport* and the *Liverpool Mercury*, and it's in the latter publication that we see the first reference in the press to Liverpool as 'The Anfielders'.

The official attendance remains unknown; however, press reports put the gate at anywhere between 200 and 1,000 supporters. Entrance had probably been free, but supporters would have to pay one penny for the official matchday programme.

Liverpool, playing in blue and white, won the toss and, after John Houlding, in his capacity as Liverpool City councillor, ceremonially kicked off the game for Rotherham, they were straight at the visitors from the first whistle. Within minutes they were a goal up through John Miller – who went on to score twice in the game – quickly followed by a brace from Andrew Kelvin. Kelvin would go on to play just six times for Liverpool, while Miller featured 24 times in that first season for the club.

Born in 1870 in Dumbarton, Scotland, Miller was something of a goal machine, firing 25 goals in 24 games, which included five goals in a single game against Fleetwood Rangers on 3 December 1892. He arrived as a Scottish champion, having won two league titles with his hometown club. He would leave as a Lancashire League Champion in April 1893 to join First Division team The Wednesday.

Newsmen of the time were aghast at Miller's wage demands. The player was demanding something of a king's ransom to stay at Anfield, and the club's refusal to bend to those demands was a factor in him leaving. The whole team had been rewarded with bonuses at the end of the club's successful 1892/93 campaign in the Lancashire League, but Miller is said to have asked for a pay rise of

£100 down and £3 per week, which was considered an 'exorbitant sum'. Nevertheless, the Sheffield club, The Wednesday, had no qualms about meeting his demands, and Miller would ultimately ply his trade in England's top tier. However, after scoring seven goals in 13 games for them, he moved back to Scotland, to Airdrieonians, in 1894. Miller was no doubt highly prized for his fearsome shooting abilities.

*Field Sport*, writing in 1892, had this to say about the player: 'J Miller is an ideal centre, and no man has earned such high praise as Miller has done since he came to Liverpool. He is a most unselfish player, feeding his forwards with remarkable accuracy, and when a chance of scoring present itself his shots are sent with a velocity that gives the goalkeeper little chance.'

Also on the scoresheet in this warm-up match was Tom Wyllie, who netted a hat-trick. Born on 5 April 1870 in South Ayrshire, Scotland, Wyllie – a full international – had been signed from Everton. He scored in almost every other game in the Lancashire League and a total of five in three FA Cup games in the 1892/93 season. When the first derby between First Division Everton and Second Division Liverpool took place on 22 April 1893 in the Liverpool Senior Cup Final, former Everton player Wyllie scored the game's only goal.

The Merseyside teams were still at odds after John Houlding had quit Everton and formed Liverpool a year earlier, a factor that would set up a particularly fractious encounter. We will discuss that in detail, in Chapter Six.

Wyllie elected to stay in the local league with third-placed Bury after Liverpool were elected to the Second Division as champions of the Lancashire League. They took the Second Division title in their inaugural season. Tom Wyllie's Bury eventually gained promotion and, as league winners, met the First Division's bottom team, Liverpool, in 1895 in a dramatic promotion/relegation decider. Bury won 1-0 and Wyllie played two seasons in the First Division before moving to Bristol City in the Southern League in 1897. He eventually retired from the game and became a newsagent in Bedminster.

Another Scot who turned out for Liverpool was centre-forward Jock Smith. Born in 1865, Smith hailed from Kilmarnock, where he met his wife, Janet. The couple would go on to have five children. Jock had two spells at both his hometown club, Kilmarnock, and Newcastle East End, before becoming a champion with Tom Watson's Sunderland in 1892. He later set up home in the North East with his family.

Smith joined Liverpool in 1892, where he played 11 games and scored five times in their debut season. At 5ft 7in, he was no target man, but as a skilful forward, known for his pace and clever dribbling, his goals helped secure the Lancashire League. However, he wasn't without his critics, described in some match reports as 'greedy'. Nevertheless, he was universally acclaimed as a 'grand acquisition' by Liverpool.

After Anfield, Smith went on to play for The Wednesday, Newcastle United and Loughborough, before hanging up his boots. Tragically, Jock fell into a terrible depression after the death of one of his children and took his own life in Newcastle upon Tyne at the age of 45. His widow was awarded the proceeds of a benefit game at St James' Park. Jock's funeral was held on 20 February 1911. This account in the *Newcastle Journal* of the efforts of the local community to render assistance to Jock's family, published on the same day, paints a picture of the affection in which he was held:

> A most encouraging attendance assembled at the Dun Cow Inn, on Saturday evening to inaugurate a movement by which assistance may be rendered to the widow and children of the late Jock Smith. Mr. J. Neylon telegraphed regret at

> inability to be present, and in his absence the chair was taken by Mr. J. Harvey.
>
> It was resolved to communicate the facts of the case to the directorates of the various clubs with which Smith had been connected, viz., Newcastle United, Sunderland, Liverpool, Sheffield Wednesday, and Loughborough. Satisfaction was expressed that the directors of Newcastle United had lost no time in forwarding a handsome donation to the widow. A prize drawing will also be held, and several contributions to the prize-list were promised by gentlemen present.
>
> Mr. J. Harvey was elected chairman of committee, and the hon. Secretary is Mr. T. Rodger, 20, Edwin Street, Heaton, who will be pleased to receive and acknowledge contribution towards the prize list before next Saturday, when another meeting will be held.

In goal for Liverpool was Sydney Ross. Another proud Scotsman, Ross was born in Edinburgh in 1869. He had two spells at Cambuslang before arriving at Anfield in 1892, keeping 11 clean sheets in 21 games before leaving in 1893. He later went on to represent Third Lanark, Clyde and Ayr Parkhouse.

*Field Sport* approved of his signing, writing the following: 'The position of goal-keeper is perfectly safe in the hands of Sidney [*sic*] Ross. His display in the practice matches stamps him as one of the finest custodians who ever appeared in a team.'

It appears that the love affair enjoyed by supporters of Liverpool and their goalkeepers had its origins as far back as 1892. The *Liverpool Echo* noted that 'it was amusing to hear Ross frequently greeted by humorously-inclined spectators behind the goal with cries of "Play up, MacRoss".'

Liverpool met Bootle FC on 11 March 1893 in a Lancashire Senior Cup encounter at Hawthorne Road. Their opponents were known locally as 'Brutal Bootle', and with good reason. Ross received an injury in the game that ended his Liverpool career, as his team slumped to a 2-1 defeat. The local press would later report on his lengthy stay in hospital as a result of his injuries, with one report claiming: 'Ross was again an absentee, being an inmate at Stanley hospital till Friday, and it is feared he has received a permanent injury.'

Ross returned to Scotland, where he attempted to rekindle his career. However, he managed just a few matches for Cambuslang before signing for Third Lanark in May 1894. There he would be mostly a reserve goalkeeper, and in the summer of 1898 he moved to Clyde.

In 1910, Ross emigrated to Brisbane, Queensland, Australia, where he would end his days at the age of 54 in 1924. He died of Hodgkin's disease and heart failure.

Liverpool finished the season with Blackburn lad Billy McOwen in goal. Despite his name possessing the 'Mc' prefix, Billy was an Englishman. He played 27 times for the Anfielders, keeping 11 clean sheets, before his contract expired in 1894. It's said that McOwen was a qualified dentist and felt that he could earn more at his trade than keeping goal. Nevertheless, he would go on to have an amateur football career at Blackpool and Nelson between 1894 and 1997.

Patrolling in front of the Liverpool goal was the tragic figure of centre-half Jim McBride. A mainstay of the team that won the Lancashire League and their successful push for promotion from the Second Division as champions in 1893/94, McBride died suddenly at home in 1899 at the age of just 28. He was a veteran of the famous Renton team and a team-mate of the incredible Andrew Hannah, of whom we'll learn more in the next chapter. He was also a Scottish international. According to lfchistroy.net, he was slight of figure and short in stature; football writers would describe him thus: 'McBride makes up by science what he loses by height. He is fearless and bold, and but a stripling.'

He managed just five league games before leaving his relegated team-mates to join Manchester City in the Second Division. City missed out on promotion, finishing second to Liverpool in 1896.

Willie Maley, Celtic's veteran manager of 43 years, regaled listeners with a hilarious story about then Renton players and future Liverpool team-mates McBride and Andrew Hannah in the *Evening Times* in 1954:

> The first League international game between England and Scotland took place on 11 April 1892 on Pike's Lane in Bolton with the English equalising 2-2 in the last minute. Hannah and McBride were in the Scottish side along with Maley, who lived to be 90 years old and was in 1954 the sole survivor of this clash. 'The Scottish players' reward for that game was 10s each with a cap and jersey,' Maley recollected. 'On the way home in the usual large saloon carriage, McBride of Renton F.C., a young lad of 17, tired out fell sound asleep – and Hannah, his club captain, relieved him of the golden half sovereign he told us he was taking home "to his mother". When morning came McBride found his gold coin had miraculously turned into a silver sixpence to the astonishment of this "laddie," who was possibly the youngest of internationalists of my experience. Hannah, of course, later replaced the gold coin.'

*Field Sport*, writing in 1892, gave us a flavour of the type of character McBride was: 'McBride, who will be entrusted with the defence of the left wing, is a player of the first water. Although diminutive in stature, he possesses a wonderful amount of strength, and never knows when he is beaten.'

Arriving at the club two months into the season was Matt McQueen, a man who would go on to play a pivotal role in a time of crisis at Anfield during the 1922/23 season. In December of 1922, with Liverpool defending the title secured under the leadership of Dave Ashworth, and riding high at the top of the First Division, their manager announced his resignation, and his plan to return to his former club, Oldham Athletic, who were ensconced in a relegation battle. The Anfield board turned to former player, and veteran of their inaugural Lancashire League campaign, to steady the ship. He would do more than that. McQueen led Liverpool to their second consecutive title, in 1923.

Born in May 1863 in Harthill, Lanarkshire, Scotland, Matt played football for West Benhar, Champfleurie, Bo'ness, Hearts, and Leith Athletic before joining Liverpool on 23 October 1892. He made his debut six days later in a 9-0 demolition of Newtown. The *Liverpool Mercury* had the following to say about the game and the debutant, McQueen:

> At Anfield, the Liverpool Club management are not allowing the grass to grow under their feet, and are kneading together a team which will take more beating than most elevens will bc able to give them. The latest captures have been very quietly effected, and in the brothers McQueen they have secured a couple of players far above the average. Their victory over Newtown was so easily gained, and the team have come on so much of late, that there is really no accurate means of gauging what they are capable of. Edwards had a most anxious time of it between the sticks, and the Newtown custodian must have heaved a sigh of relief when the sound of the whistle terminated his arduous duties.
>
> Backs and halves were fairly overplayed by the attack opposed to them, while Morgan and Pryce-Jones were the

> only forwards who could make any headway in the front line. The formation of the Liverpool eleven is now complete in every department, and it will be a question of whom to leave out. None of the players were extended, and the debut of the McQueen's must be regarded as a decided success, to judge from the lavish applause extended to them. Skipper Hannah always had the reputation of having his head screwed on the right way, and since he has thrown in his lot with the Anfielders he has given ample proof that he has lost none of his astute generalship.

Matt was from a large coal mining family and followed his father, Peter, down the pits before escaping that life for football. He had five sisters and three brothers, including Hugh McQueen, who also represented Liverpool.

Matt McQueen featured regularly for the Anfielders in their first four seasons, amazingly playing in outfield positions and 45 times as goalkeeper. He won two titles, the Lancashire League and the Second Division. He played a total of 103 games for Liverpool, scoring seven times, and keeping 24 clean sheets in his 45 run outs as goalkeeper. He was replaced as keeper by Harry Storer in 1895 – Matt was now 42 years of age.

Amazingly, he still made a further six appearances over the next three seasons under the leadership of Tom Watson, with three of them in goal. He hung up his playing boots in 1899 to become a qualified referee. Later, in 1919, he was added to the board of directors at Liverpool.

Tragically, after leading the club to its fourth top-flight title in 1923 as manager, McQueen was involved in a traffic accident that cost him his leg. In a joint Everton and Liverpool match programme comments, warmest wishes were expressed for the stricken McQueen in March 1924:

> Our opening note must be one of deep sympathy with the unfortunate and regrettable accident which occurred to Mr. Matthew McQueen a little time ago, and which has led to the amputation of a limb. We are certain that all our readers will hope that the popular manager of the Liverpool club will speedily regain health and vigour and that his physical disability will not preclude him from enjoying many years of activity in the football world.

Sadly, Matt was forced to resign from management in 1928 after his health had deteriorated. He lived with his wife Florence in Kemlyn Road, now covered by the Centenary Stand at Anfield. He continued to be a fan favourite and welcome visitor to games until his death in 1944 at the age of 81. He was laid to rest at Anfield Cemetery in a simple funeral attended by many of his former team-mates and colleagues, in which he was described as a 'relentless, stern, straight and forthright man'.

Matt's younger brother, Hugh, had died just five months earlier, in April 1944, at the age of 77. They had joined the club together. Hugh was a left-winger who scored 18 goals in 61 games for Liverpool, winning the Lancashire League and the Second Division titles. He only missed one game in the club's push for promotion to the First Division in the 1894/95 season, a campaign they finished unbeaten.

Liverpoolfc.net tells the story of how a brush with death almost cost Hugh his place in the team for the season's most important game of the season:

> Hugh nearly lost his life when he dived off a springboard at Southport baths where the team was relaxing on 27 April 1894, the day before the vital Test match against Newton Heath which would determine if Liverpool would be promoted. He was hauled out of the water, admitting later

> that he couldn't swim! Liverpool, with Hugh in the side, were promoted after a 2-0 win.

He left for Derby County after Liverpool were relegated in 1895, where he enjoyed a good career in the game. In all, he featured for six seasons at Derby, finishing second and third in the top flight in consecutive seasons. He also reached the semi-finals of the FA Cup in the same years, and the final in 1898. He was awarded a gold medal for his performance in that game, despite finishing on the losing side.

Hugh returned to Anfield as trainer of Norwich City in the second round of the FA Cup on 6 February 1909. He received a standing ovation from the home crowd. The unfancied Norwich pulled off something of a shock that day, beating Liverpool 3-2, in part due to the bizarre performance of full-back Percy Saul.

Saul, who appears to have been made captain for the game, conceded a penalty in the 35th minute, which put Norwich ahead. Liverpool levelled in the 66th minute but the visitors restored their lead with ten minutes remaining. The crowds were growing agitated, but Bobby Robinson equalised in the 85th minute. However, an 89th-minute Norwich goal broke Kopite hearts. It seems the hapless Percy Saul had been at the heart of the Reds' woes that day. These comments by club captain Alex Raisbeck relating to Percy's performance and subsequent demise as a player are intriguing:

> Norwich were considered small fry in these days and were never expected to come to Liverpool and knock the Reds out of the competition. But this is what they did. We were beaten 3-2, but, oh, the goals which the Canaries got! The first was from a penalty, which should not have been given by Percy Saul.

> Percy seemed to lose his head after giving away the penalty. He could do nothing right. He also lost the second and third goals through slackness, and many unkind things were said by the spectators that day. I felt a bit sorry for Percy, but all the same time I was also angry, for we lost a Cup-tie we ought never to have been lost.
>
> The strange thing about this game was that Percy Saul had just prior to this been made captain and the Norwich match was his last, for he never kicked another ball for Liverpool. His strange disappearance certainly caused a few tongues to wag!

No doubt his manager Tom Watson would have been apoplectic with rage, ensuring the player never represented the club again. Saul enjoyed brief spells at Coventry City, Rotherham Town and Rotherham County before hanging up his boots in 1914. The whole affair is perhaps an insight into Watson's ruthless and unforgiving nature, and perhaps his zero tolerance of players who lacked the same fierce desire, commitment and concentration that he possessed.

Another Scotsman making up the ranks of the famous 'Team of Macs' was Joe McQue. As well as being part of the Lancashire League-winning team in 1892/93, Joc scored in Liverpool's first-ever game in the Football League in 1893. Newly promoted Liverpool got the campaign underway against fellow promotion side Middlesbrough Ironopolis at Paradise Field on 2 September 1893. In fine weather, both teams are said to have played an 'exciting game', with both keepers in action. The North East groundsmen received a rebuke from the reporters at the *Liverpool Echo*, who described how the length of the grass had 'impeded the visitors'.

Despite a goalless first half, Liverpool took the game to their opponents after the interval, with Duncan McLean hitting the woodwork. Malcolm McVean eventually broke the deadlock to put

Liverpool in front. In the 89th minute, John McQue – described as a 'finely built young fellow, with superb tackling powers and excellent judgement of the ball' – sealed the points for the visitors. He would miss just two games in that all-conquering season.

His acclimatisation to the top flight was less assured, by all accounts. The *Liverpool Mercury* commented: 'Compared with last year's brilliance a great falling off is most noticeable in McQue.' Nevertheless, he made 29 league appearances that season. Tom Watson began the 1896/97 season with McQue as a regular starter, but replaced him with Robert Neill six games into the campaign. However, Neill's Anfield career was short-lived, as he returned home to Glasgow at the end of the season. This meant Joe made 14 league appearances in his final campaign for Liverpool, the 1897/98 season.

In all, Joe played 142 times for Liverpool, scoring 14 times, an impressive haul for a defender. Tragically, McQue died of complications of surgery at the Victoria Infirmary, at just 40 years of age.

We come now to Duncan McLean, born in Renton, Scotland, in 1868. McLean arrived at Liverpool from Everton in 1892 at the age of 34, where he would play 82 games, scoring four times in three seasons. He was, of course, a veteran of the famous Renton amateurs who vanquished West Bromwich Albion to become 'champions of Great Britain and the World', alongside the legendary Andrew Hannah. Both men had left Scotland for Everton in 1890, winning the First Division a year later before following John Houlding out of the club to join his newly formed Liverpool AFC. McLean was an imposing figure and hard as nails. Famed for his buccaneering style, venturing forward rather than attending to defence appears to have upset the club's directors. Programme notes from a game against Cliftonville in 1893 reveal their displeasure:

> Why will McLean persist in marring his really brilliant and effective play by getting too far away from his own goal? By

> all means back up the halves, but a full-back has no business whatever amongst the forwards, except on the defensive. If Mac will get rid of this one fault he will be as good a back as there is in England today.

Duncan left Liverpool after their first unsuccessful campaign in the First Division. He returned to Scotland in 1895. He died in 1941 at the age of 73.

John McCartney, born in Newmilns, Scotland, in 1868, a tough-tackling half-back who joined Liverpool in the October of their inaugural season. He was also 34. John McKenna had signed him from St Mirren, where he had spent two seasons. He left Liverpool in 1898 after playing 166 times for the club and scoring seven times.

McCartney featured in Tom Watson's first game, wearing for the first time ever, their red shirts and white shorts. He was one of a small band of players who had also featured in the club's debut 1892/93 season. He was now 36 years of age. However, the gentlemen of the sporting press were seemingly offended by his rough style of play. A piece in the *Cricket and Football Field*, written in 1896, seems to claim that the Liverpool boardroom were also unhappy with his tactics on the pitch:

> John McCartney still vexes his own committee by resorting to those tactics which have previously brought the club into bad repute. McCartney was though the victim of rough treatment on 21 November 1896 when Alf Milward kicked him deliberately in the Merseyside derby and was sent off. Milward later apologised but pleaded that he had been provoked by the tough Scotsman.

The article is interesting as it suggests that Liverpool had something of a bad reputation for their style of football. It's unlikely that his selectors at Anfield were too concerned about McCartney's reputation, given that he featured in 30 league games in Watson's first season, and 27 in 1897/98, his final campaign at Liverpool.

Above all, McCartney was a natural winner, fiercely competitive and, ultimately, his legacy at Anfield is that of a champion. Whatever the misgivings of the club's directors, he was certainly good enough to be selected by one of the country's most acclaimed managers.

A new era at Anfield was now underway. And, while the now 'Reds' of Liverpool would lose nothing of their desire, passion and commitment under Tom Watson, they would go on to also become renowned for the finer arts of the game.

## Chapter Four

# Captain, my captain: The Andrew Hannah story

ANDREW HANNAH is a character so colourful that he merits his own chapter. His name would have been familiar to the likes of John Houlding, William Edward Barclay and John McKenna as he had previously captained Everton to a league title in 1891, before returning to his home in West Dumbartonshire. However, his impact and character had left such an imprint that the heads of Liverpool's newest club would return to Scotland to court his signature.

Dumbartonshire had been the scene of one of Hannah's greatest moments, a true David and Goliath story, and one that epitomised the man and the spirit of his community. This is the story.

It's 9 May 1888 and we're in the small town of Renton. The skies are black and there's a smattering of rain in the air. The thunderstorms of the previous 48 hours that killed five of the area's inhabitants have now subsided. With a population of barely 2,000 souls, the loss had been keenly felt.

Despite the tragedy, a football match had just been played between the champions of Scotland and their counterparts in England. The prize at stake? The title 'Champions of the United Kingdom and the World'. And despite the recent tragedy and atrocious weather, 6,000 people braved the conditions to attend. They most likely came from all over Scotland.

Renton FC emerged in 1872 and had already reached the final of the Scottish Cup on five occasions, winning it twice, in 1885 and 1888. Their second triumph came after a campaign that saw them score 42 goals as they progressed through the rounds. Their opponents in the final were the equally high-scoring Cambuslang. With no league football in Scotland, this would have been the biggest game of the season, and it was Renton who rose to the occasion. They trounced Cambuslang 6-1 to lift the Scottish Cup.

Their victory set up a remarkable fixture with West Bromwich Albion, holders of the 1888 English FA Cup. The game south of the border was a different beast. It was more professional and funded by wealthy industrialists and businessmen. The Football League, consisting of 12 teams, had already been formed, and Albion fancied themselves as the world's finest. Flushed with pride, they challenged the Scottish 'minnows' to a World Championship match. Renton duly accepted.

It is said that, when faced with the appalling weather conditions, the English wanted to call off the game. However, the Scots were insistent it should go ahead. And so it did, with Renton FC defeating their challengers 4-1. It's still regarded as a famous victory north of the border, and rightly so, because it would have sent shockwaves through the English game.

So, after this monumental calamity for the English champions, now sent homeward to think again, Renton's heroes had one last mission. Trudging through the mud, heads still aching from the previous evening's celebrations, they ploughed on to the old pavilion at Tontine Park, home of the newly crowned kings of the world. They were following Andrew Hannah, their inspirational right-back. He was resolutely marching ahead of the group. In his hand he clutched a makeshift plaque, hastily put together the previous day. On it were the words that declared his men to be part of the greatest football team on the planet.

They reached their destination and, with chests bursting with pride, to a chorus of cheers Hannah pinned the plaque above the doorway. In that moment an incredible sporting legend was born. This group of 'Davids' had just slain the footballing equivalent of 'Goliath'. However, Andy Hannah was destined to create legends of his own on the banks of the Mersey, but not before the team he had helped to vanquish tried to snap him up first.

In a case of 'if you can't beat them, sign them', West Brom promptly completed the capture of Hannah. However, the Scot couldn't settle in the Midlands and soon returned home to Renton for another season. It would take overtures from Everton FC to persuade him to return south, in 1889. There he stayed long enough to win the First Division championship in 1891. Again, though, the call of home proved irresistible and he once more journeyed north to play for his hometown club.

Of course, while he was away, a footballing revolution was taking place on Merseyside. A new club was born and a few familiar faces would once again come calling for his services. By now, Hannah was 28 years of age and his huge personality meant he was a target for the armies of agents employed by English clubs, who preyed on Scottish football's brightest talents.

Hannah was a huge character and highly sought after. Perhaps a hint of his eye for intrigue and desire for adventure lies in the fact that he would later find employment as a dockyard detective, a profession later glamourised by author Hugh Munro, who wrote a series of novels in the 1950s about a man called Clutha, employed privately as a detective solving crimes in Glasgow's dockyards. In addition to his exploits as a 19th-century private eye, Hannah would also own a successful milk delivery business.

This article in the *Kirkintilloch Gazette*, dated 22 June 1901, gives us an insight into what a remarkable athlete and colourful individual he was:

> Andrew Hannah, at Renton Games in 1886, won first prize for hop, step and leap – distance on level ground, 47'9". At Coalburn Games, in the following year, he was first with 47'7", level ground. At Tullietudlem Games, springing from behind a board, he made 48' (first try), and at the committee's request, attempted to clear 59', but tripped and injured himself.
>
> At Dumbarton Castle Grounds he did 46'10". His best long jumps were made at Renton (20'10") and Coalburn (20'9"). Standing jump, 9'7"; standing hop, step and jump, 29'7"; hitch and kick, 8'7". Whilst in football outfit he often kicked the crossbar of the goal-posts. He carried off all the jumping events at Everton and Liverpool Games for years, and in a 150-yard handicap there, off five yards, ran second to Fred Geary, the Nottingham flyer. He was tied to jump Tom Burrows (hop, step and leap champion of the world) but the stakes were withdrawn. He won a bowling tournament of the Liverpool Club, was in the first three in several billiard handicaps; could putt a 16lb ball 33', and pole vault 9'.
>
> Hannah also had the great honour – the lustre of which he did not tarnish – of captaining the famous Renton Football Club when they won the championship of the world. He captained the renowned Everton club when they won the English League Championship, and was for three years' captain of the formidable Liverpool FC

However, for a real glimpse of this larger-than-life individual, try this fascinating article, which reveals a footballer who clearly feared neither man nor beast:

> Whilst in the latter city [Liverpool], Hannah accepted the challenge of the proprietor of a travelling menagerie to enter

> the den of lions. His reception was quite friendly. A gold medal was his reward.

The incident – most likely a publicity stunt for the zoo – occurred on 25 November 1893 and was covered widely in the Lancashire press. The *Blackburn Standard* reported that Hannah had walked into a lion's den at Wombwell's Royal Menagerie in order to win a bet with the zoo's proprietors. After he had emerged unscathed, he was awarded his wager by the owners, along with a gold medal worth £5.

Clearly, as well as being something of an athlete, he was also no ordinary man. He would therefore have driven a hard bargain when Liverpool's McKenna and Barclay came calling. Hannah persuaded them to pay him a £150 signing-on fee and a weekly wage of £5. These were big numbers for the time, and his salary would be £2 per week more than Everton had paid him. All of this gives us something of an idea of the esteem in which he was held in the 1890s.

The English media agreed that, despite the outlay, the signing of Hannah was something of a coup. The *Birmingham Daily Post* had the following to say on 6 June, 1892:

> Andrew Hannah, the famous Renton back, who played for Everton two years ago, has been engaged by the new Liverpool club for next season.
>
> Hannah will act as captain and his power of developing players is so well known that the Liverpool club are fortunate in having secured the man who did so much towards improving the all-round play of the Everton team.

*Field Sport* wrote: 'The merits of Andrew Hannah are well known both as skipper and also as a player, and his mature judgement, together with excellent defensive tactics, makes him most invaluable.'

The Anfielders had clearly signed a leader and someone who was a natural-born winner. His capture by Liverpool made him the first player to have captained both Merseyside teams, a distinction he still holds alone to this day. His impact at Anfield was immediate.

As we've already learned, the newly formed Liverpool, wearing blue-and-white shirts (quarters), took the Lancashire League by storm, even reaching the final of the Liverpool Senior Cup – which they won, defeating Hannah's former club Everton. Captaining the side, Hannah, an ever-present for two seasons, led his men to back-to-back promotions, reaching the First Division in 1894.

By now he was 30 years of age and struggling with injuries. Hannah managed just 16 games in the 1894/95 season. Liverpool finished bottom and were relegated back to the Second Division. They had lost half of their games and conceded 70 goals. The absence of their inspirational captain may well have contributed to their decline.

With the team relegated and Hannah clearly nearing the end of his powers, he returned to Scottish football. In all he played 69 times for Liverpool (40 times in the league) and scored once. He won the Lancashire League, Liverpool Senior Cup and the Second Division while at Anfield. However, it was his leadership on and off the pitch that served Liverpool well in those formative years. He must also have been an incredible character in the dressing room.

Back in his native Scotland, he turned out for teams such as Rob Roy and Barrowfield. By all accounts, despite being far from his prime physically, teams would often tempt him out of retirement with generous appearance fees. Here, the *Dundee Courier*, reporting on 22 October 1896, suggests that, despite his portly physique, he could still play:

> The demands of the business of football are about as serious as those of everyday commercial life. Here we have Andrew

> Hannah, the old Renton, Everton and then Liverpool back brought under the public gaze of football once more by the Clyde.
>
> In his day Hannah was the very picture of a back, and his reputation still lives green both at Anfield and Goodison Park, Liverpool.
>
> Returning to his native 'Ranton' three years ago Hannah gave a helping hand now and then to the club of his boyhood; but last season it was thought he had permanently retired from the ring of which he was such an ornament.
>
> Money, however, is a very powerful lover in men's lives, and Andy trotted out all gay under the colours of Barrowfield. He played a good game against the Rangers, but he has a lot of adipose hanging about him. He looked uncomfortable now and again, but in the hands of the trainer he should even yet be able to give us a sample of his former greatness.

To drive home the point, here's another match report printed a week later:

> Andrew Hannah is not exactly a spent force, although he has pretty much the appearance of being all done up. His heading lacks none of its old accuracy, and his long connection with the football ring gives him judgment second to none in the football realm.

Hannah continued to live a happy and full life in Glasgow until his death in 1940, at the age of 76. He had maintained an interest in football, even applying, unsuccessfully, for the job of manager of Clydebank in 1914. He departed the world as a celebrated figure in Scottish and English football, a sportsman of some repute, and perhaps one of Liverpool Football Club's most colourful captains. The *Daily Record* wrote this obituary on 6 June 1940:

> Another of the great old-timers has passed out. Andrew Hannah, who has died in Clydebank, was one of the famous Renton team which gained the proud title of Champions of the World.
>
> As right-back, he played for the Scottish League in the first match against the English League, in 1892, at Bolton. Referee was the late John James Bentley, who said it was the cleanest game he had ever seen – he did not have to award a single free-kick.
>
> As an Anglo-Scot, Andrew Hannah captained Everton during three seasons, and he was a stalwart in the Liverpool team, Everton's greatest rivals of the time.
>
> A noted athlete, he won numerous prizes at Highland games, his forte being the hop, step and leap, at which he had done 49'.

Andrew Hannah was clearly a remarkable man. He was a world champion, as brave as they come. Although he was never managed by Tom Watson, his exploits helped establish Liverpool as a force in the game, symbolising the club's character and ambition.

## Chapter Five

# Tom's 'Team of All the Talents'

SUNDERLAND AFC emerged out of the ferment of North East football in the autumn of 1880, having initially been founded by schoolmaster James Allan a year earlier as the Sunderland and District Teachers AFC. It was now no longer limited to teachers. Our hero, Tom Watson, was recruited as secretary on 3 June 1889, after impressing in his roles at both the Newcastle West and East End clubs. The club had gone professional in 1885. Then, a decade after its birth, and just 12 months after Tom's appointment, the club was elected into the Football League in 1890.

Their admission must have seemed inevitable and undeniable, coming after a stellar season in non-league football, in which they thrashed many a Football League outfit. However, it was the 7-2 mauling of Aston Villa that seems to have put them on the map, and handed them a nickname that would endure for decades.

Watson had become a great recruiter of footballers, bringing in players from the amateur game in Scotland, boosted by the wealth of his board of directors and able to promise decent wages. Football was still wrestling with the idea on the part of some that it was a gentleman's sport, and suggestions that players should be paid was anathema to those who wanted to keep it as a preserve of the professional class. Sunderland's board had other ideas, and their ambition was clear.

Watson's men lined up against Aston Villa in white shirts and blue shorts: William Kirkley, Tom Porteous, John Oliver, J. Stevenson, John Auld, Will Gibson, John Harvie, John Gillespie, Johnny Campbell, Jock Smith and John Scott.

The game took place at Newcastle Road on 5 April 1890 in front of a crowd of 7,000, and the Wearsiders were in imperious form, winning 7-2. A hat-trick from John Gillespie and a brace from Johnny Campbell did much of the damage, with Jock Smith and John Scott adding to their tally. All four men had been recruited from teams in Scotland. However, the most prolific among them was Johnny Campbell, one of three men signed from the famous Renton side, where he had enjoyed something of a glittering career, winning the Scottish Cup in 1887/88, the Glasgow Merchants' Charity Cup on four occasions, in 1886, 1887, 1888 and 1889, and the much celebrated Football World Championship in 1888. In 1888, this was a game played between the winners of the Scottish and English Association Cups for the title of Champions of Britain and the World. We have, of course, just learned all about this encounter and its protagonists in the previous chapter.

Joining Johnny at Sunderland from Renton were David Hannah and John Harvie. These were highly sought-after players. Eventual league rivals Everton had also had their eye on the men, and it's claimed that they had written to each of them offering £215 a week all the year round, a signing-on fee of £20 and a job.

Sunderland's wealth, built mainly on shipbuilding, meant they were capable of paying huge fees for players for a club established only a few years earlier. In 1889, they had signed Scottish centre-half Johnny Auld from Third Lanark. They were reported to have paid £170 signing-on fees plus wages. He was also given a shop in Union Street, which became a boot and shoe business. Sunderland paid to fit the shop out and paid its rent of £50 per year. Auld made 115 appearances for the Wearsiders in seven years.

For his part, the former Renton ace Johnny Campbell would go on to score 154 goals in 215 official matches and win league titles in 1891/92, 1892/93 and 1894/95, before going on to clinch another Football World Championship in 1895. By now the game was contested between the winners of both countries' top leagues. Sunderland triumphed 5-3 over Heart of Midlothian at Tynecastle.

Campbell had enjoyed a stellar career, and only the FA Cup eluded him. Johnny died on 8 June 1906, at the age of 36. Though this feels like – and is – a heartbreakingly tender age, it's perhaps worth noting that the average life expectancy for those born in Scotland around the time of Johnny's birth (1869) was, sadly, between 40 and 44 for men.

The exploits of Campbell and his team-mates against Villa in 1890 made the English football world stand up. However, the game's key movers and shakers would have no doubt been impressed by the skill with which Tom Watson had assembled this all-conquering non-league side. The League's founder, and Villa board member, William MacGregor had declared after the game that Sunderland had a 'talented man in every position'. It would be the *Sunderland Echo* that first coined a phrase that would become synonymous with Watson's men for years to come, spinning MacGregor's words into the 'Team of All the Talents'.

It was a richly deserved honorific. They contested 55 'friendly' games in 1889/90 (this includes one FA Cup game, three Durham Challenge Cup matches, and four games played on a tour of Scotland), and aside from beating Villa, they achieved impressive wins over league opponents Blackburn, Bolton, Notts County and Everton. In addition, they held Wolverhampton and Preston North End to draws. They scored an incredible 182 goals, and ensured election to the Football League with 40 wins from 56 games, drawing five and losing ten.

The local press, buoyed by Watson's confident showing in 1889/90, felt that Sunderland could finish in the top half of the 12-team league. It turned out they were justified in their optimism. While Tom's men finished seventh, they could have secured fifth place but for an apparent uncharacteristic administrative 'error' on the part of the club's secretary, Watson. Goalkeeper Ned Doig, who had signed for Sunderland, hadn't served the requisite 14 days after registering with the club before playing in a game against West Bromwich Albion in 1890. The Wearsiders won the game 4-0, but Doig was deemed ineligible, and the league punished them by deducting two points, and fining the club £25.

Doig, known as Ned when later at Liverpool, was known in the North East as Ted or Teddy. Signed from Arbroath, the somewhat colourful character received a signing-on fee of £40 and a wage of £3 per week, replacing Sunderland's keeper William Kirkley in the process. Kirkley played just 11 official games for the club, though he was a veteran of the 'Team of All the Talents'. Doig was also given an office job in the North Sands shipyard, demonstrating how keen the club was to bring him in.

Described as 'wonderfully slippery' when dealing with onrushing strikers, Doig was famed for his kicking as well as not being shy to use his fists to clear a ball. He could also be a vain man. Insecure about his bald head, he would cover it with a cap, secured additionally with an elastic band to prevent it falling off during games. Indeed, so concerned was he that nobody should see his scalp that he would prioritise retrieving his cap, if it was dislodged, rather than the ball.

For all his insecurities, Doig would prove a shrewd signing. He served the club for 14 years, playing a then record 457 games, before leaving for a healthy profit to join Liverpool for the sum of £150 in 1904. He had helped Watson's team to league titles in 1892, 1893 and 1895, and a runners-up spot in 1894. He would go on to win a further title in 1902.

Tom would experience FA Cup agony, and not for the last time – the cup would elude him entirely during a long and illustrious career – with his team being eliminated after a semi-final replay at the hands of Notts County. Sunderland advanced to within a single match of the final thanks to victories over Everton, Darwen and Nottingham Forest. The semi-final took place at Sheffield's Bramall Lane on 28 February 1891. Watson would have been forgiven for feeling a degree of confidence as he prepared his men for the game, having trounced his soon-to-be opponents 4-0 in the league fixture between the two just a matter of weeks earlier. However, this was the FA Cup, the most coveted trophy in football and, with the prize of a final at stake, Notts County would not bow out without a fight.

There was huge interest in the game back home in the North East and, perhaps believing the players could feed off that energy, Watson had them train on a local beach close to home. According to an article published on the Roker Report website, dated 26 December 2017, there was something of an exodus from Sunderland to Yorkshire for the game:

> On the day of the game, trains, which it was estimated brought 10,000 to South Yorkshire, began arriving soon after midday in Sheffield and although the kick off was not until 3.30pm, shrewd spectators set off for the ground immediately anticipating the problems in getting a good view that many latecomers experienced. Brakes, trams, and conveyances of all descriptions were soon bowling along to Bramall Lane while many thousands prepared to shank it from the centre of town. Special stands had been erected and the crowd was to total 22,000.

The game ended in a thrilling 3-3 draw, with Sunderland coming from behind on three occasions to level. However, a poor display in the replay saw County triumph by two goals to nil. It would have been a bitter blow for Watson and his players. Yet Tom had proven himself to be an able man at the helm, and his players had delivered a solid finish to their inaugural campaign in the league.

For the 1891/92 campaign, the league increased in size to 14 teams, meaning a 26-game season. However, aside from FA Cup matches – Sunderland played five times in the competition that season, reaching the semi-final again – teams could earn even more revenue by arranging 'friendly games' against less-fancied opposition. Watson arranged 27 of these fixtures during the campaign. This meant that Sunderland featured in 58 games that season. Despite this, they secured their first league title in 1892.

They had won 21 of their 26 league games, and scored 93 goals. In total, they managed an incredible 217 goals in all games, and lost just nine times in 58 outings. The club had been a professional outfit for just seven years, and Watson had been in post for three of them.

Sunderland's defence of their crown in the 1892/93 season appears to have been a relatively simple affair. They roared to their second title, finishing 11 points clear of their nearest rivals, Preston North End, racking up 48 points and scoring 100 goals. They had been unbeaten on home soil.

The league had expanded further to 16 teams, and several of Tom's men had been ever-presents in the First Division. Ted Doig, Tom Porteous and Will Gibson each featured in all 30 games, while Hughie Wilson missed just one match. Johnny Campbell accounted for almost a third of Sunderland's goals, notching 30 for the season.

The crowds were flocking to see them, with a total of between 117,000 and 120,000 people watching them at home during the campaign. Their biggest home crowd came on 17 December 1892, in a game against Preston North End, which ended 2-0 to Sunderland. Somewhere in the region of 18,000 turned out to see that match. Tom's men were also drawing huge numbers on the road too, with 20,000 in attendance for the league visit to The Wednesday on 29 October. In addition, a crowd of 20,000 came to see them play Glasgow Celtic on 6 October, in a friendly match, and a huge 28,000 were at Blackburn for an FA Cup third-round encounter on 18 February 1893.

As Watson led his team into the 1893/94 campaign, chasing their third title in a row, his stock in the English game couldn't have been higher. Only the Association Cup had eluded him, but few would have betted against adding that glittering piece of silverware to his collection at the time. Johnny Campbell missed five league games during this season, and managed 18 goals in 25 league outings. Picking up the slack was Jimmy Millar.

Born in 1871, Millar had been signed from Scottish part-timers Annbank, in 1890. Millar featured 261 times for Sunderland and scored 127 goals across two spells at the club. He left in 1896 to join Rangers, where he won two league titles and two Scottish Cups, before returning to Wearside in 1900 for a further four-year spell in which he won a First Division title.

During the 1893/94 season, Millar weighed in with 19 goals in 27 games. However, they would prove to be insufficient, and the three points Sunderland dropped to eventual champions Aston Villa would prove costly. On Saturday, 9 September, Villa visited Newcastle Road and took the lead through Denny Hodgetts in the 15th minute. Millar eventually levelled for Sunderland in the 65th minute, but the game left a sour taste after Johnny Campbell had a first-half penalty saved and a goal disallowed for offside.

Jimmy also scored in the away game against Villa, but with the game tied at 1-1 going into the final five minutes, Villa won a penalty. Jack Reynolds converted the spot kick and the Brummies won the game. It's often said, by modern-day pundits, that it's the fine margins that settle today's games. How interesting that the same held true for those at the top of the game in the 1890s. Two penalties in two games gave Villa the edge and Sunderland were unable to make up the ground. Two defeats in their final four games, against Stoke and Bolton Wanderers, meant that the Midlands club took the title, leading Tom's men by six points.

With Johnny Campbell back to fitness after his struggles the season before, Sunderland were again in free-scoring form, managing 96 league and cup goals for the season. Campbell was again an ever-present in the league, notching 20 goals in 30 games. Watson's men raced to the title, eclipsing challengers Everton by five points by the end of the campaign. They had lost just four games all season, all of them away from home.

On their way to the championship, Sunderland played out an epic encounter with current league champions Aston Villa at Newcastle Road on 2 January 1895. The game ended 4-4, and, owing to the intense rivalry between these two giants of the game, the clash was immortalised on canvas by artist Thomas Hemy, who was actually in attendance.

Remarkably, according to Sunderland historian Rob Mason, Tom Watson can be seen in the painting in his role as linesman for the day. The picture has variously been known as 'A Corner Kick' or 'The Last Minute – Now or Never', 'Sunderland v Aston Villa – Struggle for the Championship'. It's thanks to Rob that we are able to reproduce the painting – recognised as the oldest representation of an Association Football match in the world – in the plate section of this book. It can also be found in the entrance to the Stadium of Light today. There's also a smaller copy in the National Football Museum. The original is believed to be the oldest and largest oil painting of a professional football match.

As the curtain fell on the 1894/95 season, Tom was at the zenith of his game, having secured three league titles in his four years in the top flight. However, things were about to get much harder for him at Sunderland. Before that, though, Sunderland would contest their second 'World Championship' final, against Scottish champions Heart of Midlothian, on 27 April 1895. They would do so while fielding a side made up entirely of Scottish players; indeed, every player on the pitch that day, and the referee, was Scottish.

As discussed earlier, the game took place at Scotland's Tynecastle, and 15,000 people were reported to be in attendance. The idea of such a game did not find favour with everyone. Jonathan Wilson, writing for the *Guardian* on 25 April 2020, quotes the *Edinburgh News*, 1895, who wrote: 'The whole case goes to show how undesirable such events are from a sporting point of view, and what a prostitution of titles they are.'

Of course, Scottish sensibilities may well have – with some justification – been influenced by their consternation at the free-for-all of cash-laden English clubs who were raiding the flower of Scotland's young talent in the decade that preceded the game.

Sunderland won the game 5-3, thanks to a brace by Campbell, and one apiece for Johnston, Auld and Harvie. Three of Sunderland's regular starting 11 – also all Scottish – missed the game, according to Wilson, 'their captain, Hughie Wilson, whose long one-handed throw-ins caused such chaos they led to the law being changed, the winger John Scott, who was fit enough to serve as linesman, and the defender Andrew McCreadie'.

The game was played in poor conditions, with heavy rain throughout. Hearts took the game to Watson's men, but Doig was in imperious form and Sunderland were the eventual victors. At the end of the match, Harvie declared the match to be 'full of excitement and fast play'. For its part, the *Sunderland Echo* proclaimed Watson's men to be 'the premier football team of the globe'.

By now, Sunderland were an ageing team, and perhaps their opponents were beginning to get the measure of them. They slumped to a fifth-place finish in 1896. However, by now, Tom Watson had established himself as a great leader and organiser, much coveted in the English game. As we've learned, his achievements would now lead him to Anfield, and Liverpool FC. A career born in the North East, honed to a fine art at Sunderland would now be defined on Merseyside.

Chapter Six

# March of the Anfielders: Growing pains and becoming Tom's new love

A LETTER from William Edward Barclay to *Field Sport* in June 1892 signalled Liverpool's arrival on the Merseyside football scene. In it, he set out an ambitious vision that he hoped would tempt citizens of Liverpool, which had so far divided their attentions between Everton and Bootle FC, through the turnstiles of Anfield. He wrote:

> 'Subscribers' tickets will be ready in a few days at 7s, 6d, 15s and 21s, according to accommodation, and the prospects are very bright, and I anticipate a very satisfactory season on the old ground. Although we are the Liverpool club, all the old playing members of the old Everton, to whom Evertonians are much indebted for promoting the game in our midst, have been elected honorary life members. The plans for the dressing rooms and gymnasium are now under consideration, and visiting teams will be spared the trouble of dressing away from the ground, whilst our own players will not only have a clubroom, but admirable dining rooms and training quarters at the ground.
>
> In your next issue but one I hope to be in a position to give our friends a full list of our players for next season. The charge for admission to first-team matches will be 4d, and to

> second-team matches 3d, and only in very exceptional cases, when large guarantees are required, will 6d be charged. The ground is in better order now than it has ever been before at this season of the year, and is improving daily. We do not propose to lay the track this year, as it is too late, but a start will be made early next year.
>
> — Yours, W.E. Barclay.

The apparent overture of honorary membership to the 'old playing members of the old Everton' seems to suggest that the Liverpool board was keen to put the acrimony of the split behind them. In truth, there would have been little bad blood between Barclay and his ilk and the former players at Everton, a fact evidenced by the number of these who would later join Liverpool.

The first official encounter between the two sides wouldn't come until 1894. This was a First Division clash that Everton won 3-0, at Goodison Park. However, this wasn't the first time the two rivals had ever met on the field of play. During Liverpool's inaugural 1892/93 season in the Lancashire League, they made it to the final of the Liverpool Senior Cup. Their opponents were, somewhat predictably and poetically, Everton, on 22 April 1893 at Bootle FC's ground in Hawthorne Road, a site also used for cricket. Technically, this was a friendly match, so it's not recorded in official derby records by either club. However, reports show it was hotly contested and anything but a friendly encounter. The city would have been abuzz at the prospect of such an important game taking place between Everton and Liverpool so soon after their split in 1892.

Liverpool's home attendances had grown from a few hundred to nearly 2,500. However, the Blues were still by far the bigger club, averaging attendances of almost 13,000. Houlding's team were clearly seen as unpopular upstarts by their rivals, as evidenced by talk of boycotts of Anfield by Evertonians and Bootleites, as they were known. It was common back then for local supporters to transfer allegiance to their neighbours when their side was away from home. However, rumours were rife of a pact between Everton and Bootle supporters not to visit Anfield.

The *Liverpool Echo* review, written on the eve of battle, captures the mood surrounding the fixture:

> On account of the rivalry existing between the contestants – Everton and Liverpool – the game has created a vast amount of interest, and arrangements have been made for a large attendance.
>
> The game is sure to be one of the keenest and most exciting descriptions, as Liverpool are determined to try their best to dispossess Everton of the handsome trophy.

The psychological battle was in full swing in the run-up to the match and the stakes couldn't be higher for either club. Everton had publicly threatened to field a 'combination team' as they didn't see it as an important fixture. Liverpool threatened to retaliate by fielding a reserve side. This was clearly a tactic designed to downplay the significance, at least publicly, and thereby reduce the pressure on both teams' players.

In the end, predictably, both sent out a strong XI, even if some still argued that Everton fielded some of their less-fancied charges. How fascinating that such 'mind games', as they're described by today's pundits and journalists, have their origins in the very foundation of the game.

On the day, over 10,000 supporters turned up to see the game. Conditions outside the ground were described by the *Lancashire Post* as appalling, with supporters finding it difficult to get into the ground. No doubt the poor weather and torrential rain played its part, but clearly the turnstiles struggled to cope with the deluge of supporters eager to see the game.

Everton came out first, followed by Liverpool. Teams would emerge separately and run past a box placed on the pitch to allow a photographer to line up his shot. Reports suggest that both teams were given a sporting welcome by the assembled crowd packed into the old ground.

With a signal from the referee, battle commenced to a huge roar from the assembled spectators. It was Liverpool, perhaps because they wanted it more, who took the game to Everton. Clearly enthralled by the action, the reporter at the *Liverpool Mercury* gave an almost minute-by-minute account of the action: 'Liverpool had the best of the play so far, being quicker and better combined than their opponents,' he wrote.

The Everton goal was under siege, with their keeper pulling off a succession of saves to deny the men from Anfield. However, they couldn't withstand the barrage for long and in the 35th minute Liverpool took the lead. Here's how the *Mercury*'s scribe saw the goal: 'McCartney was penalised for holding, but the free kick was adroitly turned to Liverpool's advantage, as on Miller passing to Wyllie, the latter scored a goal with a low shot.'

The underdogs were 1-0 up and it stayed like that until half-time. The press couldn't make out whether they were the better team or whether Everton hadn't taken the game seriously enough. It didn't matter as far as Liverpool's new following were concerned, though.

The second half was different and, perhaps after some home truths in the dressing room, Everton emerged with more impetus. Still they couldn't break Liverpool down and, as the game wore on, they became increasingly frustrated at Liverpool's tactics. In order to weather the storm, the Anfield outfit had no choice but to resort to what could be euphemistically described as some agricultural defending. By the end of the game, Everton's fury both on the pitch and among the watching members of the Goodison board was palpable. Everton pushed hard for an equaliser. They must have been desperate to avoid a humiliating defeat to Merseyside's newest kids on the block.

In the dying moments Everton won a corner and, from the resulting scramble, they alleged a handball by one of Liverpool's defenders and demanded a penalty. In a cacophony of protests on and off the pitch, the referee, after consulting his linesman, waved away their appeals. It would be the last action of the match, and as the final whistle sounded an uproarious chorus of rage erupted. Liverpool's players and directors were jubilant.

In what many felt was a cynical ploy to prevent Liverpool receiving the trophy on the pitch after the game, Everton lodged a formal protest. The victors would have to wait to receive their spoils.

Writing in the *Cricket and Field Review*, on 29 April 1893, one journalist recorded his disappointment at the behaviour of Everton officials at the end of the game:

> I would much rather have seen the full strength of Everton on the field, and so would lots of their supporters, but the executive I suppose considered the team quite good enough to again win the cup, but when they failed it is bad form then to step in with a protest, and this on the most flimsy ground.

Everton complained that the referee was incompetent. However, the Liverpool Football Association rejected this at a hearing held at the Neptune Hotel on the following Monday. Andrew Hannah, club captain, received the trophy, described as 'a splendid specimen of the silversmith's art', the following day, at a home game against Preston. He had also lifted the Lancashire League Cup that season, completing a historic double in Liverpool's debut campaign.

However, the drama was far from over. On 1 September 1893, on the eve of Liverpool's first outing in the Second Division, both trophies were stolen from a pawnshop in the Paddington area of the city. They had been on display there, allowing supporters to view them in the shop window. The *Daily News,* on 4 September 1893, reported that 'the burglars forced open the door of the shop with a jemmy, and took away the prizes, which are of considerable value. So far the police have failed to obtain a clue to the missing cups.' Sadly, the trophies were never found. Liverpool were forced to pay the princely sum of £130 to replace them. However, it had proven to be a fine end to the club's inaugural season.

Under the stewardship of McKenna and Barclay, Liverpool had won the Liverpool Senior Cup and the Lancashire League championship, setting up a test match with Newton Heath for promotion to the Second Division. They would, of course, triumph in this game and progressed to English football's second tier at the first time of asking.

They had progressed thanks to a superior goal average, despite being outscored by their nearest rivals Blackpool. Both teams had registered identical records for the season: played 22, won 17, drawn two and lost three. To modern eyes this may seem unfair, as not only had their rivals prevailed in both league encounters, but they also possessed a superior goal difference (+51) to Liverpool's (+47). Blackpool had also scored more (82) than Liverpool (66). Nevertheless, it was the rules of the game that when teams were tied on points as both were, goal average would decide the winner, not goal difference.

If there was a little fortune in Liverpool's escape from the Lancashire League, they would prove more than ready for the challenges of the Second Division. Finishing on 50 points – eight clear of Birmingham in second – they had gone unbeaten all season, winning all 14 home fixtures and eight away games. Their six draws all came on the road and they registered 77 goals, conceding just 18 all season.

Liverpool's march to the top flight had seemed assured, and they entered the 1894/95 season in confident mood. After all, they were yet to taste failure. However, their arrival in the top flight would serve as a rude awakening to Anfield directors, as the club struggled to 22 points from a possible 60. They won just seven games all season, drawing eight and losing 15. Liverpool's attack seemed blunt, mustering 51 goals, while their defence leaked 70.

Finishing in last place, Liverpool faced Bury in a test match that they lost by a single goal, ensuring their return to the Second Division. The highlight of the season – if it could be considered so, given the results – had been the chance to compete against their neighbours in official league games.

After losing 3-0 at Goodison in front of a huge crowd of 44,000 on 13 October 1894, Liverpool went looking for revenge in the return fixture at Anfield, played on 17 November. With Everton sitting at the top of the table and Liverpool languishing in 15th place, the odds didn't seem favourable. Nevertheless, the home side put up a creditable fight.

Anfield was packed out long before kick-off, with some reports suggesting a capacity crowd of 30,000 in attendance. This would be the first time Everton had kicked a ball on the Anfield turf since the club split in 1892. This is how the *Liverpool Mercury* recorded the game:

> On Saturday Everton played their first game upon their old enclosure since the 'split,' the occasion being the return League fixture between the two great local rivals. Long before the time fixed for the kick off the ground was well filled, while upon all the roads converging Anfield wards, the people, with all descriptions of vehicles, streamed past in one continuous

> flow. When the game commenced, the ground, although extra accommodation had been provided, was packed to the utmost, the crowd being estimated at over 25,000.

Everton twice took the lead, their first coming from a penalty in the 30th minute. David Hannah, brother of former captain Andrew, levelled for the home side after 55 minutes, but with just five minutes remaining Everton looked to have clinched a much-coveted double over their neighbours, when Alex Latta put them 2-1 up at the Anfield Road end. However, with local pride at stake, Liverpool would not be beaten and, in the final minute of the game, they won a penalty in front of the huge crowd at the Walton Breck Road end of the pitch. While not yet known as the Kop, it must still have presented a fearsome sight. Jimmy Ross was given the unenviable task of taking the pressure kick, and he made no mistake from 12 yards. The game finished 2-2 and, as the *Liverpool Mercury* reported, it marked 'a most creditable performance on the part of the younger organisation'.

Liverpool once again proved to be a match for any side in the Second Division, finishing 1895/96 unbeaten on home soil, and losing just six on the road. They earned promotion back to the top flight at the first attempt, achieving a tally of 46 points. Once again, the league had been won on goal average, but this time there could be no doubt as to who were the deserving champions. Manchester City finished second level on points with the Anfield side, but Liverpool had simply been prolific in front of goal, scoring a record 106 goals for the season and conceding just 32. Their impressive goal average dwarfed that of their nearest rivals from Manchester at 3.31 to City's 1.66. Five of Liverpool's players finished the season on double figures: George Allen (25), Jimmy Ross (23), Frank Becton (19), Harry Bradshaw (11) and Fred Geary (11). McKenna's men had also beaten their challengers 3-1 at home and held them to a draw at

Hyde Road. There could be no doubt this time that Liverpool were worthy champions.

McKenna and Barclay had proven themselves to be among the game's finest administrators. They had led the club from the ashes of the split in 1892, a club with a stadium and some shirts but no team, all the way to the English First Division for the second time in just four years, but, once there, they had fallen short last time. It was time for the club to take a different direction, and in doing so they created a new role at the top of the club, that of 'team manager'. The man who would take on the mantle would have to be a proven winner, and one who had done so at the highest level of the English game.

The players recruited by John McKenna and William Edward Barclay to play for Liverpool in their opening seasons could be described as colourful characters, strong and skilful and built to compete in battlefields of football's lower tiers, the Lancashire League and the Second Division. They were all experienced campaigners, but many of them were into their 30s already.

Though the top division was no less competitive and hard-fought, they had now learned that if they were to compete for the ultimate prize, they would need to build a team with a more cultured approach to the game and, what's more, that they would need to add a sprinkling of talented and more youthful players. Liverpool, for all their battle-hardened buccaneering style, aggression and desire, had so far proven ill-equipped to truly compete at the highest level, yo-yoing between England's two divisions between 1893 and 1896.

The Anfield directors were now certain that their team needed flair, discipline and a more intelligent style of play. They believed they had identified just the man to deliver that, and they spared no expense to get him. They wanted someone capable of not only competing in the First Division, but actually winning it. Who else then, but a man who had done just that, not once but three times. Who else, but Sunderland's Tom Watson.

Chapter Seven

# Anfield punching above its weight: Ambition, vision and finance wins out as Watson joins the 'Reds'

BY 1896, Liverpool was a bustling hive of commerce, its dock system – comprising more than 30 docks and associated basins – alive with workers and, to visitors to the city, its river would have been an incredible sight, filled with boats and ships of all nations. From the centre to the suburbs, its streets were crammed. Anfield and Everton were increasingly popular suburbs. However, as we have discussed, along with economic growth, the densely packed population brought with it pollution and disease, and it would be the poorest in society who suffered most.

The city's parks were the 'lungs of Liverpool', and sport, namely football, provided physical activity for most of the year, including the dark winter months, as well as an escape from the drudgery of labour.

Whereas in areas such Sunderland and other parts of the North East, the economic picture was becoming difficult, in Liverpool, for its merchants, shipping magnates and traders, things were very different. They were enjoying the fruits of what was a roaring trade. And the men whose service-related businesses supported this growth, the brewers, landlords and hoteliers, their bank balances were also swelling.

Houlding was one such man, and his money and influence would not only prove to be pivotal in the rise of Liverpool Football Club from the Lancashire League to the First Division, but also in the recruitment of one of England's most successful club secretaries, Tom Watson – despite the Anfield outfit being widely acknowledged as Merseyside's poor relation to Everton.

Liverpool's promotion to the First Division at the end of the 1895/96 season was far from mission accomplished as far as the club's boardroom was concerned. These were ambitious men, and they had experienced promotion to the top flight before, only to see the team struggle to cope once there. Furthermore, they would have been under no illusions as to their players' level of preparedness for the challenges that lay ahead. After all, they had secured promotion by virtue of superior goal average over rivals Manchester City after a tense final game of the season in front of 25,000 people at Hyde Road on 3 April 1896.

Liverpool went into the game in first place with a healthy goal average over their nearest rival, City, in second place, but having played two games more. Their goal average had received a healthy boost thanks in part to their 7-0 thrashing of Crewe Alexandra six days earlier, on 28 March. Liverpool had scored 40 goals in their previous ten games, conceding just nine in reply.

The local press described a gloriously sunny day, and a bumper crowd that generated £800 in gate receipts. The turnstiles were locked a full 30 minutes before kick-off. For City to stand any chance of finishing the season as champions, they would have to win this game and their last two. Defeat was unthinkable and a draw wouldn't help.

The home side were at full strength, but Liverpool were missing regulars, including team captain Sydney Ross and John Holmes through injury. With Ross absent, Joe McQue deputised as captain, winning the toss and electing to kick off with the wind at Liverpool's backs. A scrappy midfield battle soon gave way to an assault on the City goalmouth. First, Allen blasted over the bar, then a scramble almost led to an opener from the visitors before the defence lumped the ball up the pitch.

Press reports reveal a febrile atmosphere and it appears to have affected the players. This was a crunch game with tackles to match. It was City who broke the deadlock, though, when Hugh Morris beat Harry Storer after the keeper had parried an initial shot on goal. Their fans were rapturous and no doubt dreaming of leapfrogging Liverpool to the Second Division championship. Liverpool laboured but were unable to equalise in the first half, heading into the dressing room at the interval a goal down.

Understandably, with so much at stake, the second half was fiercely fought. Tackles flew in and fouls were conceded as the clock ticked down. With victory in sight for the home team, the game entered the last ten minutes, then Liverpool's goalscoring hero, George Allen, stepped up to save the day. Allen had been signed from Leith Celtic in 1895. A prolific centre-forward, he would go on to score 56 goals in 96 games for Liverpool. His leveller against City came after clever play by Frank Becton and Harry Bradshaw saw a delightful ball to Allen, who was clean through on goal. He unleashed a shot that gave Charlie Williams in the home goal 'no earthly chance'. The press reports suggest that City refused to give in, being the 'superior conditioned side'; however, the final chance of the game fell to the visitors.

Liverpool launched a final attack that saw striker Fred Geary with the goal at his mercy. Geary had played with distinction for Everton, before joining Liverpool for £60 in 1895. He averaged a goal every three games while at Anfield, but this match wouldn't be one of them. He skewed his shot inexplicably wide, and with it a chance to win the game went begging. It wasn't to matter, though, as a draw would prove enough to seal the league title for Liverpool.

After finishing as First Division champions in 1895, Sunderland finished the 1895/96 season, a disappointing one, in fifth place. Aston Villa were crowned league winners after a 2-1 away victory over Bury. Sunderland and Villa were the powerhouses of England's top flight at this time, with the former winning three league titles and the latter carrying off five between 1892 and 1900. However, during the 1895/96 season, Sunderland could muster just 52 goals. Press reports suggest a combination of key players suffering a drop in form, injuries, perhaps growing complacent or tired of the same tactics, and other teams becoming accustomed to Watson's style of play.

New board members joined the club. One of them, Councillor J. P. Henderson, a wine and spirit merchant, had answered the call to become club guarantor during a period of rocketing expenses in 1892, and appears to have been more cautious in his spending. Elected on to the committee, he became vice-chairman, and when the president, Robert Thompson, resigned, Henderson took his place.

In 1896, the club's financial position seems to have deteriorated further, and there were even reports that negotiations had taken place to float on the London Stock Exchange. At the same time, press stories began to circulate that Watson was 'at loggerheads' with his directors. Even so, it appears that nobody expected that he would leave.

This report, in the *Shields Daily Gazette* dated 10 July 1896, of a meeting to discuss Sunderland's financial situation and a potential solution to it, attended by Tom Watson, gives an indication of how pressing and precarious the financial position had become at Sunderland:

> A public meeting was held in the Assembly Hall, Sunderland, last night, for the purpose of considering the proposal to form a limited liability company for

> taking over the Sunderland Football Club. This step was rendered necessary owing to the falling off in the 'gates' last season, which caused the income to be £1,400 less than the expenditure.

The board was having to fund the club 'out of pocket' with no income to cover costs, and while there was a promise to continue this for the coming season, the situation was unsustainable. A proposal was put forward to raise capital of £5,000 through the issue of shares in the new company, which would take over the running of the club. A prospectus set out the club's assets, which included two freehold houses, timber and stands with earning power given as £3,123. Liabilities were £1,742. The ground was held on lease from year to year, but a plan had been set forth to obtain the freehold, and then lay a track for cycling and athletics.

It appeared that the share issue had only limited success, and after eight days the listing closed with only £1,700 raised from a target of £5,000. The club was in a challenging position, and Watson was all too aware.

Liverpool's offer of £300 a year – double his wage at Sunderland – to make the switch to Anfield was indeed timely. Tom, who at the time owned a tobacconist's shop in North Bridge Street opposite Monkwearmouth Station, went to Grayston, the man who had recruited him, to talk it over. Perhaps he felt a sense of duty to the man whose guiding hand had led to his first big job in football. Knowing the situation at the club, and its direction of travel, Grayston advised that Tom should take the offer.

Sunderland's eventual loss of Tom Watson appears to have impacted the club's fortunes. Though they finished runners-up twice under two different managers, Robert Campbell and Alex Mackie, in 1898 and 1901 respectively, they would wait seven years for the title to return in 1902. After securing four league titles in ten years, they would now have to wait 11 for the next championship to arrive in 1913.

While it's perhaps simplistic to attribute the club's three league titles in 1892, 1893 and 1895 to just one man, there's no doubting the influence of Tom Watson and the esteem in which he was held. His loss was no doubt a massive blow to Sunderland at a critical time in their history, and consequently a huge coup for Liverpool. His decision to leave the North East for Merseyside was perceived as a huge shock to the football world.

Tom had been integral to the organisation of North East football. He had played a key part in the early history of both Newcastle United and Sunderland, and had achieved so much success on Wearside. However, it's likely that he was beginning to feel that his ambitions could no longer be met at Sunderland. Whether that was because of this new and unfavourable financial reality, or differences with the members of the new limited liability company is not entirely clear. It's more likely that a combination of both these elements, allied with the presentation of a new opportunity and a fresh start at an ambitious and young organisation, was enough to whet Tom's appetite.

Nevertheless, Liverpool, on the other hand, were regarded as Merseyside's second team, labouring in the shadow of their richer and far more successful neighbours.

These early press reports paint the picture well. On 28 July 1896, the *Liverpool Daily Post* reported:

> The engagement of Mr. Tom Watson, as Secretary of the Liverpool Football Club will probably come as a surprise to the public interested in football. Few people will hardly believe that Mr. Watson could be induced to part company with his old love, especially as just now it is being floated as a limited liability concern, but it is nevertheless correct. Mr.

> William Houlding and Mr. John Mc'Kenna, the late hon. Secretary having concluded the necessary arrangements yesterday. The 'capture' of Mr. Watson is looked upon as one of the most important – if not the most important – the Liverpool Club has made since its organisation, as 'Tom,' as he is familiarly called, will bring large and unique experience, as well as great influence, to bear on the well-doing of Liverpool football. It is just the thing the club required as it is now entering an entirely fresh career, and the cooperation of a man of Mr. Watson's views and talent will no doubt be a welcome addition to the management.

This report is fascinating for several reasons. It amply demonstrates that Liverpool were achieving something approaching the impossible here. The term 'capture' speaks of the club hierarchy's opportunistic move, and the extent of their ambition and determination. Houlding and McKenna had seen an opportunity. Clearly aware of unrest at the top of the North East club and only too aware of Watson's discontent, they had acted swiftly and persuasively to the almost universal surprise of the football world.

Another report, in the *Jarrow Express* on 31 July 1896, reveals, albeit in the understated tones typical of the period, the sense of disappointment and loss felt by all connected with Sunderland at the time, writing:

> It will be a matter of regret for all supporters of the Association game in the North, that Mr T. Watson, the well known Secretary of the Sunderland Football Club is about to sever his connection with that club. To most people it will come as a surprise. It is however some time since the Liverpool Club offered the Sunderland man £300 a year for his services as Secretary, and he has been prevailed upon to

> accept the offer. The time and the circumstances is a trying one for Sunderland, as just now they are passing through a severe trial, and can ill afford to lose such a good friend as Tom Watson has proved himself.

The offer of £300, a princely sum by the standards of the era, would have proved difficult to resist for Tom. However, beyond the promises of personal reward and remuneration, the offer would have signalled the significant ambition of the Liverpool board, an ambition he maybe felt was lacking or not possible at Sunderland.

The feeling on Merseyside was, of course, in sharp contrast to that further north. This report in the *Liverpool Echo*, published just days before the start of the 1896/97 season on 29 August 1896, speaks of the sense of excitement and optimism abroad in the city:

> With Tom Watson to run the show at Anfield, things should go on swimmingly. The new secretary should be allowed as free a hand as possible and not be hampered in his work so long as he goes all right. It should be remembered that too many cooks spoil the broth, and it would be a pity if the Liverpool soup gets spoilt for the want of foresight.

It's interesting that the journalist who penned this piece spoke of the need for Watson to be left alone to run things as he saw fit. This is perhaps a nod to the fact that he had clearly been unhappy with some of the directors at Sunderland, and a desire to see that this wasn't repeated at Anfield. Liverpool's hierarchy was filled with strong characters, and men regarded far and wide as exceptional administrators. It would take quite the sacrifice of ego for such men to hand over the control of team affairs completely to Watson.

At most clubs, the man at the helm was not a manager (or head coach) as we understand it today. Teams were run by club secretaries who had responsibility for recruitment and administration, with selection, tactics and formations decided often by a committee of board members. The day-to-day preparation of players was the responsibility of trainers, and during a match the club captain would make decisions, as the secretary would often not be present. The role of secretary often involved scouting missions, so, as every team played on the same day and at the same time, the secretary would rarely be at one of their own team's games. This was the case for McKenna and Barclay, and, despite the role evolving under Watson, it would remain so for him too.

In the wider football world the move was viewed as a signal of Liverpool's ambition to cement their place as one of English football's top clubs, and to directly challenge their nearest neighbours, Everton. See this report in the *North Devon Gazette*, published on 22 September 1896 with the football league season already underway:

> The fact that Mr. Tom Watson has accepted the secretaryship of the Liverpool Club – at a salary of £300 a year – suggests that the Liverpudlians mean to leave no stone unturned to retain their position in the First Division; and that they started the season well by beating the English Cup holders is synonymous with saying that genial Tom is sanguine of making his new team equal to, if not actually better than, the big local opposition in Anfield Road – Everton, the wealthiest club in the country. The growth of the game in Liverpool is startling, for it is not many years since the dribbling sport would be introduced into the Mersey port, and now the two teams are in the First Division, with such an organiser as Tom Watson at the head of the weaker team, the prospect of the English Cup or the League Championship going to Liverpool was never better.

The reference to the growth of football on Merseyside is significant here, and was clearly a factor in shaping Watson's decision. Tom was given a taste of the passion of Merseyside's supporters, and the great potential at Anfield, when he served as linesman for the visit of The Wednesday in March 1895, in which he witnessed a crowd of 20,000 turn out to see new signing, and former Preston North End striker, Frank Becton line up for Liverpool. An exciting game saw Liverpool win 4-2, with Becton on the scoresheet twice.

Tom could clearly see huge potential at Anfield, a desire on the part of the board to compete at the very top of the league, factors that clearly energised him, if this report in *Pearson's Weekly* on 10 October 1896 is anything to go by:

> During the summer a rumour was current that the Sunderland team would be removed en bloc to London. As a matter of fact there were some negotiations with that end in view, and it is well known that that Mr. Tom Watson, who had great influence with the players, was at loggerheads with some of the other officers of the club. The negotiations came to nought, however, and the Sunderland cracks remain for the most part on the banks of the Wear; but Tom Watson has left them to their own devices, and accepted service at the Liverpool club, whose team he says he will make the strongest in the country.

There's an intriguing postscript to the saga, however, for it wasn't only Liverpool who were alerted to Tom's growing dissatisfaction at Sunderland. A report in *Sporting Life* on 16 September 1896 claims that the newly reorganised Newcastle United had made an offer to Watson to return to his old stomping ground as secretary. However, they had balked at the figure of £300 that Liverpool were now willing to pay.

It seems the die was cast and it would be farewell to the North East, a monumental decision for the man.

Watson had been the northern representative at the English FA, a role he was immensely proud of and that was key to his stature in the wider game. However, his move south to Liverpool would mean he was no longer eligible to fill the position. There was clearly a lot for him to consider and weigh up in making this decision, not to mention the emotional wrench of leaving the players and members of the local press with whom he clearly enjoyed a great bond.

A report in the *Scottish Referee*, published on 24 August 1896, described the gifts bestowed on Tom by Sunderland's football press and his former players. He received a 'golden carbuncle scarf pin, and a silver matchbox' from reporters. His former players showered him with a 'handsome clock and a pair of brasses'.

Backing up reports that Tom left with the goodwill of many in the North East, the *Sheffield Daily Telegraph* wrote, on 25 August 1896:

> Mr Tom Watson left Sunderland on Saturday morning, for Liverpool, where he commenced his duties as secretary of the Liverpool Football Club yesterday. A large crowd, including the Sunderland players, assembled at the station to see him off, and much good feeling was displayed. A handsome timepiece and bronzes have been presented by the Sunderland players to their ex-secretary, who has been the recipient of many other handsome farewell gifts.

Tom and his family set up home at 106 St Domingo Vale, Liverpool. He and Kate now had four children: Ralph, Ethel, Tom and Winifred. Tom's profession, listed on the 1901 census, was 'Secretary of Football Club'.

The Watson revolution at Anfield was about to get underway in 1896. However, his appointment wasn't the only sweeping change at the club. McKenna and the board were about to make a monumental decision that would forever change how the team looked, and in doing so they ushered in a new nickname that would serve them until this day. Liverpool FC, the 'Anfielders' or the 'Livers' as they had previously been known, were about to become the 'Reds'.

In 1892, Everton had walked out of Anfield and decided to set up a new club at Goodison Park. John Houlding, as we have learned, quickly set about building his new team, recruited mostly from Scotland. There had been just one problem: there was no money left over to buy a kit.

Everton's new board had decided to change their shirt to 'ruby red', so Houlding was left to go rummaging in the Anfield storeroom, where he found Everton's old blue-and-white shirts. So these became Liverpool FC's official kit. For four full seasons, until 1896, Everton played in red and Liverpool ran out in blue. However, at the end of the 1895/96 season, with John McKenna moving into the boardroom and Tom Watson taking over, Liverpool decided they needed a change of kit. The last time the team played in blue was in a 2-0 test match defeat to West Bromwich Albion at Stoney Park in the Midlands.

For their part, Everton had decided to ditch the red shirts and opted instead for royal blue. Houlding quickly saw his opportunity and immediately purchased 20 red shirts from Jack Sugg's clothing store in the city centre. It turned out to be a masterstroke, because red and white were the municipal colours of the city. This meant his club now bore both the city's name and its colours.

There's some confusion over the colour of the shorts, or knickers as they were known at the time, though, as they were originally intended to be black. However, as the team kicked off the new season away to The Wednesday on 1 September 1896, the *Liverpool Daily Post* reported that they were wearing red shirts and white shorts for the first time.

Liverpool FC were now officially the 'Reds'. They won their first game wearing the new shirt 2-1 and the first player to score for Liverpool wearing a red shirt, white shorts and red socks was George Allen. He netted twice. Sadly, though, the first game in red at Anfield was a 2-0 reverse against Bolton Wanderers. The Reds faced similar disappointment at Goodison when they faced the Blues for the first time, with both sides in their new kits. The game ended 2-1 to Everton, with Jimmy Ross scoring for Liverpool. Liverpool's first victory over Everton while wearing the red shirt came on 25 September 1897. The Reds won 3-1 in front of a crowd of 30,000 people.

The shirt was a simple one, with a 'dark red or black stand collar and buttons down the front'. There was no badge, though. Liverpool players didn't wear a Liverbird upon their chest until the 1950 FA Cup Final against Arsenal. It disappeared after that game, which the Reds lost 2-0, and wouldn't be seen again until 1955. Eventually, though, Bill Shankly would oversee the change to the all-red kit in a game against Anderlecht in the European Cup, during the 1964/65 season.

With Liverpool seizing of English football's most successful manager, they had potentially weakened one of the First Division rivals. However, that still left Sunderland's main rivals, Aston Villa. They had been a force in the English game since the 1880s and had been pioneers of the passing game, in which short, quick passes had been imported from north of the border by Scottish manager George Ramsay, who was appointed as the world's first professional football manager in 1886. Did the Liverpool board want to emulate this style of appointment, which had proven so successful for Villa?

Ramsay managed the club for 40 years, and led the Midlands giants to six league championships and six FA Cups in that time, earning Aston Villa their status as the most successful club in England. Their supporters could hold on to this proud boast until the 1970s.

Watson no doubt enjoyed a rivalry with Ramsay and Villa, and his desire to compete on the same level makes his move to Liverpool all the more interesting. While cynics may point to the money involved in terms of his signing-on fee, it's worth noting that Watson is highly regarded for his character and integrity as much as his abilities as an organiser. It's therefore not unreasonable to suggest that he wouldn't have made the move had he not seen at least the potential to build a worthy rival to Ramsay's Aston Villa. He clearly felt this wasn't going to be possible at Sunderland.

## Chapter Eight

# Scouting for champions, creating a new culture: Tom proves himself a class act

IT HAS long since been recognised that the role carved out by Tom Watson in the North East went beyond the club secretary job typical of the game during that era. He was probably the closest thing to what we call a manager today.

Arriving at Anfield, aged 37, in 1896, he was taking the reins at a club that had spent the first four years of its life struggling to cement its place in England's top division. A talented team had been assembled at Liverpool, but he would need to add to it if he was to take them to the next level.

With John McKenna now firmly back at the directors' table, Tom was given the freedom to become more involved in recruitment, team selection and tactics. *The Cricket and Football Field* noted at the time that Liverpool had never had a 'boss off the field and there have been too many on it', perhaps a hint that the players were viewed, at least by journalists, as the ones calling the shots up to this point. If this had been the case, they were about to meet their match in Watson.

Supporting Tom in the boardroom were a powerful group of men who had nursed the club into existence in 1892, and carried it to this point. They were, of course, John McKenna, William Edward Barclay and James Ramsay. In addition, according to newspaper reports, George Patterson would join the club's administration with the backing and support of Watson. Ramsay, it seems, would become a great ally and close colleague of Tom. According to this snippet, published in the *Liverpool Echo* after Ramsay's death, and dated 4 October 1918, the two men often worked at close quarters:

> First information is here given of the death of Mr James Ramsay, ex-director of Liverpool F.C. He had been connected with Liverpool ever since the club was born, right away to the Houlding days. In later days he spent most of his time alongside Mr. Tom Watson in, first the old hen-pen which served as a secretarial office, and, later, in the palatial office. The Sandon and Anfield were his 'home' and his all.

Of Patterson, we can confidently say that he would become a trusted pair of hands at the club, with the club turning to him on two occasions after they had lost a manager. After Tom's death from pneumonia in 1915, the club immediately turned to George and asked him to take the reins. His credentials for the role of succeeding such a legend of the game are difficult to judge, given the sparsity of information about his qualities. It's true that there are some comical references to his clumsiness – he once walked into a tree and injured himself severely – and there's also a reference by the legendary football reporter Ernest Edwards, or Bee, writing in the *Liverpool Echo*, of his 'wriggling bones' and 'big frame'. Here's the full quote, written in 1915:

> I am glad that Mr. George Patterson has been appointed secretary of Liverpool FC. He is a practical man, unobtrusive, and shows wisdom with pen and in football matters. He is following one of the best in the late Tom Watson, but has been well schooled, and will make good. In his football days

> he played a deal of football with Orrell and other clubs, but from an army point of view his big frame is useless – he has an extraordinary number of wriggling bones that have been broken. Here's to him!

Patterson's record in terms of on-pitch results is, of course, mixed, at best. But he was clearly a very able administrator, trusted and safe. He would be called upon again in the late 20s, when Matt McQueen left the manager's position. Patterson was still involved at the club as late as the 1950s and early 60s.

Liverpool's new 'manager' was a believer in football 'science' and, backed by an able group of men, he set about putting his mark on the club. He understood the importance of diet and exercise – though some of his methods and ideas would raise eyebrows today. As a powerful and well-known figure in football, Tom is unlikely to have struggled to win the respect of the dressing room. However, whatever his new charges had become used to in the past, things were about to change dramatically for everyone at the club.

According to contemporaneous reports, sourced by Arngrimur Baldursson and Kjell Hanssen, and published on lfchistory.net, the players' day started early, with them reporting to Anfield at 7.30am. Once there, they would complete a 30-minute stroll. It's not clear where they would have done this, but it's possible that locals would have seen them walking around the neighbourhood of the stadium or in Stanley Park.

Breakfast was served at 8.30am and consisted of 'weak tea, chops, eggs, dry toast or stale bread'. Apparently, Tom didn't want his players indulging in butter, sugar, potatoes or milk. As in the modern game, training was split into two sessions, the first beginning at 9.45am and the last at 3.30pm. As was his custom at Sunderland, Watson allowed his players a glass of beer or claret for dinner and encouraged them to be sparing with their use of tobacco. The day would be a long one, though, as they would end it with a stroll at 7.30pm, before presumably being told to get an early night.

It's not known how much this differed from what the players had become used to under Barclay and McKenna. But, with them spending much more time tending to the administration of the club, it's likely that such a decision would have been ceded to the club's trainers. No doubt, in order to convince players of the need to modify their diet and pay special attention to their physical wellbeing, Tom would have had to deploy his legendary communication skills, natural authority and charisma. Football was rapidly developing, both in terms of the commercial and organisational side of the game, and also with reference to the management of players. And Tom Watson was at the forefront of all of that, having been described as both progressive and as a moderniser.

There's some evidence that Tom's influence stretched beyond the English game, however. Among several articles that testify to his exploits overseas, this tantalising line in a *Liverpool Echo* tribute to Watson, written after his demise, is fascinating: 'Mr. Watson was in the habit of spending his holiday abroad, and it is not too much to say that he had a distinct influence in popularising the game on the Continent.'

Watson himself attributed much of his success as a manager to recruitment. In an article he wrote in 1899, entitled 'Hunting for Men', and published in the *Leicester Chronicle*, he gives yet more amusing accounts of his exploits north of the border in pursuit of footballing talent. Interestingly, Tom claimed in the piece to have no preference for Scottish players, pointing out that half his Liverpool team had their roots in England. He simply believed they were the best to be found 'at the time', by which he was referring to his time in the North East. However, Scotland remained a place he frequently went to in search of players. Of the two players Watson brought in after his arrival, during the 1896/97 season, both were Scottish, although Alex Latta (from Dumbarton) was signed from Everton. The other was Andrew McCowie, brought in from Cambuslang Hibs.

As we know, when tracking a player, Tom often employed cunning and subterfuge to outwit the secretaries of the clubs whose players he was 'stealing'. Success, he suggested, hinged on several factors: his friends and allies in Scotland, the owners of Liverpool, who were committed to financing the best football team in the land, and the club chaplain. The latter would be necessary to convince the parents of his targets that Liverpool FC had their sons' moral and spiritual wellbeing at heart. However, they weren't always successful in their pursuits, as his account here suggests:

> Sometimes our experiences were less edifying. The 'chaplain' on one occasion had need of all his prayers for his own safety. It was in Glasgow, and we three had made our headquarters at a hotel there while hunting for a celebrated player. Our presence became known to his club, and a plot was laid to entrap us.
>
> The club secretary himself called at the hotel, pretending he was the player whom we wanted. He was rather shy of coming to close quarters; so we made an appointment to meet him the same night at a house in Govan-hill and settle terms. I thought it cruel hard lines that at the last moment I had a raging attack of toothache. It was a blessing in disguise. I escaped the unpleasant adventure of my two colleagues, who went without me.
>
> They were attacked in a low part of Glasgow by a mob of footballers, vowing vengeance on the 'poachers'; ancient eggs flew right and left, likewise bags of yellow ochre, and more dangerous missiles still, and at last, they had to take refuge in a friendly doorway and knock for admission to the house. Here they passed an anxious time until the arrival of

> the police, who had been drawn to the spot by the row; half a sovereign rewarded their kindly host, and then, escorted by a large body of Glasgow police, they arrived back at the hotel, not without a parting salute of eggs and ochre from the disappointed mob.
>
> The 'chaplain', I must say, bore a very unclerical appearance. It was rumoured afterwards, at home, that I was the 'chaplain' having disguised myself with his clothes; but, as I have said, I was saved – saved by the toothache, probably the only instance on record in which the toothache ever did anybody any good. I would go through it again under the same circumstances.

The encounter with an angry mob in Glasgow seems to have altered Watson's tactics, and they became even more devious as a result. He continues:

> After that, when in Glasgow, we adopted different tactics. Each of us stayed at a different hotel. The trick was simple enough, but it never failed to work at night. I would then call, in a cab, on my colleagues, pretend to take each of them up in turn, and drive off, followed by a crowd of angry Scots vowing vengeance on the English thieves who were stealing all their best players. When the enemy were out of sight the other two gentlemen set about business unmolested. I engaged the attention of the crowd till it was time to return and 'CAPITAL BAGS, OLD MAN,' was the news that saluted me when I went to inquire next morning how the ruse had worked.

Tom was an engaging man, witty and urbane. He was also quite the storyteller, and among the many articles he wrote are amusing anecdotes of his life and times in the game. This one, from the *Football Gazette (South Shields)*, dated 29 September 1906, reveals something of his eye for a joke and smart wit:

> I have often had a good laugh over a visit to London to see an Army Cup Final, attended, of course, chiefly by military men. As it so happened Mr J. J. Bentley was present at the match, and he and I were fortunate enough to be searching after two different players. We sat next [to] two non-com officers, and during the match an incident occurred on which I made a passing remark to Mr Bentley. '! ! ! ----- fool,' said the army man, 'What do you know about football?' I meekly replied 'Nothing: it's my first match.' My soldier neighbour muttered 'Thought so, you ------ fool.' These kind expressions did not quite meet with my approval, and I told him so. Then Mr Bentley came in for a rub, and he, too, informed the soldier that though it was his first match he had paid his money and had a right to express an opinion on the game.
>
> Peace reigned supreme till [*sic*] half-time, when we went to the bar to lubricate our voice tubes. For the joke of the thing we invited the two soldiers to join us in drink, and on the way to the refreshment the abusive officer cooly consoled us by saying that he was sorry 'and all that,' but he could see we had never been to a match before. We told him not to bother because we didn't mind.
>
> As we entered the bar – at great difficulty because it was well filled – we were met by several well known football officials, and were accosted this wise: 'Hello Johnnie Bentley. Hello Tom Watson, what are you doing here?' The soldiers we had invited to gargle with us saw the blunder they had made, and in a trice – after the drink – slunk away.

When he wrote this article, Tom was 47 years of age and already an elder statesman of the game. His views, anecdotes and musings seem to have been sought out by many in the game and also those in the various journals and newspapers who covered it. By 1906, the date of the above piece, he had won league titles with two different clubs – five in total, and clearly had many tales to tell.

At Tom's side at Anfield between 1898 and 1903 was the trainer James Chapman, who was part of Watson's backroom staff when Tom led Liverpool to their first league title. Born in 1855, Chapman was from Uphall, West Lothian. He had achieved league and cup success at Heart of Midlothian FC, and no doubt was well known to Watson. Often pictured in team photos wearing a suit and a bowler hat and sporting a fine moustache, Chapman came with a considerable reputation, as this article in *Athletic News*, dated 17 November 1902, spells out:

> Amongst the numerous official positions which the League system has brought into being and importance is that of trainer to our leading organisations. Success on the field can easily be achieved by players who are physically fit, hence the responsibility attaching to the man whose duty it is to prepare the team for all engagement. Of those at present thus employed throughout the country, few can boast a record equal to that of James Chapman, of Broxburn, as he is more familiarly known, who for the past four years has acted as trainer to Liverpool.
>
> His career, from boyhood, has been connected with athletics, and in his time he has performed valiant deeds on the running-track. In early youth, he displayed a fondness for running and hurdling, and played a prominent part in the highland games and other festivals in the Edinburgh district. Before reaching 17, he won the Half-Mile Flat Race at

> Broxburn, as a professional, which was but a prelude to some striking successes gained during the following eleven years.

Chapman first became involved with football in 1885, at Cowdenbeath. His next club was Broxburn Thistle, before he left to join Dunbarton in 1887. He spent eight successful years there. He joined Hearts of Edinburgh in 1896. *Athletic News* had the following to say of his achievements there:

> For three years he continued the work of developing the prowess of would-be champions on the running track and the famous Edinburgh club won the League Championship twice during this period, the Scottish Cup, Rosebery Charity Cup twice, and the East of Scotland Championship – not a bad three years' work.

He was known to eschew smoking, and boasted that he only occasionally sampled wine. His ideas on the subject would therefore have been in sync with his new manager at Liverpool, Tom Watson. It was said that players looked up to Chapman, himself the image of physical fitness and highly respected for the results he achieved in terms of preparing them for games.

Looking back on his career, legendary Liverpool captain Alex Raisbeck relayed a charming story about Chapman that gives us something of an insight into his personality, and perhaps how he was viewed by his players. The article is principally about the various stunts and practical jokes his team-mate Johnny Walker got up to. Raisbeck explains:

> While I am on this subject of practical jokes and of Johnnie [*sic*] Walker in particular, I must tell you another incident which took place at the same hotel and which was

responsible for upsetting the equilibrium of our genial trainer Jimmy Chapman. I met Johnnie out on the sands one day picking up small pebbles. I didn't think he was anything of a geologist, so I wanted to know what he was doing, but he put me off and refused to tell me. That night, however, he let me into the secret. And when we all went upstairs that evening none of us could get into our bedrooms. Johnnie was not among us – and I only knew the reason why – but as his door appeared to be locked too nobody thought anything about the matter at first.

Well, I can assure you a fearful rumpus arose in that hotel that night. None of the bedroom doors would open and sixteen angry men stood on the landing threatening all sorts of vengeance on the 'idiots' and 'fools' who had locked them out. Nothing on earth was apparently able to move these doors. The row was tremendous and the proprietor of the hotel appeared on the scene anxious to know what all the racket was about. But the most comical figure of the lot was Jimmy Chapman.

By the time we had been standing on the landing for over half an hour and Jimmy's wrath was rising with every passing moment. He was a strict disciplinarian and was putting us through a rigid training, so that the fact that we were being kept out of bed all this time was very irritating to him. Jimmy was a very decent, dour, good-living man, but I rather think he recalled all the profanities of his boyhood days as he breathed out threatenings and slaughter on the 'blithering asses' who had 'done' his players in this way. I, who was in the secret, was beginning to feel uncomfortable, for the joke had just gone far enough, yet Johnnie, lying in his bed behind the only door that was really locked, chuckled silently, but never said a cheep!

Walker had jammed all the doors but his own with tiny pebbles. It would soon become apparent who the culprit was, and we're not treated with the information on Walker's comeuppance, but we can bet it was severe.

A reported move by Chapman back to Hearts in 1899 appears not to have come off. As reported in *Athletic News* in 1902, he had seen Liverpool claim the league title in 1901 and was looking forward to achieving more at the club.

In March of 1899, an article appeared in the *Evening Express*, which shed some light on how the team prepared for an FA Cup Final, and Chapman's training methods. The newspaper spent time with the club and its players at their training base in St Anne's-on-the-Sea, on the west Lancashire coast. Tom Watson was apparently taking care of some neglected 'clerical work', yet still found time to regale the *Express*'s reporter with details of the players' training regime:

> They rise at eight, and partake of breakfast an hour later. At half-past ten they all take a quick walking exercise, and baths are ordered by the Trainer James Chapman according to the physical condition of each man. Dinner is served at one o'clock, and at half-past three the only severe training of the day takes place in the shape of sprinting exercise in a field belonging to the St. Anne's Cricket Club. The party sit down to tea at half-past five, and the evening is ordinarily spent in quiet walks, billiards, cards, and other harmless amusements.

Interestingly, the players were forbidden from training with a football during the camp. The players for their part appeared to be in fine shape. This is how the article described their condition:

> They are bronzed almost like African travellers, and have all benefitted palpably by their stay at St. Anne's. They sprinted like greyhounds round the cricket field, and several of the men have appreciably increased their pace. At the same time no attempts has been made to render the training too severe. The players have rather been held in check in this respect, and the consequence is that any symptom of staleness is altogether absent.

Chapman went on to work for Leeds United in 1908. He had been widowed after the death of his wife, Mary, and by 1911 – the year of his death – he was living at Parkfield Mount, Beeston, Leeds. In addition to his son – who was also a footballer – James Chapman was also survived by his daughters Barbara and Margaret. His death was recorded in the *Evening Telegraph*, 14 August 1911, with the following words:

> Followers of Association football throughout the country will learn with regret the death of James Chapman, trainer of the Leeds City team. Chapman was at the ground only a week ago, when he took suddenly ill. He consulted a specialist, who ordered his removal to Leeds General Infirmary, where he died from an internal complaint early yesterday morning. As a trainer Chapman was very successful with Scottish international teams, Dumbarton, Heart of Midlothian, and Liverpool clubs. He was fifty-six years of age and a widower. His son George Chapman plays at centre half for Glasgow Rangers.

Joining Watson's backroom team after Chapman had moved on, in 1903, was William 'Billy' Connell. He would spend 25 years at Anfield and was a key figure in the famous 'Untouchables' team who clinched back-to-back league titles in 1922 and 1923, along with Wilson. His loyalty and contribution to the club's success would be rewarded in 1924 with a testimonial game played against Rangers, which Liverpool lost 2-0.

Born William Downing Connell, in Heaton Norris, Stockport, on 8 May 1863, he was the son of a blacksmith, John Connell, and Martha. His siblings were Herbert, Allat and Bertha. At the age of 20, he married Miranda Chandley on 18 May 1883, in St Peters Church, Levenshulme. The couple lived at two addresses, numbers 10 and 70 Lloyd Street in Heaton Norris, Stockport, between 1883 and 1903. Billy's occupation is recorded in census documents during this period as 'Hatter' and 'Felt Hat Blacker'.

However, Connell had developed a passion for football and alongside his day job had taken up the role of trainer at Stockport County, working alongside Charlie Wilson. The two men were good friends and Wilson would recommend Billy to Liverpool. He joined the Anfield outfit in 1903 and quickly developed a considerable reputation in the game.

He and Miranda lived at 27 Clapham Road, Anfield, where they raised their four children, and at this point the 1911 census records Billy's occupation as a 'Trainer of Professional Footballers'. Now earning a living from the game, his stock was such that several commercial brands sought his endorsement. In 1904, he was featured in a newspaper advert for a product called 'Zam Buk', an ointment for cuts and bruises, and later, in 1914, an advert for 'Bovril', a beef-flavoured drink, which appeared before the club's appearance in the FA Cup Final, and carried a quote from Connell: 'During the training of the team for the "English Cup" competition, they have consistently taken "Bovril," which they have found gives them great staying powers. W Connell, Trainer.'

His continued contribution after being replaced by Charlie Wilson was recognised in the *Liverpool Echo*, which, after the club had retained the title for the first time in 1923, wrote: 'Liverpool's fine consistency both this year and last pays silent tribute to their silent trainer.'

Furthermore, a letter to the *Echo*, penned in 1925 by a local referee in the amateur Zingari League, a Mr Charles Taylor, joined in a chorus of praise for Connell, who he claimed was 'an expert in manipulating tired muscles'.

Connell was also credited with a major role at Anfield during the First World War, where he helped steer the club through the loss of Tom, after his death in 1915, and while navigating the uncertainties and challenges of wartime football. His death in 1940, after the outbreak of the Second World War, was recorded in the *Evening Express* on 23 January, with the following somewhat perfunctory words:

> The death took place early today of Mr. William Connell, of Clapham-road, Anfield, Liverpool. Mr. Connell was for 40 years chief trainer to Liverpool Football Club, which he joined from Stockport.
>
> He retired about ten years ago, being succeeded by Mr. Charlie Wilson. He leaves two sons and a daughter, all of whom are married.

His funeral, three days later, appears to have attracted many prominent figures in the game. The *Evening Express* was again on the case:

> Prominent footballers past and present attended the funeral in Liverpool today, of Mr. William 'Billy' Connell, the former Liverpool F.C. trainer.
>
> Liverpool Football Club was represented by Mr. William Harvey Webb, director, and Mr. George Patterson, secretary;

> Everton F.C. by Mr. Ernest Green (Chairman) and Mr. Theo Kelly (secretary).
>
> Others who paid their respects were Messrs. Jack Parkinson, Charlie Wilson, Walter Wadsworth, Donald Mackinlay, Ephraim Longworth and William Cockburn.

Upon his arrival at Anfield in 1896, Tom Watson would set about rebuilding the Anfield playing staff, equipping his new club with the steel, skill and cunning necessary to not just reach the top flight, but to stay there. He was aided and abetted by a loyal board who appear to have given him both the funds and latitude to carry out his work. He had more than earned that respect. However, he could also draw upon the services of some of the finest backroom staff in the game in James Chapman and Billy Connell.

## Chapter Nine

# Tom takes charge and the crowds flock to Anfield

THERE WAS huge excitement around Anfield in July 1896 as Tom Watson swept into the club. With the club newly promoted, and looking forward to another season in the First Division, the arrival of such an important and successful figure would no doubt have set hearts racing and tongues wagging. It seems football was continuing to grow in popularity and average home attendances would grow to 12,400 for the season, almost double those of the previous campaign.

Such was the surge in crowds that in November the landlord of local pub the Albert Hotel (now known as simply The Albert) located in front of the Spion Kop, a Mr Lewes, applied to the licensing bench to install a window from which his establishment would serve half-time beers to spectators, who would rush out of the Kop for a drink. Supporting the application, a Superintendent Tomlinson told the chairman that he felt the addition of the window and alterations to the hotel, namely blocking a staircase, would alleviate what he described as the 'bedlam' he had witnessed there during the season. The application, reported in the *Liverpool Mercury*, was, of course, granted.

Work in Liverpool, particularly on the docks and in factories, was precarious, tough and often dangerous. Football would have provided an important outlet for the working class. However, the two-day weekend was some years away, and many would leave their employment in the afternoon on a Saturday and head straight to the ground, travelling by horse-drawn tram or on foot. Some would take the train.

Meanwhile, the Anfield directors had wasted no time in making preparations for the new season, and several players had been brought in and others moved on before the new boss arrived. Alex Latta arrived in September from Everton, and Andrew McCowie joined him in October from Cambuslang Hibs, though it's not known whether those deals had already been lined up by the club.

Tom's first game in charge of Liverpool, however, was an away fixture against the current FA Cup champions, The Wednesday, at the Olive Grove, on 1 September 1896. A crowd of between 2,000 and 3,000 turned out to see the game, with several travelling from Liverpool. According to the *Liverpool Mercury*, an even bigger crowd went to Liverpool's Central Station to wish the team well as they prepared for their 'invasion of smoky Sheffield'.

Watson's first-ever line up was as follows: Harry Storer, Archi Goldie, Tom Wilkie, John McCartney, Joe McQue, Tom Cleghorn, Malcolm McVean, Jimmy Ross, George Allen, Frank Becton and Harry Bradshaw.

This was also Liverpool FC's first game wearing red shirts and white shorts, according to the *Liverpool Daily Post*. Their opponents were wearing blue-and-white-striped tops with black shorts. The game kicked off in heavy rain, which no doubt impacted upon the attendance. Only 1,000 people stood on the terraces as the game got underway, with more drifting in during the match. The weather also meant that the game was played in dim light, but this would have been something the players of the day were accustomed to. The game was end to end, with reporters describing Liverpool's forwards as 'resplendent in their sodden red shirts' and the home crowd chanting, 'Play up Wednesday'.

Liverpool took the lead through George Allen with a 'clever header' on 13 minutes, but the home side hit back just five minutes later through Harry Davis, with the crowd now reported to have swelled to 3,000. With half-time imminent, Allen struck a 'regular daisy-cutter' straight into the net to put Liverpool ahead at the interval. With conditions deteriorating significantly in the second half and the light 'exceedingly bad', Liverpool hung on for victory.

The press appeared impressed with their display, with the *Liverpool Mercury* remarking that, should they maintain their form, they may well bring the championship to the 'village of the Mersey'.

After a promising start to the season, Watson's men slumped to consecutive defeats to Blackburn and Bolton. They recovered to beat Derby County and Bury before drawing 0-0 with West Bromwich Albion at Anfield to remain in second spot. Next up was a game against sixth-placed Everton at Goodison Park on 3 October 1896. It would be Tom's first experience of the Merseyside derby.

With Everton sporting light-blue shirts and white shorts, this would be the first derby that could be referred to as Reds versus Blues, as 45,000 people packed into Goodison. With excitement at fever pitch, gate receipts approached a record £1,150. The local papers reported on streets swarming with spectators as the game approached, with thoroughfares blocked and turnstiles struggling to cope with the influx.

The atmosphere within the stadium was unprecedented as both sets of supporters raised the roof in support of their respective teams. Such scenes modern supporters would easily identify with, but to the watching world of football journalism this was completely unique, and they marvelled at the spectacle of hundreds of supporters locked out as the stands reached capacity. Inside, supporters greeted their teams with a roar, described as 'simply deafening', as they entered the field of play at 4pm, before falling into silent concentration as battle commenced. It was all enthralling stuff for the reporters in attendance.

Match reports refer to the teams as Evertonians and Liverpudlians, and there is again reference to Liverpool as 'the Reds'. The opening exchanges were frenetic. Everton raced into a two-goal lead through Alfred Milward and Abe Hartley in the 11th and 13th minutes respectively. Watson's men, stunned into life, took the game to Everton and almost halved the deficit but for a fine save by Henry Briggs. Tackles were flying in now, and numerous free kicks were conceded by both teams as the Reds fought to get back into the game. Allen hit the bar and another chance went begging, before Liverpool went into the changing rooms two goals down at the break.

With Watson's words ringing in their ears, Liverpool roared into the second half, halving the arrears six minutes later. In the stands, the crowd surged and swayed as McCartney squared the ball to Bradshaw, who immediately sent Jimmy Ross racing in on goal. His shot struck the outstretched arm of Briggs and flew into the net. Liverpool's 'partisans' erupted in celebration – it was game on.

Both sides exchanged blows and, for Liverpool, Goldie saw his shot hit the bar. It wasn't to be, and it turned out that the Reds had given themselves too much to do by half-time. A highly creditable second-half display meant that supporters of Watson's men could go home with a degree of consolation. However, the arguments and banter in workplaces and schools would continue for weeks.

Next up was a home match against Nottingham Forest, which Liverpool won comfortably. Two goals from McVean and a late 88th-minute strike by Bradshaw sealed the victory. Now all eyes would be on Tom Watson's return to the North East, and his first game against former club Sunderland, at Newcastle Road. It was a thriller, but Liverpool once again gave themselves a mountain to climb, before mounting a second-half fightback that fell just short.

The Wearsiders were well motivated for the game, and their players keen to put on a display for their old boss. A crowd of 7,000 watched as Jimmy Hannah put Sunderland in front after just two minutes, before Andrew Hamilton made it 2-0 on the quarter-hour mark. On the stroke of half-time, Hannah popped up again, and Liverpool went into the interval three goals down.

In the 72nd minute, Archie Goldie grabbed his debut goal, and hope flickered for Watson's charges. It was quickly extinguished, though, when Hamilton made it 4-1 just four minutes later. However, Liverpool were far from finished. Fine pressing led to an own goal by Sunderland's Donald Gow. With five minutes still remaining, the score was now 4-2. The home crowd grew nervous, and Liverpool pushed hard, earning their reward two minutes from time when George Allen made the scoreline a more respectable 4-3 to the home side. It was all too late, though, and Liverpool slumped to another defeat,

They won two of their next three games and drew the other, before getting their chance at vengeance when Sunderland arrived at Anfield on 7 November 1896, as 10,000 people turned out to watch a fine display by the Reds, hampered by torrential rain and, in the second half, thick fog.

Two goals by David Hannah – who had replaced Bradshaw – either side of the interval and one from McVean in the 55th minute gave Liverpool a three-goal lead before heavy fog descended on the pitch in the final 15 minutes. Facing certain defeat, Sunderland's officials attempted to get the game abandoned. However, after consulting his linesmen, the referee, a Mr J. West, opted to see the game out.

Liverpool had now gone top of the league, although the position was somewhat artificial given that second-placed Preston North End – just one point behind – had played three games fewer. Watson's men remained in and around the top spots in the table throughout the Christmas fixtures and well into the New Year, fluctuating between second and third.

They were also ensconced in a fine run in the FA Cup, reaching the semi-final against Aston Villa on 20 March 1897, at Bramall Lane. Their 3-0 defeat in that game appears to have hit them hard and they struggled to recover. Liverpool lost the following home match against Burnley at Anfield 2-1, and drew the remaining two games of the season, also at Anfield. They had dropped to fifth place in the league. Villa went on to be league and FA Cup winners, beating Everton 3-2 at Crystal Palace in the cup final.

Nevertheless, his first season in charge gave Tom much food for thought. He carried out sweeping changes, saying farewell to top scorer George Allen, at least for a short spell. The striker joined Celtic for £50 before returning to Liverpool at the start of the 1888 season, for the same fee. Malcolm McVean and Frank Becton did depart permanently, though, and Tom brought in no fewer than 13 new players between 1897 and 1898, including arguably one of the club's greatest, and a future captain, Alex Raisbeck. The Watson revolution was now well underway at Anfield.

## Chapter Ten

# Rise of the Reds and Tom goes close, but no cigar ... yet

THE YEAR of 1897 was a diamond jubilee in Britain, with the monarch, Victoria, beginning her 50th year on the throne. This was also the year when readers were first introduced to such supernatural delights as Bram Stoker's *Dracula*, and H. G. Wells's *The Invisible Man*, Marconi sent the first wireless communication and, in football, Aston Villa moved to the newly built Villa Park. Meanwhile, at Anfield, ground improvements would ensure 20,000 covered spaces for supporters.

However, for Liverpool this was set to be a season marked by inconsistency and a forward line that failed to make a significant impact. The Reds' highest scorer would be Becton with 11 goals, and the nearest to him was McCowie with six. The problem was clear – Watson's attack was just too blunt. With so much churn in the squad, players coming and going, it's unsurprising that Tom struggled to identify the right blend. They ended the season in ninth place, in a 16-team league, and exited the FA Cup in the third round. The eventual champions were Sheffield United, with Watson's former club Sunderland finishing runners-up. Everton ended their campaign in fourth place, and the FA Cup winners were Nottingham Forest, who beat Derby County 3-1 in the final.

Despite the early growing pains, there's evidence that Tom had established himself as a fan favourite on Merseyside. Aside from the steadily growing home attendances, up to an average of just over 13,000 for the season, supporters went to extraordinary lengths to get into games, sometimes claiming to be associated with Tom or having a delivery for him.

In a retrospective review of the old days, published in the *Liverpool Echo* in 1934, the author recalls a supporter with the probably fictional name of Bob Caruthers, dressed in a grey macintosh and sporting a flat cap, who never missed a game home or away back in the Watson era. On one occasion the poor guy was turned away at the turnstile, which had reached maximum capacity. Not to be deterred, after attempting to enter via several other gates, he eventually gained access via another entrance to the ground by carrying a sack and claiming to have a delivery of 'coal for Mr Watson'.

Tom's popularity stemmed as much from matters off the pitch as those on it. He was acknowledged as working hard to develop junior football in the city. He was described by scribes of the time as 'personally very popular', and his determination to create a pool of local talent and thereby reduce the club's dependence on Scottish footballers drew admiration from the local community, with many young kids offered a route into the game. Such was the esteem in which he was held that a campaign begun to award him a testimonial gathered so much momentum that it made the newspapers in 1902 – just six years after he joined the club.

The faith placed in him by supporters and directors alike would eventually be amply rewarded, of course, and in the 1898/99 season Watson took the Reds agonisingly close to the promised land. In a season that went down to a heartbreaking final day, newcomers such as Alex Raisbeck, Bill Goldie, Tommy Robertson, Jack Cox and Charlie Wilson made a huge impact.

Watson had now brought in 18 players between 1897 and 1898, and the excitement levels at Anfield had reached new heights. A season preview in the *Lancashire Evening Post*, published on 27 August 1898, illustrates the point nicely:

> Liverpudlians are awaiting the forthcoming season with eagerness and confidence, and unless Tom Watson is a false prophet Liverpool will achieve fame and honour before many moons have passed. No expense, no effort, has been spared in the attempt to get a first-class team together; and Mr. Watson has every reason to feel proud of his handiwork.

The Reds roared into the season, with a 4-0 thrashing of The Wednesday at Anfield. A huge crowd for the period of 18,000 packed into the ground for the campaign opener. No doubt supporters were eager to catch a glimpse of the new stars, and they were treated to the debut run outs of Raisbeck and Goldie, the latter grabbing the opener in his first outing as a Liverpool player. Hugh Morgan and two goals from Robertson, who had made his debut the season before, completed the rout.

Tom had reduced the age of the Liverpool team to around 24 years of age. The new arrivals introduced flair and energy, while losing none of the Reds' famed steely approach. More importantly, Watson had bonded them together as a real team. As Raisbeck would later say, perhaps too modestly, as individuals they were average talents, but their strength lay in their commitment to each other.

No doubt the highlights of the season were Liverpool's two wins over their neighbours Everton. The rivalry between Reds and Blues had grown to new heights. With both teams in England's top division, games now had added spice, and attendances were huge by the standards of the period. In all, a combined 75,000 people watched the games at Goodison and Anfield, with 45,000 attending the game at Goodison and 30,000 at the smaller Anfield.

In glorious sunshine and cloudless skies, Liverpool travelled across Stanley Park on 24 September 1898, and were greeted by a record attendance and a fierce atmosphere. In order to cope with the deluge of supporters, Everton opened their gates at 2pm for a 4pm kick-off, and the *Liverpool Mercury* reported that the ground was approaching capacity a full hour before the commencement of hostilities. Gate receipts reached £1,250. The *Liverpool Mercury* beautifully captures the nature of the rivalry in 1898:

> Meetings between Everton and Liverpool, whatever the occasion may be always productive of more than ordinary interest, but when the respective forces are opposed to each other in the League tournament the local feeling is focused to fever height for then it is a stern case of Greek meeting Greek. For weeks prior to the all eventful day arguments pros and cons are indulged forth by the respective partisans of the two clubs, and thus the interest increasing until the actual meeting which brings trump to the one side and comparative despondency to the other.

Interestingly, despite Everton being the more experienced outfit and the more successful club, Liverpool started the game as favourites in the opinion of many, largely due to the influx of new talent. To this point, Liverpool had never even mustered a draw at Goodison, and had only secured a win on home soil once.

For this game, both sides were without key men. Liverpool had lost George Allen to injury, while Everton's prolific inside-left, Edgar Chadwick, was also sidelined. Musicians entertained the throng of supporters as they waited for the teams to enter the fray, and a huge roar rose, as Everton, dressed in 'deepest blue' shirts, were described as looking tiny when contrasted with the giant crowd in attendance. No sooner had those cheers died down than Liverpool entered, 'robed in red', and the noise erupted again. One local scribe penned the following words: 'The contrast was magnificently picturesque, and no finer sight on a football field could be imagined than the few seconds prior to the signal for starting.'

Goalkeeper Harry Storer captained the Reds and won the toss. With the early exchanges favouring Everton, Liverpool's defenders struggled to keep the Blues at bay. A powerful shot from Ellis Gee was palmed wide by Storer, only for John Proudfoot to score with his head from the resultant corner.

Everton, through Gee and Jack Kirwan, went close to adding to their tally. Eventually, though, Liverpool grew into the game and Walker initiated a movement towards the home goal, and home keeper Willie Muir was kept busy. The Reds won a corner on 25 minutes. Robertson sent in a delightful ball, and an unmarked McCowie chested the ball into the net. The Blues protested fiercely, claiming the ball had gone out of play instead of entering the goal, but their appeals were waved away by referee J. Lewis.

The teams went into the changing rooms level at half-time, as the band struck up a song entitled 'Will Ye No Come Back Again'. The second period saw the game settle into a cautious and tense affair, before Everton goalscorer Proudfoot had to leave the field injured. He eventually returned but it was clear he was struggling and the Blues were effectively playing with ten men. To make matters worse, they soon were, when Gee left the pitch with a 'strain', which meant the Blues were effectively down to nine.

This was a derby, though, and with so much at stake in terms of local pride, Everton were not about to give up. They took the fight to the visitors, forcing Storer into a fine save, after a 'magnificent shot from Kirwan'. Then, in the 75th minute, Everton's William Balmer conceded a penalty, fouling Liverpool's Tommy Robertson. McCowie stepped up and placed the ball neatly past Muir. The goal won the game and undoubtedly ensured misery for Evertonians as they eventually traipsed back into work. They would no doubt argue, as did the local press, that a draw would have been a fairer result. However, not then and never since has anything but the result in a Merseyside derby ever mattered to the two rivals.

Liverpool failed to win their next four games, drawing one and losing three, including a costly 3-0 reverse against Aston Villa. They had slumped from third to 12th in the league. They would recover to a large extent and, by the time January 1899 arrived, they had navigated a run of 12 games, winning seven, drawing two and losing three. They were now in fourth place.

Everton arrived at a wintry Anfield on 21 January. The Blues were in second spot, with Liverpool hot on their heels in third. Two points separated the teams, with the Reds boasting a superior goal average. A win for the home side would see them leapfrog their neighbours.

Again, a bumper crowd was in attendance, with every vantage spot filled long before kick-off. The battered pitch was in poor condition, described as a 'mud heap', and freezing rain beat down incessantly in the run-up to kick-off. Miraculously, the clouds gave way to the sun just in time for the start of the match. Most felt the condition of the pitch would favour Liverpool. Despite that, Everton, perhaps stirred on by a burning sense of injustice still smouldering from their defeat at Goodison, again took the game to Liverpool, creating many chances. For their part, Liverpool failed to take advantage of the chances that came their way in the opening exchanges. Robertson missed an easy chance, and the Reds seemed to grow into the game. In the 12th minute, Liverpool's Johnny Walker broke the Blues' resistance to open the scoring and send most of Anfield wild with delirium. It remained 1-0 at the interval.

Winter sunshine greeted the players as they entered the pitch for the second half and, with Everton playing with the sun in their eyes, Liverpool looked to drive home their advantage. The game ebbed and flowed, with the Reds having the better of it. Still, Everton had their chances too, but the Liverpool defenders stood resolute. Then, in the 89th minute, Robertson ended all hopes of an Everton revival. This is how the *Liverpool Mercury* described the goal: 'A minute from time [Jack] Cox dribbled past Hughes and Molyneux, to a short distance from goal, when he sent the ball across, and Robertson put it past Muir. This was the last point scored, and Liverpool, who had played better football won by 2 goals to nil.'

The press were in agreement on this occasion that Liverpool were worthy winners. They had outfought and outfoxed Everton, and in the process they had climbed above them into second place after completing what was at the time a historic double over their nearest rivals. Despite the rivalry, reports suggested that both matches were played fairly, without the usual rough tackles. Liverpool supporters would have no doubt enjoyed their 'bragging rights' for the rest of the season. Well they might. Their team would not enjoy another victory over Everton at Anfield until 1919.

A run of 11 victories, one draw and two defeats saw Liverpool top of the table going into the last game of the season against second-placed Aston Villa. Both teams were level on 43 points. Liverpool had to win. Lose or draw, and Watson's men would hand the title to the Midlanders. Villa, having scored 94 goals to Liverpool's 69, had a vastly superior goal average.

The omens were not good going into the game, and Villa held a psychological advantage over the Reds. They had won the game at Anfield comfortably. Nonetheless, the *Liverpool Mercury* reported that many supporters made the journey from Liverpool to Birmingham and the attendance at Villa Park was a huge 41,357.

The game was reported to have the feel of a cup final rather than a league encounter. Both teams entered the field to tumultuous applause, with Villa coming out first. Imagine those hopeful Scousers taking up their places in the ground, hopelessly outnumbered, bellies full of ale and trying their damnedest to shout the lads to glory over a cacophonous Villa din.

However, their hopes were cruelly dashed. While it's possibly the case that the occasion got the better of the Liverpool men, Villa were in imperious form. They were out of sight by half-time. The local press was damning, stating that 'the Anfielders lost heart and were outplayed'. Two goals from Jack Davey in the first 20 minutes set Villa on their way. Then Billy Garraty and Jimmy Crabtree grabbed a goal apiece in the space of a minute, before Fred Wheldon sealed the five-goal rout in the 44th minute. Liverpool mounted a fightback in the second half, but it was a case of too little, too late. All that was left was for that merry band of Liverpudlian supporters on their 19th-century away day to make their way home to Merseyside, heartbroken.

They returned to unwelcome and damning headlines in the *Liverpool Echo*, words that, though cruel, captured perfectly the scale of their disappointment:

FIGHT FOR THE LEAGUE CHAMPIONSHIP
AGONY FOR LIVERPOOL
ASTON VILLA MAKE NO MISTAKE
ROUT OF THE LIVERPOOL MEN

Imagine the misery of those red pioneers as they passed those words, emblazoned on billboards at Central Station, before making their way home. They would face another season of disappointment, as the 1899/1900 campaign ended with Villa as champions once more, and Liverpool slumped to tenth place, exiting the FA Cup in the second round.

Watson's struggles to find a title-winning blend would soon end, though. A further six players, including the veteran and future manager Matt McQueen, would leave the club. And two signings would set pulses racing and create havoc in opposition defences, as Tom's Liverpool stormed the gates of the promised land in 1901. Those men were the potent strikeforce of Sam Raybould and Charlie Satterthwaite, signed either side of Christmas 1900. With the Reds flirting with relegation in December, it was their goals – Raybould with seven and Satterthwaite with six – that helped Liverpool climb to tenth place in the table. There was no doubting their contribution, and the press agreed they had made the difference, with more than just goals: 'Since the inclusion of Raybould and Satterthwaite in the team, matters have gone ahead with a smoothness which had almost become foreign to the play witnessed before their arrival, and the utility of a decent centre has never been more forcibly exemplified than in the case of the Anfield eleven this season.'

The stage was now set for a historic title charge, and Tom was about to become the first manager in football history to win First Division titles with two clubs. The Liverpool directors would receive a hefty return on their £300 investment, as Watson's men turned the town red.

## Chapter Eleven

# 'Owd Tom' and his Reds reach the promised land

UNDER THE headline 'Liverpool At Last!', the *Daily Telegraph* on 29 April 1901 declared Tom Watson's men champions for the first time in their history. In doing so, they singled out one man as key to the team's ultimate triumph, Alex Raisbeck. This is how the paper saw the centre-back's contribution:

> With only 59 goals, Liverpool have nevertheless broken the First Division scoring dominance of Aston Villa, who finished well down the table with 45. But their real strength has been in defence, with Scottish international centre-half Alex Raisbeck outstanding in the middle.

Liverpool went into the campaign after disposing of a further six players, and bringing in four. These included, John 'Tom' Robertson, bought from Stoke for £400, and John Glover from Blackburn Rovers for £350. These were not insignificant fees for the time. Joining them at Anfield were Andy McGuigan from Hibernian and Maurice Parry from Brighton United. It's fair to say that the club struggled to demonstrate a return on their considerable investment, however.

Robertson featured 27 times for Liverpool in the championship-winning season before, much to the annoyance of Liverpool's directors, leaving for Southampton in 1902, despite appearing happy at Anfield and earning the maximum available wage. Liverpool's other big signing, John Glover, failed to make the breakthrough until the 1901/02 season, managing just ten games in their championship-winning campaign. His Anfield career would end in controversy when he was found to have accepted illegal payment to sign for Portsmouth. As a result, he, along with team-mates Bill Goldie and Sam Raybould, was banned from football until 31 December 1903. None of the men would ever be able to sign for Portsmouth. Glover turned down a maximum wage contract in January 1904, leaving for Small Heath.

Parry would go on to play 221 times for Liverpool, and, although he was a debutant in their victorious 1900/01 season, only managing eight appearances, he was still presented with a winners' medal on 27 August 1901. Happily, he would play a much greater role for the Reds in 1906. McGuigan, having started 14 games, also earned a title-winners' medal in his first season.

As the football world geared up for the first season of the 20th century, the *Liverpool Echo* featured a cartoon depicting an ebullient Tom Watson on a hunting trip. He's engaged in a witty exchange with another man, who appears to symbolise Liverpool's rivals that season. Holding up the results of his quarry – a bird he has shot – the man asks, 'Good morning Tom, what do you think of these?' Chugging away on a fat cigar, Tom replies, 'Good day to you. I'm doing about the same as yourself. Looks a promising season, don't you think?'

Perhaps for the first time since their inception, Liverpool appeared to see themselves as the equal of all rivals in the top division. The confidence engendered by the near miss of 1899 had not dissipated, despite the mid-table finish in 1900. Watson felt he had assembled a side capable of challenging at the top, and he had corrected the flaws that saw them fall short the season before.

The 1900/01 campaign got underway against the backdrop of the ongoing Boer War in South Africa, along with other overseas conflicts. Many Liverpool men were involved. At home, there were improvements in the lives of working families. A law had been introduced banning children from working in the mining industry, and the rise of trade unionism would see more improvements to come.

In football, West Bromwich Albion began the campaign at a new ground, moving to The Hawthorns on 3 September. Of course, this was a venue that would provide the backdrop to Liverpool glory in the final game of the season on 29 April 1901.

In a hard-fought league campaign, Liverpool began and ended in first place. However, they would spend none of the games in between in the top spot. They failed to beat Everton at two attempts, drawing the home fixture and losing the game at Goodison 2-1. They also exited the FA Cup in the first round.

The season started with a run of 11 matches that saw Liverpool lose three times, to Sunderland, Notts County and Wolves, winning seven and scoring 26 goals (more than anyone in the league). They had risen to third place in the table and were four points off the top with a game in hand. That run had included a creditable draw at Goodison Park, a 5-0 home demolition of West Brom and a 5-1 rout of Aston Villa. The latter would have given Tom great satisfaction. He had enjoyed a burgeoning rivalry with Aston Villa, and in particular their manager, George Ramsay.

The sunshine brought out 18,000 supporters, eager to see the contest. They were certainly given great value for money as Liverpool raced into a three-goal half-time lead. The Reds were in the lead after just five minutes through Sam Raybould, before Andy McGuigan (15) and Johnny Walker (25) gave Watson's men a comfortable lead at the interval.

Liverpool's second goal was a thing of beauty. Satterthwaite, with the wind at his back and the uproarious encouragement of the supporters in the stands, raced down the wing before delivering a delightful centre, which was met by Robertson, who headed the ball on to McGuigan, who in turn directed a bullet header past Billy George in the Villa goal.

Villa fought back, but were wasteful in front of goal. Liverpool's third came from a brilliant counter-attack. The visitors had wasted a corner, then Robertson raced away, curling in a cross to Walker, who barged his way through the defence, blasting the ball into the net.

Robertson was now having a fine game, and in the second half he again provided an assist, this time for Raybould, who netted Liverpool's fourth goal in the 63rd minute. For the supporters crammed into the stands, this was a treat, and the crowd lapped up the performance, along with the men in the press box. Two minutes later, Liverpool were 5-0 up. Villa conceded a free kick in a dangerous area, and Johnny Walker unleashed a terrific shot that sailed high into the goal, giving the keeper, George, no chance. Villa were soundly beaten, but there was still time for a consolation. Five minutes after going five goals down, they won a corner. The resultant scramble in the Liverpool penalty box saw George Johnson poke the ball past the Reds' keeper, Bill Perkins. It mattered little, though, and Watson would have left the ground full of satisfaction.

After the rout of Aston Villa, the *Liverpool Echo*'s resident cartoonist captured the mood of the Liverpool boss perfectly. It depicted an Evertonian as a thin stooped character in ill-fitting kit, attempting to congratulate a smiling Tom Watson, who's chugging on a huge cigar and appearing like a giant by comparison with his Blue companion. The caption reads:

LIVERPOOL'S WHOLESALE SLAUGHTER OF THE VILLANS.
Everton – Ok-er-may I congratulate you on-er-your-um-what shall I say –
Liverpool – Tut, dear chap! Don't mention it.

> Assure you it was a-er-very simple smash up – no exertion – dear me, no.

The Red juggernaut was hardly cruising but they were still in the fight. Then the wheels appeared to have come off altogether. The Reds' manager Tom Watson and his men will have been brimming with confidence as they embarked on the all-important winter schedule. However, a disappointing 3-2 defeat away to The Wednesday, in Sheffield, heralded a Liverpool slump. After they had taken the lead within three minutes, the home side raced into a 3-1 lead with 33 minutes on the clock. Liverpool pulled one back four minutes later, and, despite them huffing and puffing in search of a leveller, they couldn't find the breakthrough. The Sheffield side held out and sent the Reds home with nothing to show for their struggles. That defeat was the beginning of a miserable run of 13 games. The Reds lost six of them, drawing three and winning just four. One of those defeats was a chastening 2-1 reverse at home in the Merseyside derby.

The game took place in mid-January 1901, in terrible weather conditions. The *Liverpool Mercury* reported that the match was almost abandoned. However, it would eventually get underway at 2.45pm with huge pools of water collecting on the pitch, which by this stage was reportedly giving way underfoot.

The Blues took full advantage, lofting long balls into the Liverpool box, and by all accounts the Reds' back line was struggling to cope. Jack Taylor put Everton in front after 18 minutes and the home side were in trouble. Still, they somehow managed to rally and in the 37th minute Jack Cox levelled for Liverpool. It would remain that way until half-time.

The game was now being played in almost swamp-like conditions, and the result could have gone either way. The team that wanted it most would emerge victorious, and that, sadly, was Everton. In the

62nd minute, Taylor grabbed his and Everton's second and the points returned to Goodison. Liverpool had now been leapfrogged by the Blues and the sense of humiliation and disappointment in the Red half of the city would have been palpable.

Another defeat followed at home to Bolton, and Liverpool were now eighth in the league, nine points off the top and facing a grim trip north to second-placed Sunderland. Few would have relished the encounter, but it would prove to be something of a turning point.

There were just 12 games remaining. If Liverpool were to get anywhere near the league title – and few on Merseyside or anywhere else gave them a chance – they couldn't afford to lose another game. And they didn't. Their improbable 1-0 victory over Sunderland at Roker Park was like a slap in the face for the slumbering Red men. It seemed to wake them up and instil some fight back into this punch-drunk outfit. A tough trip to Preston North End followed, and they battled their way to a 2-2 draw, despite leading twice in the game. Despite giving up their advantage in the game on two occasions, the Reds seemed to have drawn strength from the result.

They arrived at Sheffield United on 22 April 1901, in fourth place. They had won 16 of their 31 games, drawing seven and losing eight. They were two points behind the leaders, Sunderland, with 39 points. They had played a game less, however. The leaders had been in a wasteful mood, dropping points in an earlier game against The Wednesday on 13 April. Liverpool had climbed the table by beating Manchester City 3-1. Crucially, though, Sunderland now only had one game left, and Notts County, who were in second place, had none.

Sunderland then went on a tour of five friendly matches before their final league game of the season, a local derby away to Newcastle United, on 24 April, which they won 2-0. The victory took them two points clear at the top of the table. However, Liverpool were now breathing down their necks, after earlier beating Sheffield United 2-0 in blustery conditions, and with two games still remaining.

The Reds' next game, against Nottingham Forest at Anfield on 27 April, was being billed by the press as a title decider. However, in truth, Liverpool still had work to do. They needed a win to draw level with Sunderland, of course. The Wearsiders had a vastly superior goal average, which meant the Reds would need to also win their final game of the season at The Hawthorns to be guaranteed the title.

In the run-up to the game with Forest, there were fears that the scheduling of the FA Cup Final replay on the same day, at Burnden Park, Bolton, would lead to a 'boycott' of Anfield. Spurs and Sheffield United had fought out a 2-2 draw at the first attempt before a record crowd of 110,000 at Crystal Palace. The Londoners would go on to win the replay, and their first Association Cup, in front of a vastly reduced crowd of just 20,470.

Suggestions that many Merseysiders would flock to Bolton to see the cup final replay proved unfounded, and the 20,000 crowd that turned out in bright sunshine at Anfield for the visit of Forest delighted many. It's perhaps testament to the prestige of the FA Cup that so many thought Liverpool supporters would miss such an important game for their team in favour of the final involving two rival teams.

The weather would prove fickle, though, with bright sunshine giving way to dark clouds as the first half wore on. Forest ran out first, in all white, and were afforded a friendly welcome by the home crowd. They were far from a match for the Reds, though. Goals from Jack Cox in the 25th minute and Sam Raybould ten minutes after the interval sealed the win for Liverpool. The crowd hailed Raisbeck's fine defensive play, cheering every interception. However, while the forwards appear to have bombarded the Forest goal, it seems Jack Cox was the subject of many dissatisfied murmurings from the home support as he wasted chance after chance in front of goal.

Liverpool were comfortable winners, nonetheless, and not even the heavy downpour in the middle of the game could dampen dreams of a first top-division league title. The Reds would now travel to The Hawthorns on 29 April to face lowly West Bromwich Albion, who were languishing at the bottom of the table in 18th place. All Watson's men needed was a draw and the title would be theirs, at long last.

West Brom's manager may have been called Frank Heaven, but their supporters had been treated to a hellish season. The prospect of entertaining Liverpool, who were looking to be crowned champions, may as easily have been perceived as either the highlight of a doomed campaign or the final nail in its coffin.

With over 4,000 spectators turning out to see the game, it seems that the home side made a decent fist of it, at least in the opening exchanges. Tom Robertson shot narrowly wide, before Ben Garfield was knocked off his stride just as he was about to shoot from close range. Then a diving header from the Reds' Johnny Walker put the visitors in front after 20 minutes. They needed just a point, and if they could hang on for two points, the title would be comfortably in the bag. However, Albion went close to levelling almost immediately after, but Abraham Jones squandered the opportunity.

The second half was a tense stalemate, with both sides weak in front of goal. Perhaps the pressure was beginning to tell on Watson's men. Nevertheless, they hung on for the win and, with it, the championship was theirs for the first time.

Back in Liverpool, it was now sunset, and on Ranelagh Street a huge crowd – some estimates say 60,000 strong – had assembled in front of Central Station. There was a faint drizzle of rain in the air. Nobody cared about the weather, though, as they stood on tiptoes, their faces caught in the glow of the streetlamps and their necks straining for a glimpse of the newly crowned league champions, Liverpool Football Club.

Tom Watson and his players were travelling back from Birmingham, and the crowds were desperate to show their appreciation for their conquering heroes. It's certain that, among the great throng of mainly Liverpool supporters, there would have been a generous sprinkling of Evertonians.

Today's visitors to Liverpool's Central Station may view it as something of a nondescript building, almost hidden by the shops that cover its once grand Victorian frontage. At the turn of the 20th century, however, it was an impressive and imposing sight, complete with a tall brick structure standing 65 feet in the air and covering the great arched shed that lay behind it. In front of that, tall pillars, 20 feet high, held aloft the iron signage that carried its name. Beneath that archway the champions of England would soon emerge on a horse-drawn cart and, if they could find a path through the bustling masses, they would be carried all the way to Anfield, and the Sandon Pub, for an evening of celebration.

What emotion must have been unleashed in the hours after it became clear the Reds had delivered their first-ever league title. Civic pride, yes, but there were also local bragging rights at stake here too, and not just for the Liverpool board and their players. A keen rivalry between supporters of the Reds and Blues had already been cemented, and cartoonists of the day had already noted its fierce nature. Now they would draw even greater inspiration from Everton's discomfort at playing second fiddle to their neighbours across Stanley Park.

The championship had been secured by great players such as Scotsman Alex Raisbeck, the club's giant golden-haired captain, and Johnny Walker, a man who looked like a Wild West gunslinger, and who had scored the goal that won the league. Both men would undoubtedly have earned the Reds an army of new admirers in the city.

Imagine the scene, as a terrific roar fills the air. 'They're here, the champions are home,' people shout. Eager children, their clothes scruffy and some with their feet bare, dart between the legs of men and women dressed in their best 'clobber'. Some will have come straight from work; others will have dodged the night shift to catch sight of the title winners.

Then, they emerge. The men who would be forever immortalised in the history of Liverpool Football Club ride out of the station on the back of a cart, or 'brake', pulled by horses. They are immediately swamped. Raisbeck is hoisted aloft and the crowd sing and shout for him to make a speech. He declines, and the players continue their onward journey towards the revelry that will surely last way into the small hours. This is how our first championship-winning captain recalls events:

> What a night after the match! We got a great send-off at Snowhill Station by the Brummagen folks who were good enough sports to cheer us off as League champions, but we were unprepared for what was waiting us at Liverpool. I should imagine there was a crowd of between 50-60,000 packed in front of the Central Station, and right along nearly as far as Lime Street.
>
> The street was literally black with people and in the time-honoured way, the horses were dispensed with, and our brake practically carried along by willing hands to our headquarters at the Sandon Hotel. As we went along the crowd yelled for me to make a speech from the brake. I was not to be found, however, as I found it convenient to lie low behind some of the others. Speechmaking was never in my line.

What must it have felt like for Watson to usurp his old club with Liverpool. His achievements and status in the game were beyond doubt, having led two clubs to the championship, claiming his fourth league title as football manager. To Liverpool supporters, he would have been every bit as revered as the men who followed him, men like Shankly, Paisley and Klopp. Yet, in terms of his Anfield reign, he was only just getting started.

Watson, his trainer and players received their medals at a ceremony held at the Sandon Public House in Anfield, in the presence of the club's directors, shareholders and the gentlemen of the press. Presenting them was Councillor William Houlding, Liverpool FC's chairman, who declared the season 'the most satisfactory that the management of any club could possibly have'. In a speech, Houlding described the league championship as 'the blue riband of the football world'. He was challenged by reporters, who asked, 'If the championship is the blue riband, how would you describe the English Cup?', a reminder of how valued the FA Cup was, and how much pressure there was to win it.

Houlding heaped praise on the players and the public, describing their loyalty as key to the club's eventual success, after many ups and downs. He expressed great optimism and his hopes that he could keep the team together. However, Houlding saved his highest accolades for Watson, clearly satisfied that Liverpool FC's directors had managed to prise the great man away from Sunderland in 1896.

For his part, Tom Watson accepted his medal with great modesty, claiming the success was all due to Houlding and the board, who, he said, 'had done more for football than most'. Of course, success has many fathers, to coin a phrase. However, there was now no denying that the Liverpool manager was at the peak of his powers, having secured four league titles with two separate clubs in under a decade. His stock on Merseyside and across the football world could not have been higher.

## Chapter Twelve

# Liverpool FC's first champions: Portraits of Red heroes

AS THE United Kingdom said farewell to the 19th century, the Second Boer War was still raging in South Africa, and concerns about the way it was being executed helped to secure a general election victory for the Conservative Party, in what was dubbed the 'khaki election'. Winston Churchill was elected to represent the Oldham constituency, and the newly formed Labour Party saw two of its candidates elected to Parliament: Keir Hardie in Merthyr Tydfil and Richard Bell in Derby.

In January 1901, the death of Queen Victoria was an event of huge cultural and political significance. The monarch had been on the throne for 63 years and seven months, and would have dominated the headlines and political discourse at the time. She was succeeded by Edward VII.

Meanwhile, in the North West of England, arsenic poisoning of beer was responsible for the death of 70 people. And in football, Liverpool were just one year away from becoming champions of England, at last.

There's no question that the team that won Liverpool FC's first top-flight league title in 1901 was Tom Watson's. Of the 18 players who made up his title-winning team, only Billy Dunlop had been recruited before his arrival. In just five years, Watson had completely revolutionised the club on and off the pitch, and the complete transformation of the squad speaks to the support he received from an ambitious board of directors.

The club had spent over £2,000 on ten players in the five years following Tom's arrival (fees for seven of the men are unknown, while one was a free transfer). Of course, this figure doesn't include wages paid to the men.

At Sunderland, Tom Watson developed a reputation for recruiting his footballers from Scotland. However, while at Liverpool, although he didn't completely abandon scouting players from the country, he certainly seems to have taken a more balanced approach.

His champions, for example, contained an even split of players hailing from north and south of the border.

Indeed, when we look at who Tom preferred to select in his starting line-ups, of those who started more than half of the games, five were English and six Scottish. Goldie and Robertson, both Scots, were ever-presents in the league, and Englishman Perkins would be Watson's No. 1 throughout the campaign.

Below, we provide pen portraits of the 11 men who earned a league winners' medal in 1901. As you'll see, while they were all footballing heroes, they were human beings, some of whom faced many challenges in life. We do not shy away from these, as to do so does them an injustice. Their struggles make their achievements all the greater, and we see each of them as ordinary men living extraordinary lives.

## Alex Raisbeck

*Captain, and half of Tom's team*

Our story now moves to Edinburgh. It's 1898, and a 19-year-old Alex Raisbeck is waiting in the home of the chairman of Hibernian Football Club, Phil Farmer, for the arrival of Stoke City secretary

Horace Austerberry, to discuss joining the club where he had so far been on loan.

In truth, the young Raisbeck isn't sure what the next step in his career should be. He has been impressing on loan at Stoke, and wouldn't mind staying on. However, he sees his long-term career back home in Edinburgh. As the second hand on the elaborate gold clock, perched on the mantlepiece in the drawing room, ticks loudly, an appointment that was but minutes late is now more than an hour overdue, and still there's no sign of the eminent Mr Austerberry.

Alex isn't sure whether he should call time on the meeting, but then there's a knock at the door. He sits nervously as Farmer gets up to answer it. Then, with a sweep of the door, in steps the imposing figure of Tom Watson. His frame fills the doorway and, as he steps into the room, he covers the light entering through the window. In his right hand is a cigar, and he offers the youngster another with his left.

It would take no time at all for old Tom to convince Raisbeck that his future lay on Merseyside, with Liverpool. He will be paid £6 weekly, all year round.

That's how the man who would go on to be arguably the club's first superstar describes meeting his future manager, in an eight-part serialisation of his life story, first published in the *Weekly News*, March 1915:

> At the appointed hour no Stoke secretary appeared, and in Phil Farmer's house I met instead Tom Watson. I had never seen the gentleman before, and I shall never forget him. He made me an offer which I could scarcely refuse. If Mr. Austerberry had kept his appointment – which probably was no fault of his own – I would in all probability have been a Stoke, instead of a Liverpool player. It was a fortunate thing for me.

Liverpool paid £350 for his services, and Raisbeck never looked back. He regarded his time at Anfield as some of the best of his life and career. Here, in his own words, he lays out his feelings on Liverpool:

> In a very real sense I was one of Fortune's footballs, and probably the luckiest and most profitable of any transaction to which I was a party was when I shook Tom Watson, of Liverpool, by hand, who in turn, in his own peculiar genial way, asked me for a sample of my handwriting, which, in effect, tied me to Anfield for eleven of the happiest years of my life.

He described his new club and the team-mates he fought alongside as 'a sanctum, the comforts of which I had hoped but never expected to enjoy'. And of the team and the club:

> We as a club had our ups and downs. If we were not perilously near the foot of the table, as Tom Watson used to say, we were very near the top of it.
>
> We marched right from the Second Division to the leading position of the First in successive years, which will demonstrate to you what sort of side we were. You perhaps expect me to follow on with the suggestion that we were a 'team of all the talents'. We were not. Some of us were perhaps better than others, but taking us all over, we were only a little above the average as a combination. As a team we were as one man, and therein lay the secret of our success.

Born on Boxing Day in 1878 in Wallacestone, Stirlingshire, Scotland, Alex moved around a lot as a young boy, and eventually settled in Spittal, a small hamlet in East Lothian, where he went to school. He would later joke that he kept the local shoemaker in business, as he wore out his boots playing football, which amounted often to kicking a tin can around the streets.

Raisbeck soon joined a Boy's Brigade team, established and 'sponsored' by a local church. Football was his love but, even at 12 years of age, he was acutely aware of the need to obtain a trade. He duly followed his father and brother down the mines, explaining, 'No matter how skilful you may be in playing the game, the first duty of every player is to make sure that he has a trade or profession to fall back upon when his playing days are done.'

Alex was blessed with skill from an early age, claiming that the ball 'acted like a magnet to me'. His natural position was at centre-half and it was there that his career would blossom, with Alex claiming that 'no other place on the field suited me better'. Raisbeck believed he was 'born to be a centre-half'. Though a few disagreed – as evidenced by one short piece in the *Lancashire Evening Post*, dated 6 January 1900, which asked whether Alex (often referred to as Alec in the media) would be better suited to full-back – Tom Watson had absolutely no doubt about his gifts in the middle of the defence. While lambasting Scotland's selection committee for not picking Raisbeck enough, Watson would have this to say in 1900: 'I don't know what your selectors have been thinking. Alec has been the best centre-half in England for long enough. He's half our team.'

The manager's comments were recorded in a retrospective entitled 'John Allan's Sporting Memories', published in the *Daily Record* on 8 September 1942. In it, Allan recalls how 'Old Tom doted on Alec'. Little wonder, as Raisbeck was a fierce competitor who took the game incredibly seriously, and rarely gave less than his best. Here, again, in his own words, we get an understanding of what the player himself felt set him apart in the game:

> If I were asked what was my chief peculiarity while I was an active participant in the game – League match, Cup tie,

> or International, I should say it was the seriousness with which I viewed the prospect of every match, the continual dread that we should be on the losing side.

In addition to his mentality, which marked him out as a winner, Raisbeck's physicality often drew the attention of journalists and supporters alike. These comments by the *Liverpool Echo*'s Ernest 'Bee' Edwards are a case in point: 'A man of Raisbeck's proportions, style and carriage would rivet attention anywhere. He was a picture at five feet nine inches and fully 12 and a half stone; a fine and beautifully balanced figure.'

Despite this, he was a shy young man when he first entered the dressing room at Anfield, and opted to keep his powder dry when it came to giving his views and speaking out. His integration was, of course, made easier by the healthy sprinkling of Scots in the squad: 'There was Geordie Allan at centre and Barney Battles, two of the finest-built men who ever figured on the football field [...] Then there were the brothers Goldie, and Billy Dunlop, all Ayrshire callants; Hugh Morgan, Robertson, Cleghorn and Matt McQueen. Last, but not least, was Johnnie [*sic*] Walker, my special pal,' Alex would recall later.

If he had one weakness that he would admit to, it was being 'lazy in the morning'. On one occasion he almost missed a match during the 1907/08 season. The Reds were due to kick off at 3.30pm. After lunch, Alex decided to have a nap on the couch, and in an attempt to set an alarm he accidentally set his clock an hour earlier than the actual time. Soon he had lapsed into a deep sleep and had to be dragged away from his resting place with just 30 minutes to go before kick-off. 'If the Germans invaded my house tomorrow I could not spring with greater alacrity from my couch than I did that day. I was in time, but had my friend not called, I should have been snoozing away for half-an-hour or more after the game had begun,' Alex remembered.

Raisbeck's recollections to the *Weekly News* in 1915 are fascinating. They give us a genuine sense of the man, his personality and just how important the game of football was to him. Packed with stories, what stands out is that even as far back as the early 20th century, players like him were hero-worshipped, with fans regularly visiting his home and the training ground. We get an insight into how difficult that was at times, especially when those calls came asking for more than just an autograph. Alex and his team-mates would regularly be persuaded to part with a shilling or two by fans claiming to be down on their luck, or even impersonating old pals or relatives in order to gain favour.

In 1901, Alex married Elizabeth Maxwell Stewart in Larkhall, Scotland, and the Raisbeck family grew to include 14 children. They lived near to Anfield until his death in 1949; he was 70.

Alex was a pivotal figure in the Watson era, helping the club to their first two top-flight league titles, and captaining the team with distinction. He was idolised by supporters, fellow professionals and those who wrote about the game. An article published in the *Liverpool Echo* by Victor Hall on 8 November 1924, under the headline, 'Alex Raisbeck, who raised Liverpool's prestige', waxes lyrical about Raisbeck, speaks of his importance to the club and, frankly, makes us envious of all those fortunate enough to have watched him in the flesh:

> What a trier he was! Who that ever saw him play can forget the unmatchable enthusiasm he displayed in the sheer love of the game. He not only put body and dash into individual games he played, but more importantly he helped to create the soul, that inward sacred fire of zeal without which no club can thrive and live.
>
> Let us recall his characteristics. Tall, lithe, sinuous, and yet gifted with muscular and physical development beyond

> the ordinary. Active to a degree, speed either on the turn or in flight, and with niche, at the addition of resourcefulness and judgement that would have been all sufficient in a other player, without those added gifts, methodical in training, painstaking in preparation, genial with his players and considerate with his committee. With a perfect blending of the qualities that to make a really great player!

Alex left Liverpool in 1909, at the age of 30. He had played 341 times for the Reds, scoring 19 goals. He spent five years at Partick Thistle, where he made a further 121 appearances and scored seven times, before finally hanging up his boots aged 36. Some 10,000 people attended a benefit match for him in 1914, at Firhill Park in Glasgow, with gate receipts of £300.

Alex went on to have a career in football management, at Hamilton Academicals, Bristol City, Halifax Town, Chester and Bath City, although Liverpool was never far away from his thoughts. He unsuccessfully applied for the Liverpool manager's job, which had been vacated by Dave Ashworth in December 1922. However, he would eventually return to Anfield in 1947 as a scout.

For those who saw him play, he was quite simply one of the greatest centre-halves in the game. Surely the greatest signing Tom Watson ever made.

## Sam Raybould

*Watson's 'Prodigal Son'*

Born in 1875 in Chesterfield, Raybould was already something of a veteran at the age of 24. He had by now played for six different clubs, including Derby County, before arriving on Merseyside. And, he was something of a goal machine. The young Raybould was attracting the attentions of Liverpool scouts while playing for New Brighton Tower as an outside-right in the Second Division. In just 13 league games for New Brighton, he had scored ten goals. Tom Watson had seen enough, and the Liverpool board was persuaded to pay £250 for his services.

Tom knew he needed a goalscorer, after being pipped to the title in 1899, and seeing his team and his shot-shy strikers slump in 1900. He clearly saw something in Raybould, who was contributing goals as a winger, and knew his goals were much needed at Anfield. His capture would prove a masterstroke.

Standing at 5ft 9½in and weighing 12 stone, Sam made 11 appearances for Liverpool during his first season at the club, the second half of the 1900/1901 campaign, scoring seven times. His first game came in a 2-0 win over West Bromwich Albion at Anfield, on 13 January 1900. Hugh Morgan scored both goals for the Reds that day, and, unfortunately, Raybould had been noticed for all the wrong reasons. He endured a wasteful outing in front of goal, and, in a report featured in the *Lancashire Evening Post*, the match reporter had detected a hint of nerves, and suggested this may explain his apparent profligacy in front of goal:

> Raybould did not make an altogether successful first appearance for Liverpool against West Bromwich Albion. He missed two glorious open goals – worked for them hard, worked his way right up to Reader, and then failed to score in the simplest fashion. It is that final touch, though, that shows the true artist.

The step up to Liverpool and the First Division was a big one. Sam, like many players before and after him, was adjusting. However, the last sentence of the above article suggests they had spotted real potential. Indeed, the remainder of the match report is somewhat sympathetic, with favourable comparisons to the great George Allen, who had scored 56 goals in 96 appearances for the Reds:

> He is the most likely successor to George Allan that Liverpool have yet had. He will not make the local public forget Allan – they cherish his memory too much for that. But I rather think the recollection of the Kyles and Hunters has been blotted out, and that Raybould will prove to be that centre-forward for whom Liverpool have been searching high and low.

The *Liverpool Mercury*, meanwhile, overlooked Raybould's wastefulness and preferred to focus on his contribution to the team overall, suggesting that he had helped his team-mates to completely 'overrun' the visitors. The fact that Liverpool had scoured the country for a new forward, only to discover that he had been lurking across the water, on the Wirral, the whole time, was not lost on the local press, with more than a little irony.

He was clearly a player of some ability, and the following week he lined up against Everton at Goodison Park in front of 30,000 people. Unfortunately, Liverpool succumbed to a 3-1 defeat, but Raybould bagged his first goal for the club, in the first minute of the game. The goal came after a shot from Alex Raisbeck was parried, and Raybould profited from the resulting goalmouth scramble. Liverpool held on to their lead for 68 minutes, but three goals in six minutes saw Everton take both points.

Sam's real breakthrough would come in the 1900/01 campaign, which, of course, ended in championship glory. He made 31 appearances that season, as the Reds battled to their first-ever league title, scoring 17 goals. From a nervy newcomer, Raybould had grown into a league champion, and a firm favourite among the Anfield faithful too. However, there was more to come in a career that would yo-yo between the First and Second Divisions.

In the 1902/03 season, Sam took his goalscoring exploits to another level, bagging an astonishing 31 league goals in 34 games – his best for the Reds. However, sadly, his career would become mired in controversy and scandal. Sam was accused of accepting an illegal contract from Portsmouth, along with fellow Reds John Glover and William Goldie. After a lengthy argument, it was decided that the move was illegal and Raybould received a seven-month football ban and, along with his team-mates, he was prohibited from ever signing for Pompey. In addition, the FA fined Portsmouth £100, and suspended their manager from taking part in football until 31 December 1903.

Liverpool missed Sam and his goals. By the time he had served his ban, which ended on New Year's Eve 1903, they were locked in a fight for survival. Little wonder, then, that the club seemed willing to forgive his apparent disloyalty. An extract from an article in the *Illustrated Police News*, published on 12 December 1903, suggests that Tom Watson had ensured that rival clubs wouldn't be able to take advantage of the situation, convincing the board to re-sign the player with great haste:

> There has been some secret rejoicing in Liverpool over the recapture of Samuel Raybould, who signed on again for Mr T. Watson last Tuesday, so that any other club would have to be very early astir to have 'captured' him again. Parkinson is admittedly a promising substitute but he is no Raybould.

The reference to 'secret rejoicing' hints at the fact that the club was attempting to maintain something of a dignified stance on the deal, perhaps conscious that Sam's reputation had been tarnished somewhat by the whole affair. However, it's easy to understand why Liverpool were so willing to forgive and forget. He had been an integral part of their success to date and Watson would have seen that he had no ready-made replacement in the wings. The reference to Jack Parkinson being 'no Raybould' in the above snippet is certainly evidence of that fact.

In truth, with football in its infancy, rules on transfers appearing to be vague, and wages precarious and relatively low, attitudes among players and managers to players jumping ship may have been different at the beginning of the 20th century. Watson, himself, was no stranger to poaching players from other clubs using methods so clandestine that books could be written about them. As we've seen, he would even refer to activities north of the border between England and Scotland as 'hunting for men'. It's possible that Tom would have regarded the controversy surrounding Raybould as just part of the game.

It appears, though, that supporters and others in the game of football saw things differently, as evidenced in a biography of Raybould published in a Liverpool matchday programme on 17 December 1904. The opening paragraph talks of Raybould receiving a huge amount of criticism: 'We know of no other player who has been so adversely criticised, and in our opinion so unnecessarily so, than Sam Raybould.' Furthermore, a cartoon published on 11 January 1904 in *Athletic News* imagines a tearful Raybould in his football kit, receiving a consoling hug by his boss, Tom Watson. Underneath is a caption, which reads: 'Mr T. Watson and Raybould in the touching Anfield drama. The "Prodigal's return"; or "O dry those tears."'

The sketch perhaps hints at how troubling the whole affair was for the player, and maybe suggests an almost fatherly relationship with his manager. It may, of course, have been little more than artistic licence. Whatever the case, it must have taken very broad shoulders for Sam to have returned to a club he had sought to leave, and to weather the barrage of criticism that came his way. Surely, the support of his manager and team-mates would have been critical. And, as we can see from the above quote, the club threw its full weight behind him.

Raybould managed four goals in 15 games after his return. However, by now the team were in freefall and suffered relegation in 1904. It appears that, for Sam, life was crashing down all around him.

Perhaps in sympathy, and despite his previous transgressions, the club held a benefit game for the player at Anfield on 4 December 1905. The opponents were Aston Villa, and some 25,000 attended. Sam received the gate receipts. He had made his first-ever league football appearance for Derby County, in a match against Villa, a game in which he scored the only goal.

At home, his marriage to wife Selina was in trouble. The pair had three children, and she was said to have been an alcoholic, an issue faced by many in this period of history. We can speculate that his domestic problems may have played a part in him accepting an inducement to move to the south coast, but we will never know for certain. He would successfully sue for separation from his wife in 1910, on the grounds that she was a 'habitual drunkard'. Sam won custody of the children, while agreeing to pay Selina 15 shillings a week. This was, of course, an incredibly testing time for the couple and their children, and we get a sense of Raybould's sense of responsibility and his love for his children. As for his poor wife, we know nothing of what happened to her, though she's likely to have endured a very difficult time.

Liverpool, with the help of Raybould's exploits up front, bounced back from the pain of the previous season by winning the Second Division title in 1905. Sam's appearances and goals significantly contributed to that outcome. In all, he made 32 appearances and scored 19 goals. In doing so, he set the club on a path that led to their second First Division championship in 1906.

Sam featured 25 times for Liverpool in that title-winning team, and still weighed in with a very creditable 11 goals. The following season would be his last at Anfield, with Sam featuring 35 times and scoring 15 league goals. Tom Watson transferred the player, who was by now 32, to Sunderland in 1907. He would continue his exploits in the North East, and undoubtedly Liverpool missed him. According to LFChistory.net:

> Raybould was a strong and powerful striker with a wonderful turn of speed, good ball control and was praised for his daring rushes up-field and judicious distribution of play to the wingers, but first and foremost, his deadly scoring capacity.

Sam Raybould was an extraordinary player, who managed to light up football despite his troubling personal life. We could say that he was so good that Tom Watson signed him twice. The club clearly forgave him for wanting to leave Anfield for what he saw as greener pastures. Perhaps there was an understanding of the difficulties he was navigating at home.

He should be remembered as the first Liverpool player to score 100 goals, a feat he managed in just 162 games. In all, Raybould scored 130 times for Liverpool in a career that spanned 226 appearances, winning two First Division titles as well as the Second Division championship.

Sam died on 17 December 1953 in Chesterfield. He was 78 years old. For the final word on Raybould, we leave it to *Athletic News*, which on 4 December 1905 wrote this: 'There are few inside forwards superior to Raybould.'

## Thomas 'Tommy' Robertson

*Watson's 'sprightly' wing wizard*

Born on 17 October 1876, in East Benhar, Fauldhouse, Linlithgowshire (now West Lothian), to parents Andrew and Jane, Tommy Robertson joined Liverpool in 1898 for a fee of £175. His home village had been built by the Benhar Coal Company to support those working at the colliery. The area, consisting of a row of 160 dwellings either side of the main thoroughfare, also boasted a school and numerous shops.

Tommy's father worked down the mine, and at the age of 14 his son followed him into the pit. Football would provide Robertson with an opportunity for exercise and he soon earned himself a reputation as a pacy winger, physically strong and with an eye for goal. His junior career began with East Benhar Heatherbell.

Motherwell took a look at him, but he would eventually sign for Heart of Midlothian in 1896 at the age of 20. Known more for providing crosses for his team-mates, Tommy was also a fine finisher, famously netting four times in a 5-0 victory over Clyde. That game saw him go on to taste glory for the first time in his career, winning the league championship with Hearts in 1897 at the age of 21.

Robertson quickly established himself as an exciting and dependable player at Liverpool, missing just one game in two seasons and contributing 15 goals. As an ever-present in the title-winning 1900/01 campaign, he scored nine times.

However, there are more than a few hints in the records to Tommy's inability to settle outside Scotland and some suggestions that his lifestyle was getting in the way of his career. Throughout his time at Anfield, he lived the single life as a 'boarder' in a house in Everton. After the title win in 1901, his form seems to show signs of decline. He featured in 25 games in 1901/02, netting six times, but press reports note that his performances were 'lacking just that little bit of something "extra" – especially in shooting'.

Liverpool made a profit on Tommy, returning him to Hearts for a fee of £200 in May 1902, for what turned out to be a relatively brief spell. His appetite for drink meant that he would fall out of favour with his new club, after missing several training sessions. Hearts' patience eventually wore thin, and he was transferred just five months later to Dundee.

He appears to have resolved his issues while at Dundee, where he played 76 times for the first team and scored 26 goals. In May 1903, he again made the move south, this time to Second Division Manchester United, where he played three games before his old problems resurfaced. Sadly, United cancelled his contract when he and Sandy Robertson arrived for training drunk.

Tommy headed homewards to Scotland, and enjoyed a spell at Bathgate FC, where he also returned to the mining industry to earn his living. He died at Harthill, Lanarkshire, on 13 August 1941. He was 64 years of age. As an undoubtedly proud Scotsman, capped once by his country, and enjoying his status as a Scottish league champion with Hearts, Robertson also gave great pleasure to Liverpool supporters, and his legacy is that he was a winner both north and south of the border.

## Bill Perkins

*Watson's ever-present champion between the sticks*

William Henry Perkins was born on 26 January 1876 to parentsh George and Sophia. The family lived initially at Rockingham Road, Kettering, Northamptonshire, but by 1881 they had moved to Doggett's railway huts in East Grinstead, Surrey. They had moved presumably because his father gained employment there as a blacksmith with a railway gang.

Bill's entire childhood was spent in Surrey, where he went to school before they followed George back to Northamptonshire, where he found another job as a blacksmith. At the age of 15, Bill, one of three boys, found employment as a shoe finisher. However, sport and particularly football had become his first love.

He played in goal for teams such as Burton Latimer Temperance FC, before moving on to play for Kettering Town and then Luton Town, who he joined in 1898. It was there that he attracted interest from Watson at Liverpool. He signed for the Reds a year later, in

1899, for £200. Bill remained at Anfield until 1903, and was one of three ever-present players in the title-winning side of 1901.

During his time at Liverpool, he's recorded as living as a lodger with the Cole family at 220 Salisbury Road, in the civil parish of Everton. He was said to be earning his living as a 'professional footballer'.

Bill took the place in goal of future championship-winning manager Matt McQueen, who had himself taken the place of Harry Storer towards the end of the 1898/99 season. Matt, who also played in outfield positions, made just two appearances before giving way to Perkins. Eight successive defeats at the beginning of the 1899/1900 season saw Bill replaced by Harry Storer after a 2-1 defeat to Bury on 14 October 1899. It must have been a huge blow psychologically for Bill, as he had effectively shouldered the blame for the team's poor run of results.

Nevertheless, he somehow managed to stay in Watson's thoughts, and returned to the side against Stoke at Anfield on 30 December 1899. He kept a clean sheet and his place, becoming a Liverpool mainstay until 1903. At this point, Watson was rotating between Bill and Peter Platt, and eventually replaced Bill with Platt on 30 March 1903. According to an article in the *Lancashire Evening Post* dated 4 April 1903, Perkins would eventually lose his place in the team due to a severe case of 'nerves'. The piece goes on to claim that:

> He is a singular case of degeneration; a player usually improves with experience. He is really an intelligent chap, but he suffers from 'nerves,' and it is really his self-distrust that has brought about his succession once more, and for the last time.
>
> He cannot complain, for he has had lots of chances; and if he thinks meanly of himself, it is very natural for others to

> take him at his own valuation. It is especially true of goalers that they ought to have a good conceit of themselves.

Football then, as it is now, was a ruthless business, it seems. Bill left Liverpool to play for Northampton, where he remained until 1906 when he hung up his gloves at the age of 30. He then went into partnership with a Mr T. E. Fox, and the pair opened a bootmakers and repairers shop in the town.

He married his wife, Clara Agnes Hobbs, on 15 October 1911 at St Mark's, Regents Park, London. The couple had two children: Mabel, born in 1912, and Joseph, who arrived in 1914. Soon after the birth of his son, war broke out, and Bill served as a gunner with the Royal Garrison Artillery. After the war, he returned to Kettering, where he found employment in a factory with Buckby Brothers, and lived in a house named 'Aston Villa' at 64 Station Road.

Sadly, Bill's wife passed away in 1934, and the former Liverpool keeper lived out his days as a boot repairer, living with his daughter in Burton Latimer in Northamptonshire. He died at the age of 73, in 1949.

## William 'Bill' Glover Goldie

*Watson's wrought-iron wing-half*

Bill Goldie was a powerful weapon in Watson's armoury, tough in the tackle and solidly dependable. Born to parents Alexander and Christina in 1878, in Hurlford, Ayrshire, Scotland, Bill was one of three children. By 1891, the family had grown, and Bill now had seven siblings. At the age of 13, he was employed as a coal miner. Away from the colliery, he played football for his local team, Hurlford Thistle.

Some sources suggest that Goldie spent time at Clyde. However, extensive research by Liverpool FC's official archivist, Jonny Stokkeland, has revealed no evidence that he featured in their first team. While it is possible (but not confirmed) that Goldie had a trial with them, it appears that the move to Anfield was a direct transfer from the Hurlford club.

Goldie signed for Liverpool on 25 November 1897, at the age of 19, having followed in the footsteps of his brother, Archie, who had also played for Clyde, and arrived at Anfield in 1895. However, Bill didn't make his debut until 2 April 1898, a 3-2 defeat to Notts County. He seems to have settled in the city quickly and was married to Martha (Margaret) Hunter on 30 April 1900, at St Bridget's church in the Wavertree area of the city. Interestingly, his marriage certificate records his occupation as coal miner.

Bill and his wife lived at 315 Tinsley Street, Anfield, which no longer exists. The site of their home has long since been demolished as part of the expansion of Anfield stadium and is now covered by the club's official store.

Goldie held his place in the side from 1900 to 1903, a span of 102 consecutive league games. He also made 16 appearances in the FA Cup during the same period. In all, Bill spent six seasons at Liverpool.

His Scottish accent often proved difficult to follow for non-Scots, and after he was charged with 'discourteous language' following an FA Cup semi-final against Sheffield United, Bill was suspended for the last three games of the 1898/99 season, which meant he missed the title run-in as Liverpool missed out on the championship to Aston Villa. The chairman of the FA disciplinary panel was forced to employ an interpreter as nobody present was able to understand what Bill was saying, so impenetrable was his accent.

Sadly, this wouldn't be the only time Goldie found himself in trouble with the football authorities. Along with Sam Raybould and John Glover, he was found guilty of accepting an offer of a one-year contract from Portsmouth FC in 1903, despite being offered the maximum wage of £208 per annum at Liverpool FC. This was against the rules. The case was heard on 10 June 1903 at the Grand Hotel, Manchester, with the secretary of the FA presiding over a five-man panel.

The players argued that they had wanted a change, and should be free to join any club they pleased. The panel was not impressed and found against them three days later. They were banned from football until the end of the year.

However, unlike Raybould, Goldie was not re-signed by Liverpool when the ban concluded, and joined Fulham in January 1904. Bill went on to play 215 games for Fulham, winning two Southern League championships and he played in the Cottager's first campaign in the Football League in 1907/08. By 1911, Bill and his wife were living in Leicester, where he ran a pub. He continued to play football, for Leicester Fosse and Leicester Imperial.

Bill died on 3 February 1952 at the age of 74. He played 174 times for Liverpool, scoring six times. He was also one of the men who brought home the club's first league championship.

On 1 January 1910, a letter written by Bill was published in *Cricket and Football Field*. It makes interesting reading, and we've chosen to give Goldie the last word by reproducing the letter here:

> For six seasons I played for Liverpool without missing a match; although, of course, I was in the reserve team a good lot. Well, when I got my benefit it only totalled £109. At that time players were getting £300 and £400 for their benefits. So I wasn't satisfied at all, at all.
>
> I signed on for Portsmouth seven seasons ago, and for doing that I got suspended for six months for doing nothing at all. John Glover and Sam Raybould were suspended along with me (both of them are now keeping 'pubs,' although Sammy still plays for Chesterfield). We got 'tried' at Manchester. S'help me. I thought I had got off. I

> had the Commission who tried us laughing until their sides were sore.
>
> Ye see. Ah ha, never cheenged ma tongue sin Ah left Scotland, and they couldna understand me avall. But I could not understand them when I heard my sentence, six months hard labour without the option.
>
> That was rather a slap on the nose to get when leaving a club you have been with for six years.

Bill Goldie was clearly quite a character.

## William 'Billy' Peden Dunlop

*The crowd cried, 'Boot it, Dunlop!'*

Born on 11 August 1874, in Hurlford, Ayr to parents Alexander and Jane, Dunlop would go on to spend 15 years at Liverpool but, first, the son of a coal miner, he followed his father down the pit.

The family lived at 211 Riccarton Road, Hurlford, before moving to 124 Academy Street in the same district. In 1894, Billy moved south to Liverpool after a spell at Kilmarnock, for a fee of £35. His address on Merseyside was 29 Arkles Road, which, as we know, lies in the shadow of Anfield stadium. He was boarding there along with fellow Liverpool player John 'Sailor' Hunter. Meanwhile, another player, Maurice Parry, was a boarder next door, at number 27.

Dunlop suffered an ankle injury at the end of October 1895, which kept him out of the team for four months, returning to action in late February the following year. Despite this, his team-mates maintained the push for promotion back to the First Division in 1896.

He faced stiff competition from the likes of Tom Wilkie and Archie Goldie at left-back in the following season, but regained his place in the team towards the end of the campaign. He would go on to become a regular starter for the club over the next decade and captain the team between 1899 and 1900. He would also be a key member of both of Liverpool's championship-winning teams in 1901 and 1906. He was a firm favourite with the Anfield crowd, playing with a non-nonsense style, making left-back his speciality. Famed for taking no chances in defence and frequently launching the ball upfield, he would regularly be serenaded by supporters chanting, 'Boot it, Dunlop!' A matchday programme summed up his value to the team with these words:

> Always keen and watchful on the field, he betrays his over-anxiety to repel the invader by his terrific lunges, and on his day, there is no more brilliant player than this same Dunlop. A better servant no club ever possessed, and though we may occasionally differ from him as to the methods he employs on the field, on one point we must all agree, that for downright single-mindedness of purpose Dunlop's tactics have never been questioned.

Before his move to Sunderland to take up the role of assistant trainer, in July 1911, Billy was living at 140 Walton Breck Road, where he owned a tobacconist and newsagent shop. Two Liverpool players, and future stars, were boarding there with him. They were Donald McKinlay and John McConnell.

Dunlop remained at Sunderland for many years, where he was employed as a trainer and masseur until 1939. At this point he was living at 31 Dene Lane, Sunderland, with his wife, Elizabeth Jane Dunlop. He died two years later on 28 November 1941.

## John 'Jack' Thomas Cox

*The Scouser in the team*

Jack was born in Liverpool on 21 December 1877. His parents, William, a bootmaker, and Sarah, were from Monaghan and

Armagh, in Ireland. The family seemed to have moved around the city during his early life. They first lived at 266 Vauxhall Road, but soon moved to Robson Street in Everton before settling in Vienna Street, a stone's throw from Anfield stadium, by 1885. Jack had three siblings: Ellen, Catherine and William.

By 1891, Jack, his mother and brother, William, had moved to Blackpool. He was 14 years old. His father and sisters were no longer with the family. While at school, Jack learned to play football and later played for South Shore, before joining Blackpool in 1897.

Liverpool came calling that same year, and, with Blackpool vulnerable as a result of financial difficulties, they agreed to the transfer of Jack to Tom Watson's team on Christmas Eve for the very generous fee of £150. However, despite training and playing in Liverpool, he appears to have continued residing in Blackpool for his whole life, at least according to official records.

At the age of 20, Jack made his debut in a game against Notts County on 12 March 1898. He made a great impact in front of a 12,000-strong crowd, having a hand in Liverpool's first goal and scoring their second in the 85th minute.

Cox was part of the side that enjoyed a fine run to the semi-final of the FA Cup, and finished runners-up in the league in 1899. Sadly, though, the season would prove a false dawn for Jack and the Reds, with 1899/1900 seeing them finish tenth. However, he featured in 32 league matches, scoring ten goals during their championship-winning campaign, as a winger.

According to lfchistory.net, Cox appears to have been unhappy at Anfield, and on numerous occasions sought an exit from the club, with both Fulham and Everton attempting to sign him. However, due to the fact that he was contracted on the maximum wage, there was no way for him to legally make a move.

Thankfully, from a Liverpool perspective, he stayed at the club until 1909, becoming a double title winner, after the Reds won the league for a second time in 1906. Remarkably, he and his team-mates had won the Second and First Divisions in consecutive seasons.

In 1902, Jack took part in a 100-yard footballers' race, which had been organised by Dundee FC. He won it that year, and in 1905 he finished second to Liverpool's Jack Parkinson. Cox was also a capable greens bowler, and later won two tournaments in Blackpool, the Talbot and Waterloo in 1925. He became the first player to do so.

After leaving Anfield, he returned home to Blackpool, where he became player-manager of the club, spending two years there. In 1910, Jack married Elizabeth Barrett, on 27 April. The couple lived at Oxford Road in Blackpool, where they appear to have employed a 'servant'.

Tragically, Jack's brother, William, died in Birmingham in 1915 as a result of injuries sustained while fighting in the Dardanelles during the First World War. He had previously been a talented footballer for Bury, Preston, Dundee and Hearts.

By 1921, Jack was working as a 'commission agent' and the family had two daughters, Ada and Mollie, the latter serving in the Women's Voluntary Service Mobile Unit in 1939. She would have provided catering support to those affected by the war.

On 11 November 1955, Jack died. He was 77 years old, and he left his wife the sum of £8,205 11s 10d. To a generation of Liverpool supporters, Cox was a champion, winning two First Division titles and the Second Division during a Reds career that spanned 12 years and included 360 appearances. He scored 80 goals from the wing, a great legacy.

## Johnny Walker

*Watson's practical joker, and splendid fellow*

Johnny Walker would mature into the epitome of a working-class gentleman footballer. However, he seems to have indulged in somewhat ungentlemanly conduct during his early Reds career.

Born on 24 August 1873 in Shotts, Lanarkshire, his life and that of his family was intricately woven into the life of the local colliery. His father, Thomas, was a 'Pitheadman' and he provided for his wife, Elizabeth, and their 12 children with the £5 per month he earned from the mine.

Thomas Walker Sr, Johnny's father, was a deacon in the local Presbyterian church for 30 years. He appears to have been regarded locally as a great man, and would have undoubtedly ingrained into his children a strong work ethic and a sense of service. His obituary provides us with a sense of how others regarded him, including these words: 'Strength and independence of mind. Fiercely impartial, ruled by a sense of duty, aimed high in all he did, left behind an honoured name.'

At the age of 20, Johnny was playing football for a team called Armadale, before joining Hearts in 1892, where he stayed for five years. While there, Johnny won the Scottish league twice, in 1895 and 1897, and lifted the Scottish Cup as captain in 1896, in what was a hugely successful spell.

Watson signed Walker, now capped by his country, in March 1898, paying £175 as part of the same deal that also brought Tommy Robertson to Anfield for a combined £350. He made his debut on 4 April 1898 against The Wednesday, which Liverpool won 4-0.

In an incident on Oakfield Road, Anfield that his father would have certainly disapproved of, Johnny and his team-mates,George Allan and Hugh Morgan were charged with breaching the peace and obstructing a police officer, just a few months into the 1898/99 season. A report in the *Dundee Courier*, dated 15 November 1898, describes how Johnny and Hugh Morgan attempted to prevent a constable from arresting George Allan, with Walker shouting, 'Let's show him some Scotch blood.' The police officer – who clearly recognised the players – was reported in another newspaper article to have retorted, 'You think you can do as you like with your £5 or

£7 a week.' Their defence lawyer argued that 'it was after a match, and they had won', arguing the men were sober. The court appears to have been sympathetic, stating there was 'no violence', and advising the men to 'turn in a little earlier on a Sunday morning', before dismissing the case.

In the 1901 census, Walker is recorded as living as a boarder at 108 Herschell Street, Liverpool. He shared this abode with fellow Liverpool team-mate Tommy Robertson, and the head of the household was Liverpool FC trainer John Chapman.

Johnny famously scored the deciding goal against West Bromwich Albion on the final day of the season, which clinched the league title for Liverpool. He left the Reds at the end of the following season to play for Glasgow Rangers, having played 120 times for Liverpool and scoring 30 goals.

Alex Raisbeck described Johnny as a practical joker, sharing many of his team-mates' japes in his 'life story', which he relayed to *Athletic News* in 1915. Describing Walker as his 'special pal', Raisbeck had the following to say:

> Johnnie [*sic*], I make bold to say, was the most splendid fellow I met during the whole of my professional career. As a practical joker Johnnie took the biscuit. He was simply unique and up to all manner of tricks.

In 1910, Walker emigrated to Manitoba in Canada with his older brother, Thomas. Johnny found work there at Manitoba Government Telephones. With the outbreak of war, the brothers were keen to enlist. Thomas was among the first Canadian citizens to join up with the 1st Canadian Division in 1914. He served overseas throughout the war, and fought at the 2nd Battle of Ypres, the Somme, Vimy Ridge, Hill 70, Passchendaele, Amiens, the Drocourt-Quéant Line, the Canal du Nord, and Cambrai. He was awarded the Distinguished Conduct Medal in 1918.

However, for Johnny, a knee injury had resulted in a case of 'drop-foot' and a wasted calf muscle, which would have prevented him joining up. Nevertheless, he was so determined to get into the army that (at least according to family lore) he taped putty to his leg to fool the recruiters. It seems unlikely that they would have fallen for this, but he was eventually accepted in March 1916. He had also apparently lied about his age, recording his birth date as 1895. This would have made him 22 years younger.

Johnny was assigned to the Signal Corps of the Canadian Engineers. He was stationed with the 5th Reserve Division from 1916–1918, in England, before being sent to France with the 1st Tramways Company. His work was crucial in building and repairing railway lines and bridges necessary to resupply the front lines during the final 100 days of the war.

In 1919, after the war was over, Johnny returned to Winnipeg, Canada via England and resumed his work with Manitoba Telephones as an engineer for six years. In 1925, he moved to Pilot Mound, Manitoba, where he took up farming with his brother Thomas and his two sisters, Mary and Elizabeth.

Tragically, he died in 1937 after a wood-cutting accident on the farm, when a pulley belt slipped off and struck him. He was 63 years of age. His obituary paints a picture of a modest, strong and well-respected man:

> John Walker grew to a sturdy manhood through exemplary conduct and preserved intact, his powerful physique, and made him outstanding in the world of sport. He quickly rose to fame as a professional football player, and in the early years of this century his name was a household word in Great Britain; his prowess earned for him International recognition – than for which there is no higher honour in football.

> He was noted as one of the most gentlemanly of players, and off the field, he was modest and retiring to a degree. All who knew him were struck by the solid strength of character and esteemed highly his fine personality. He was the type of citizen that can ill be spared in any community.
>
> And to many here, it was never known that he once was so illustrious a figure in the Old Country, 'Big League' sport.

Johnny is buried in Greenwood Cemetery, Pilot Mound, Manitoba, Canada, Plot 334. His legacy is one of service, of a strong work ethic and powerful sense of duty. He threw off the wildness of youth to carve out a new life for himself on another continent, but for a brief spell he was well known as a champion of Scotland and England, a 'most splendid fellow'.

## Charlie Wilson

*Watson's centre-half and Liverpool trainer-in-waiting*

Born on 27 April 1873 in Sutton, St Helens, Charlie would go on to play a pivotal role in Liverpool's first four top-flight league titles. As a player, he won a league championship medal in 1901. He was a member of the backroom staff when the club won the league in 1906. He was awarded a medal for that season, despite not playing for the team. He would also be a key part of Dave Ashworth's and Matt McQueen's coaching team that helped the Reds win back-to-back titles in 1922 and 1923.

His parents were Charles James and Elizabeth, and he had one sibling, Eliza, born in 1874. Tragically, she died before her second birthday in 1876. Wilson's father was employed as a 'Stationary Engine Driver', and there is reference to Charlie being employed as a mechanic, before football took over his life.

He had joined the Reds from Stockport in 1897, and played 92 times for Liverpool. He would therefore become something of a living legend at Anfield, with a reputation as a talented defender and something of a student of the game. However, his playing career was blighted by a horrific injury, which saw him break his leg in the first minute of a game against Middlesbrough on 28 February 1903.

Alex Raisbeck once recounted a story of how Wilson had dreamed that he would suffer a break the night before the game. The injury put him out of the team for eight months and he would manage just nine appearances for the club afterwards. A matchday programme, dated 15 December 1906, laments the loss to Liverpool and Wilson's career:

> Before he broke his leg Wilson was a sound centre half, who studied the game, and played it accordingly. Indeed, there are many who think that he would have disputed pre-eminence with the great Raisbeck himself but for the unfortunate accident which practically stopped his First League career. He can score goals, and his offensive work was always splendid. Especially dangerous was he when corner kicks were taken. The juniors can learn much from Wilson if they will. He is bulky now, and must be one of the weightiest men playing in Combination football.

Wilson played his last game in the first team in 1905 and continued in the reserves until 1908. He remained a fixture at Anfield until his eventual retirement in 1939.

Charlie worked at the club throughout the First World War, while spending leisure time 'filling shells with Ernest Peake, and training lady footballers'. In 1922, the club awarded him £500 in lieu of a benefit match.

Wilson's capture from Stockport was something of a coup, with Manchester City also in the reckoning for his signature. However, a lump sum of £100 was enough to stave off their interest and seal his move to Anfield. There is some doubt as to whether this money was ever paid, with journalist, author and oral historian Stephen F. Kelly, recalling a conversation with Charlie's son, Doug, that suggests the money, though promised, was never forthcoming. A biography of Charlie, published in another Liverpool matchday programme, dated 26 November 1904, gives us a flavour of his attributes as a player: 'A sturdy, vigorous, and well-built youth, he plays football with all the energy he possesses, and his very exuberance of vitality is often mistaken for roughness by biassed individuals.'

Wilson played 92 times in defence for the Reds, scoring three goals. His final game came in the Second Division, and ended in a 1-1 draw with Bolton Wanderers, on 1 April 1905, with 25,000 people there to see it. The result saw Liverpool at the top of the league. They went on to win their remaining five games, clinching promotion to the First Division.

Charlie died on 9 June 1947 at the age of 74. Sadly, he just missed out on seeing George Kay's Liverpool win the club's fifth league title, their first after the Second World War. There are surely few greater servants than Charlie Wilson, who spent four decades at the club, serving them on and off the pitch with distinction.

## Thomas 'Tom' Robertson

*Watson's wandering full-back*

Not to be confused with his team-mate, 'Tommy' Robertson, 'Tom' was born on 6 June 1874, in Lesmahagow, Lanarkshire, Scotland, before his family moved to Newton Mearns, near Glasgow. Alex Raisbeck, in his 'life story' published in *Athletic News* in 1915, describes how the rest of the team differentiated between the two men by referring to one as Tommy and the other as Tom. Both men had been known as 'Tom' at their previous football clubs.

Tom's early football experiences came at an amateur team, Newton Thistle, in his local village. He then went on to join St Bernard's of Edinburgh. His professional career began at Stoke in May 1894. Tom returned to Scotland, at Hibernian, for two years from 1895, before returning once more to Stoke in 1897, where he played as a half-back.

A shy and retiring young man, he signed for Liverpool in 1900 for a fee of £400, and spent two years at Anfield before deciding he needed another move, swapping Merseyside for Southampton in 1902. He had been part of the Liverpool team that suffered a shock 4-1 defeat at the hands of Southampton in an FA Cup second-round tie at The Dell on 8 February 1902.

A precision tackler, Robertson was also famed as a powerful kicker of the ball. During the championship-winning season, Tom made 22 consecutive appearances from the start of the season, but was replaced by John Glover for the following nine matches. Robertson regained his spot in the final three games of the run-in, earning himself a winners' medal.

His move to Southampton frustrated Watson, particularly as they had paid a significant fee for him, and he was leaving for the Saints, who were playing in the Southern League. A piece in the *Evening Telegraph*, dated 22 May 1902, set out the club's position:

> Liverpool are anything but pleased at Tom Robertson, their late full back, migrating to Southampton. It cost them close upon £400 for his transfer from Stoke, and they have not had two years' service out of him. So far as they are aware, Robertson had no grievance, and as he was offered the maximum rate of wages, some very unpleasant things are being said in Liverpool as to the inducement for him to journey south.

There is a pattern, during this period, involving young players who sought to move around frequently, perhaps seeking new adventures in different places, or being tempted by the promise of signing-on fees and wages at their new club. It will have done little to endear them to supporters.

Robertson would win the Southern League in back-to-back seasons with Southampton, before his wanderlust took hold and he transferred to Brighton in 1904. He would become a publican in retirement.

In all, he played 47 times for Liverpool. Tom died on 8 December 1923. He was just 48 years of age.

## Charlie Oliver Satterthwaite

*Watson's powerful inside-forward*

The year is 1895, and a report appears in the *Lancashire Evening Post* about an assault that took place on a football pitch in Workington. A Mr John Hayton was walking across the pitch, when he decided to take a shortcut through the goalposts. A group of youths took exception to him disturbing the game, and one of them, an 18-year-old labourer, launched the ball in his direction, and it struck the man with force. From this moment on, the man was targeted every day as he walked across the field.

The youth in question is Charles 'Charlie' Oliver Satterthwaite. He was born in Cockermouth, in England's Lake District, in 1877, and he would go on to be a league champion with Tom Watson's Liverpool FC.

Football was a passion for Charlie, and his skill and powerful shot drew the attention of many local clubs, including Black Diamond, Workington, Bury, Burton Swifts and Moss Bay. On 12 December 1899, Charlie signed on at Anfield. This is how the *Lancashire Evening Post* reported the news of his capture:

> The Liverpool Football Club have secured a new forward named Charles Satterthwaite, who has been playing recently for Moss Bay, a club in the vicinity of Workington. He is a powerful-built young fellow, and can play either inside or outside left. He makes his first appearance for Liverpool to-day in the Combination match with Turton.

He made his debut just eight days after putting pen to paper, in a 1-0 defeat to Nottingham Forest. The game was evenly contested, and Charlie would have left the field disappointed that he had missed a golden opportunity to level for his team after being set up by Tommy Robertson.

Satterthwaite was a tall lad with a powerful shot. Although his contribution to the team was about more than goals, he did score a hat-trick in his second-ever appearance, a 5-2 victory over Glossop at Anfield. However, a report in the *Liverpool Mercury* suggests he had to leave the pitch injured before the end of the game. Still, he had more than done enough to win over the 5,000-strong crowd, and no doubt his manager. His injury wasn't serious, though, and he would go on to make 18 appearances in the league during the remainder of the 1899/1900 season. As we've learned, the addition of Charlie and Sam Raybould to the team was regarded as the main reason for the team's improvement and ultimate survival in the division.

During Liverpool's title-winning season of 1900/01, Satterthwaite made 21 appearances, scoring five goals, earning a winners' medal. However, he would lose his place in the team the following season, making just four appearances.

He left Liverpool in 1903, after playing 45 times and scoring 13 goals. He moved to West Ham for one season. His fearsome shooting is claimed to have broken the net in one game. In another match, against Sheffield United, it's claimed that the ball hit a goalkeeper in the head, knocking him out before going over the line.

Charlie's next move was to Woolwich Arsenal, where he became the first player to score a Football League goal for the club. Charlie would go on to establish himself as an important player for the London club, scoring 70 times in 178 games.

He returned to Workington in 1910. The *Newcastle Journal* reported the move on 31 August:

> The Workington Club has gathered together a very strong combination indeed, and with the inclusion in their ranks of Charles Satterthwaite, a forward scintillating with Woolwich Arsenal last year, and Richard Smith, a centre forward from Burnley, it will readily be seen that the Cumbrian mean business.

A year later, in 1911, the now 34-year-old Charlie was living with his wife, Mary, aged 44. The couple had two children, John and Stanley, aged four and 11 respectively. The family lived at 64 Derwent Street, Workington. Satterthwaite was by now a publican in a brewery business.

Charlie died on 25 May 1948. He was 71 years old. After a long and distinguished career in football, in which he made a significant contribution to Liverpool FC's first top-tier title, he had become a devoted family man, a far cry from the cheeky young ruffian who stood before the magistrate all those years earlier.

## The nearly men

*They each played their part*

In addition to the above first-team regulars, there were seven men who played minor roles in the squad. All of those who made at least one league appearance were awarded a winners' medal on 27 August 1901. They each played their part, and they were, along with the number of appearances:

Andy McGuigan – 14
John Glover – 10
John Hunter – 8
Maurice Parry – 8
Rab Howell – 2
John 'Jack' Hunter – 1
John Davies – 1

## Chapter Thirteen

# The fall and rise of Tom's champions

LIVERPOOL MADE several signings during the 1901/02 campaign, with one key player leaving the club also. Charlie Satterthwaite joined New Brompton in 1902, and would go on to feature for West Ham and Woolwich Arsenal. Watson brought in seven players, with many of them destined for the reserves. In terms of financial outlay, the two more significant acquisitions involved the double capture of George Bowen and George Fleming from Wolves in May 1901, each for £215.

While Bowen returned to Wolves in September 1902, Fleming went on to play 83 times for Liverpool between 1901 and 1906, scoring six times. His best season came in the club's push for promotion from the Second Division during the 1904/05 campaign, in which he featured 29 times in the league, and twice in the FA Cup. However, he would figure just three times in the title-winning season of 1905/06.

Another significant capture, both in terms of outlay and his contribution to the club's success, was Arthur Goddard for the sum of £460. Goddard went on to play 414 times for Liverpool in the league and cup, and scored 77 goals. He featured 28 times in the promotion campaign and twice in the FA Cup, and was a league ever-present during the 1905/06 First Division championship-winning season.

Despite the optimism generated by the 1901 title win, Liverpool struggled in the following season, finishing 11th in the league. They won just two of their opening ten games, beating Birmingham 3-1 and Manchester City 3-2. Of the other matches, they drew six and lost two, to The Wednesday and Stoke.

One of those draws came at Anfield against Everton. Though the sun was shining, it was cold on Merseyside. Liverpool had gone to great lengths to ensure they could accommodate what was predicted to be a bumper crowd, and actually placed seats alongside the pitch. Gate receipts indicate that there were around 30,000 in the ground before kick-off.

Everton won the toss and were the first out of the blocks, launching a salvo of attacks. However, Liverpool struck first. Making his debut in the game was Bill White, who had been signed before the season started and only went on to feature six times for the Reds. He opened the scoring, and this is how the *Liverpool Courier* recorded his one and only goal for the club:

> The visitors were the first to get going and Sharp was very dangerous, when Wilson fouled him. The free kick was worked away, and then the Liverpool forwards dashed off, Raisbeck checked a return by Proudfoot and then Bowen dashed along the wing. He finished with a beautiful centre. The ball flashed past McGuigan and Raybould, but White received it, and slammed the leather into the net – a beautiful goal. This success was met with howls of joy by the Liverpudlians and encouraged by the cries the home side kept up a rattling attack.

There was just two minutes on the clock, and as Liverpool debuts go, White could not have asked for a finer one than this. Scoring a goal against Liverpool's biggest rivals in the Merseyside derby should herald a great Anfield career. Sadly for White, this would prove to be the singular high in an ultimately disappointing spell. The Scot transferred to Dundee in 1902, where he would enjoy greater success, before several clubs south of the border attempted to sign him. He would eventually choose Middlesbrough in 1903, though could have had his pick, as evidenced by this report in the *Evening Post*, dated 5 February 1903: 'William White, Dundee's crack inside right, has been transferred to Middlesbrough. It has been an open secret for some time that White contemplated joining a leading Southern club, and intended signing for them on 1st of May. Middlesbrough and other League clubs were also anxious to secure him.'

With the crowd offering its vociferous support, Liverpool continued to take the game to Everton, but the Blues slowly grew into the game and, in the eighth minute, Everton's Jack Sharp levelled from close range. With barely ten minutes gone, the crowd began to sense that it was in for a classic.

McGuigan had the ball in the net for the Reds, only to see it ruled out, and Liverpool continued to threaten but failed to add to their tally. Everton began to gain some measure of control midway through the half, and one attack saw Jimmy Settle shoot high over the bar. Then a Liverpool counter-attack saw White injured and led off the pitch 'for a rest'. With Liverpool temporarily down to ten men for the final few minutes of the half, Everton took full advantage. John Proudfoot handed possession once more to Settle, who unleashed a fierce shot that gave Liverpool's Bill Perkins no chance. It was 2-1 to the visitors after 42 minutes.

In the second half, Bill White moved into the forward positions and excelled. From an advanced position he was able to bring Jack Cox into the game more, and Liverpool looked hungry for an equaliser. Just three minutes after the restart, they got it. Dunlop launched the ball upfield, where Raybould won possession, turned sharply and shot. The ball sailed past Muir, who, according to one report, should have done better. Liverpool supporters cared little, though – the score was 2-2 and hopes of a third were high.

However, the game appears to have descended into a scrap, with Raisbeck going down for several minutes and White continuing to feel the effects of his injury of the first half. He was seen to be holding his shoulder, in pain, throughout the closing stages of the game. Despite this, the teams had fought each other to a standstill and the game ended 2-2.

The season was failing to live up to expectations and by the New Year the Reds were in an uncomfortable 13th place. The December fixtures were particularly damaging, with three defeats and a single victory from four games. As they prepared to welcome Stoke City to Anfield on 4 January 1902, the Reds had won just five of their 17 games, had scored 21 and conceded 20. Expectations could not have been lower going into the game.

What followed was the most remarkable game imaginable. The Stoke team had dined on fish before kick-off and to say it didn't agree with them is an understatement. The match was recalled in the *Liverpool Echo* in 1915, and although it was clearly no laughing matter for the visitors, it would have no doubt raised a smile or two among the Anfield faithful. Liverpool ran out the winners by an incredible seven goals to nil, and had scored four of those in the first half. However, as the *Liverpool Echo* put it, 'Stoke were not well. They were ill before the game, during the game, and afterwards. They had had fish.' So bad was the bout of food poisoning that the City players were forced to leave the field periodically to 'heave to'. The bouts of vomiting throughout the game meant that at one point Stoke were reduced to just seven players. Liverpool, for their part, showed no mercy at all. And, benefitting most from Stoke's digestive woes was Andy McGuigan, who became the first Liverpool player to score five goals in a single league game. Sam Raybould added the others.

The victory did little to improve Liverpool's league position, and in the following game the Reds received a pummelling of their own from Everton, losing the game 4-0 at Goodison. The humiliation at the hands of their neighbours was somewhat assuaged by then defeating the Blues in the first round of the FA Cup, 4-2 in a replay at Goodison, after a 2-2 draw at Anfield.

It would prove small consolation, however, with Liverpool going out in the next round to Southampton. As disappointing as this season was, but for a missed penalty in the final game of the season against Blackburn Rovers at Ewood Park, the Reds could have finished as high as seventh.

In that final match, Liverpool went a goal down on 15 minutes but fought back hard. With Blackburn down to ten men in the second half, thanks to an injury to Bob Crompton in the first half, Liverpool levelled through Johnny Walker in the 75th minute. The game finished 1-1, but Sam Raybould missed a penalty. Had it gone in, Liverpool would have finished level on points with seventh-placed Aston Villa, with a slightly better goal average. Football has always been about fine margins, it seems.

The year of 1902 was marked by a horrific footballing disaster, which occurred at Glasgow's Ibrox Park on 5 April. In a British Home Championship match between England and Scotland, a stand collapsed, resulting in the tragic deaths of 25 people and injuries to more than 500 others. Elsewhere, Hibernian won the Scottish FA Cup, Newton Heath changed their name, becoming Manchester United, and Norwich City was formed as an amateur club in June.

During the 1902/03 season, Tom Watson handed debuts to five players: Edgar Chadwick, George Livingstone, Don McCallum, Peter Platt and John Carlin. Of these, only John Carlin would go on to feature in the championship-winning season of 1905/06, during which he managed 14 appearances. The others had all moved on before that campaign.

Peter Platt, a goalkeeper, was signed from Blackburn Rovers, who held his league registration after he left to play for Oswaldtwistle Rovers in 1901. He played 44 times for Liverpool, keeping six clean sheets. He made way for Ned Doig and went on to play for Luton Town and Nuneaton Town. He died in 1922 of pneumonia after a bout of influenza. He was 40 years of age and the popular landlord of the White Swan Inn, Nuneaton.

Liverpool opened the 1902/03 season at home to Blackburn Rovers with six veterans of the 1901 title win, including Bill Perkins in goal, Billy Dunlop, Charlie Wilson, Bill Goldie, Arthur Goddard and Sam Raybould. In addition, Maurice Parry and John Glover had featured but not enough times to win a medal.

The Reds won the game 5-2 in front of a crowd of 20,000. However, Blackburn played the final hour of the game effectively with ten men. Defender Bob Crompton left the pitch for treatment to an injury. Although he returned after treatment, he was described in one match report as merely a 'passenger' for the rest of the game. The scoreline could have been higher, but for a wild penalty kick by Jack Cox with Liverpool already leading 2-0. His spot kick went yards wide of the goal, ultimately denying him a hat-trick. The scorers for Watson's men were debutant George Livingstone, Sam Raybould (2) and Jack Cox (2).

The win saw Liverpool open the campaign in fifth place, as some teams had by now played twice, and that's where they would finish. Watson's men would again experience misery in the Merseyside derby, losing the game at Goodison 3-1 and fighting out a goalless draw at a gloriously sunny Anfield on 10 April 1903. The *Liverpool Courier* covered the game, and reported on another huge attendance – some 30,000 rattled through the turnstiles, a capacity crowd – amid great expectations.

Liverpool lined up with captain Alex Raisbeck in the side. The Scot missed seven league games during the campaign, including the opening two games of the season. It would prove another case of 'what might have been' for Liverpool, with Raybould wasteful at the death. The reporter at the *Liverpool Courier* was particularly scathing of Sam's miss: 'Raybould absolutely threw a goal away by a ridiculous miss under the bar. Liverpool were undoubtedly having the best of matters, but the shooting was bad.'

At this stage, Liverpool were eight points behind league leaders The Wednesday, having played two games less, with four games to go. Raybould's miss had squandered the chance to close the gap and to maintain their tenuous grip on the race for the championship.

With hopes of winning the title evaporating, attendances at Anfield dipped, with 15,000 and 10,000 seeing the games against Aston Villa and Bury, respectively. Watson's men finished in a creditable fifth place, demonstrating some recovery from their hugely disappointing defence of the title in 1901/02. However, as had been the case throughout their history thus far, an up would soon be followed by a down.

Liverpool were relegated after the 1903/04 campaign, just three years after being crowned champions of England for the first time. It would be a body blow to Tom Watson, who was visibly upset at the experience. This story from Alex Raisbeck in *Athletic News* in 1915 paints a picture of a man 'on the edge':

> There's one incident I shall never forget in this memorable year and it concerns my late manager. We were at Molineux Grounds playing Wolverhampton Wanderers and we badly needed to win the match. In fact, had we won it, it would have gone far to help to keep us in the First Division. But we lost.
>
> When we got to the station that evening we all got seated quickly, I can tell you. Jack Addenbrooke, the Wolves manager, came down to the train with Tom Watson and I

> recollect the conversation that passed between the two. The tears stood in Tom's eyes as he shook hands with Mister Addenbrooke. 'Goodbye,' he said. 'I didn't think you would have done what you did this afternoon. I thought you'd remember what I did for you.'
>
> Of course, this was only sentiment and Jack simply murmured something about being sorry and all that sort of thing, well knowing that Tom referred to the help Liverpool had been in getting the Wolves into the First Division.
>
> We in the carriage had our hearts full enough, I can assure you and to see Tom taking it on like that made us feel very uncomfortable. To ease the tension one of the boys started to sing and we all joined in. I shall never forget the look on our manager's face as he turned in the carriage. 'How can you have the heart to sing tonight, lads?'

Watson cared deeply about the game, and took results personally. He was a natural-born winner but, along with that, the pain of defeat could sometimes prove too much. We'll learn later how his sometimes fragile temperament got the better of him, and how, at times, he would be unable to watch games due to the tension.

Liverpool finished the campaign second from bottom. It had been a miserable season, with all of the joy and optimism of 1901 completely gone. The Reds had won just nine games all season, drawing eight and losing 17. They had actually scored three more than the division champions, The Wednesday, but the defence had leaked an incredible 62 goals.

Watson's team finished a point behind Stoke, who had battled Liverpool for safety during the campaign. After a 1-0 away defeat to Middlesbrough, on 2 April 1904, Liverpool's players and Watson had been hoping for a favour from their neighbours. Everton were to play Stoke a week later, and, if they won, the Reds would have a shot at achieving safety. Alex Raisbeck describes the significance of the game for both Liverpool and Everton supporters:

> The match which sealed our fate, however, was one in which we were not engaged. Stoke, who were running us neck-and-neck, as it were, for relegation had to play Everton at Goodison Park. It ought to have been a pinch for Everton as they were well up in the League and were very hard nuts to crack on their own ground. To the surprise of everybody, however, Stoke won the match and our fate was sealed.
>
> The result did not please everyone, as you will imagine, and I heard at the time that a great number of Everton's ticket-holders tore their tickets up after the game and swore they would never go to Goodison again.

Raisbeck reveals something of the spirit among supporters at Anfield, however, who, despite Liverpool's travails, had, according to him, stood by the team. 'It was a remarkable thing that, despite the fact that we were sailing so near the wind, that season our support never failed us,' he wrote.

Indeed, during what was a catastrophic season for the club, Liverpool's average Anfield attendance had been a very reasonable 15,411, with 10,000 turning out to see their relegated heroes beat Bury 3-0 on the last home game of the season.

As Liverpool supporters got used to the idea of once again navigating their way through games in the Second Division, the Anfield hierarchy showed no signs of losing faith with their manager. Not surprisingly, they backed the manager by signing defensive reinforcements in Tom Chorlton, David Murray, James Gorman and goalkeeper Ned Doig, for whom they paid £220 to Sunderland.

While both Chorlton and Murray would feature 12 times, Doig would be an ever-present as Liverpool escaped the second tier as champions, playing 34 times in the league and turning out twice in the FA Cup. Meanwhile, James Gorman made just 23 appearances for Liverpool between 1904 and 1908, leaving them for Leicester Fosse.

The year of 1904 was significant in the city for the opening, on 12 March, of Britain's first surface electric trains, which ran from Liverpool to Southport. Meanwhile, anyone fortunate enough to be able to afford a motor car would have to license it with a number plate for the first time, and they would be limited to 20mph on the roads. In football, Brentford FC opened their Griffin Park ground in West London, and, in the same area, Loftus Road opened as the home of Shepherd's Bush FC.

Liverpool's promotion push got off to a slow start, with a win and two draws in their opening three games. The season opener was a 2-0 home win over Burton United on Thursday, 1 September 1904. Ned Doig became Liverpool's oldest debutant at 37 years of age, as two first-half goals from Bobby Robinson secured the points. However, the performance was far from convincing. A report in the club programme was particularly scathing, and bemoaned the fact that Liverpool had failed to add to their tally in the second half, with the following words: 'Are you satisfied with Thursday's game? Well if you are, my friend, I assure you, I am certainly not. Liverpool met the weakest team they will meet this season, and instead of winning by ten goals, they annexed a solitary two.'

Anyone claiming that modern football's culture of instant gratification is a new phenomenon should perhaps think again. After taking four points from a potential six in their opening three games, our disgruntled author in the matchday programme continued, suggesting that the patience of supporters was wearing thin:

> It must be confessed the followers of the club are not quite at ease. The three opening matches were fully expected to realise six points, instead of only four have accrued.

> We are waiting patiently. I hope our waiting will not be too long deferred. At all events, the men are absolutely determined to show the populace that they can still play the game.

It seems the players were listening, or our scribe was being somewhat impatient, depending on what way you look at it. Liverpool went on to win their next ten games in succession, scoring 29 goals, and conceding just five. They were now unbeaten in their first 13 games, and sat four points clear at the top of the table.

The Christmas schedule was marred by two defeats on the road to Bolton Wanderers and Manchester United. And, as they closed out the year, Liverpool were in third place, four points behind leaders Bolton, and behind United in second, by virtue of goal average.

In the New Year, Watson's men crashed out of the FA Cup to Everton after a replay at Goodison Park, but they had battled their way to the top of the table by March. A 4-1 victory away to Doncaster Rovers saw them go top by virtue of goal average, with Bolton in second place, level on 45 points. United were now in third, three points adrift.

It seems that Sam Raybould, who had struggled in the early stages of the campaign due to being moved out wide, was now starting to adapt to his new role. He had clearly been receiving considerable criticism from Liverpool supporters, as evidenced by this report in the club programme following a 5-0 victory over Grimsby Town in October: 'Parkinson missed, but the ball came to Raybould who scored with a beautifully judged shot – the best goal of the day. His success was cordially received, and perhaps the crowd will now give him fair play and encouragement instead of barracking him.'

He would go on to score an impressive 19 goals in the season, with Bobby Robinson scoring 24. However, it would be Bootle-born Jack Parkinson who caught the eye, with 20 goals in 21 games. The club programme praised his contribution, if a little half-heartedly, on 18 March 1905:

> There is no doubt that Parkinson is a coming man. If he is fortunate enough to steer clear of injury, he should receive the highest honours. He may not be a great centre forward – such a phenomenon only comes once in a generation – but he's a good one, for all that. He has gone on improving ever since he made his first appearance; he combines pace with a capacity for keeping his wings moving, and only wants a little steadiness to make him even more dangerous than he is. His success is most gratifying as he is a local youth.

The goals scored by Liverpool forwards would clearly play a huge part in securing promotion. Liverpool scored 93 league goals in the 1904/05 campaign. However, the defence had also done its part. Goalkeeper Ned Doig and their centre-half and captain Alex Raisbeck had considerably steadied the back line, and by the end of the campaign they had only shipped 25 goals in 34 league games. Doig had kept 16 clean sheets, and deserved all the plaudits that came his way in the club programme, dated 12 November 1904:

> The defence of the Livers away from home has been wonderful. This speaks well for Doig whose advent into the team was a master stroke. The veteran has displayed all his old ability, and although he has seen so many years' service he is as agile and clever as ever. To have such a player between the posts must give those in front of him every confidence, and if he keeps fit and well there is no doubt but that at the end of the season it will not be his fault if the team does not go top.

Liverpool's rivals for the championship were Bolton and Manchester United. With six games remaining, Liverpool played out a 1-1 draw with Wanderers at Anfield in front of 25,000 supporters. The result did Bolton no favours, and they slipped to third place behind United. However, the gap couldn't be tighter, with goal average separating the top three sides.

Watson's men looked to improve their goal average in their next outing, a home game against Burslem Port Vale. Liverpool ran out 8-1 winners, with goals from Jack Cox (2), Jack Parkinson (2), Sam Raybould and Bobby Robinson (3). The result moved Liverpool a point clear at the top, with United in second place, and Bolton – who didn't play that day – two points behind in third.

After victories over Bristol City and Doncaster Rovers, each by a single goal, Liverpool faced Manchester United at Anfield on 22 April 1905. Bolton had won their game in hand 4-0 against Gainsborough on Wednesday, 12 April. They then beat Burslem Port Vale 3-1 and West Brom 1-0 to draw level on points with the Reds, so Liverpool had to beat United.

A capacity crowd turned up to see what was to be a pivotal game in the season for both teams. United brought a great number of supporters, with many of them carrying red-and-white umbrellas. And, with every seat and space in the ground taken, the roofs of the local houses were said to contain local supporters anxious to catch a glimpse of the game.

The opening exchanges were fierce, and United took the game to Liverpool. Ned Doig, battling the dazzling sunshine, struggled to keep out two 'scorchers' from the Manchester forwards. However, Liverpool soon gained the upper hand. Jack Cox got the first goal, before Raybould made it 2-0 before half-time, and Liverpool were comfortable. As the players left the field of battle, those in the stands and on the roofs of houses, looking in intently, would grow ever more confident of promotion.

United defender Jack Fitchett didn't appear at the start of the second half. He had sustained an injury to his ankle and was receiving treatment. He did manage to return, but struggled to contribute anything to the game. He went off for the last time after Raybould had scored his second and Liverpool's third.

Raybould also had to depart before full time due to injury, but not before he had scored his third and Liverpool's fourth. Both teams finished the game with ten men. The club programme offered 'sympathy' to United, but declared with great satisfaction that they had been outplayed, and suggested that Liverpool had gone easy on them after Fitchett had been forced to retire.

The win set up a tense affair on the final day with Liverpool facing Burnley at Anfield, on 29 April. Liverpool and Bolton were still level on points, but Wanderers had lost 2-1 to Barnsley on Monday, 24 April. Their season was over, and the Reds edged top spot on goal average, while United had fallen away. Watson's men needed only a point to escape the Second Division at the first time of asking.

Sam Raybould had recovered sufficiently from his injury against United to start the final game at home to Burnley. However, he twisted his ankle early in the match and had to hobble on during the first half. Despite carrying a player, Liverpool took the lead through Jack Parkinson on 40 minutes. Raybould could barely walk as the players left the pitch and Watson would only be able to field ten men after half-time.

Things went from bad to worse on 55 minutes when defender George Fleming went off with concussion. Liverpool would have to defend their slender lead with just nine men. Amazingly, Bobby Robinson put them 2-0 up. But before the crowd could allow themselves to breathe again, Burnley won a penalty. The 10,000 supporters inside Anfield could only chew their nails and pray.

Just as he had done all season, the great Scottish keeper, Ned Doig, came to their rescue, saving the spot kick to an almighty roar.

Buoyed by this, Liverpool somehow managed to extend their lead in the final minute of the game, when local lad Jack Cox scored their third. It sealed a courageous victory and secured the Second Division title for Liverpool. Watson was overjoyed. Liverpool's 58-point tally was a record for the Second Division.

The Reds' improvement was based on the Herculean efforts of many key men. However, there was no doubting that the performances of club captain Alex Raisbeck had been pivotal. The *Liverpool Echo* would later have the following to say of his performances and overall contribution to the club:

> Ten years have passed since the Liverpool Club fought its way into First League circles, and during this period, Alex Raisbeck has commanded his forces with wisdom and energy. A player of amazing vitality and strong personality, he has won many games by his individual efforts. His early training was among Scottish cracks, and the highest honours have been his. It is very largely down to his individual efforts that the Liverpool team has returned to the First Division.

The *Liverpool Daily Post* felt that the Reds had achieved promotion in style, after waging 'warfare' for eight months. Claiming they should never have found themselves in this position, they gave Liverpool huge credit for navigating such an arduous campaign. It's also worth commending Liverpool's board for keeping their trust in Watson. They could easily have taken a different direction after the club's humiliating relegation of the previous season. Their decision to back the boss speaks highly of his reputation and the manner in which he conducted himself. However, it's also testament to the sense of stability and assuredness at the top of the club. They would be amply rewarded for their patience in the campaign to come.

## Chapter Fourteen

# Tom secures second title after uneasy start

THE YEAR 1905 was a momentous one in many respects, with King Edward VII into his fifth year on the throne, following the death of Queen Victoria in January 1901, and a Liberal Government in office. The country continued to face numerous challenges at home and abroad. In Ireland, Sinn Féin would be launched later in the year, with a commitment to full Irish independence in a direct challenge to the UK. The Suffragettes, led by Emily Pankhurst, would stage their first public protests in Westminster. And, in a reminder of the perilous conditions endured by British workers, a National Colliery disaster at Wattstown in the Rhondda, Wales, resulted in the tragic deaths of dozens of miners. The news would have shocked the nation, and with several of Liverpool's players coming from mining communities, the losses would have been felt keenly at Anfield.

In football, February 1905 saw Alf Common become the first £1,000 footballer after he joined Middlesbrough from Sheffield United. He would be at Goodison Park for the opening game of the season, playing in torrential rain that waterlogged the pitch. A goal he scored from 18 yards even drew applause from the home crowd. In March, Chelsea Football Club were founded, and took up residence at Stamford Bridge after Fulham had declined the opportunity to move in. Three months later, Charton Athletic were established.

Liverpool supporters grabbing their copy of the *Liverpool Echo* on the eve of the new season would undoubtedly skip to the team arrangements section to see the line-ups for the following day's matches. On the same page, a reassuring advert regarding the *Football Echo* describes the investments made to ensure the best and most detailed reports for the coming season, with information hitting the newsroom via telephone, telegraph and pigeon.

Watson's men opened the season in the capital, and were pitted against Phil Kelso's Woolwich Arsenal. Kelso was something of a maverick, hailing from the Scottish seaside town of Largs, and he ensured that Woolwich Arsenal adopted professionalism, and match preparation was a key component of his approach. The Anfield party departed Lime Street station the previous afternoon. Tom and his team were joined by vice-chairman John McKenna and directors John Asbury and W. R. Williams. Their accommodation in London was to be The Manchester Hotel. A popular establishment with travellers from the north, it was a self-proclaimed hotel for sportsmen, providing 300 rooms, electric lighting, lifts and a nourishing breakfast. Liverpool arrived shortly after nine o'clock, retiring early in readiness for the opening day.

Cloudy conditions failed to prevent some 20,000 supporters from packing into the Manor Ground, a venue not famed for its accommodating nature, particularly when it came to the northern opposition that dominated the First Division places. The support was partisan, to say the least, made up from a variety of backgrounds, including workers from the Woolwich Works. The atmosphere could be intimidating and the language colourful.

To one end of the ground was a large sewage pipe, which provided a free vantage point of the pitch. The embankment on to which the pipe abutted was screened off with a cover, to prevent supporters enjoying proceedings for free. Following their promotion in 1904, this embankment had been developed into terracing, which was christened Spion Kop by Boer War veterans who formed many of the regulars at Arsenal matches. Of course, this was some two years before Anfield's new terrace was christened Spion Kop by Ernest 'Bee' Edwards.

As the crowd settled in for the game, they were entertained by the boys of the Lewisham Industrial School, who carried out a series of physical drills, which appears to have kept the waiting supporters entertained. Pre-match entertainment is not considered acceptable by many supporters of the modern English game, especially supporters of Liverpool. It's more associated with the American game. However, it was commonplace at all grounds in the early days of the game here.

Included in the Arsenal line-up was inside-forward Charlie Satterthwaite, a member of Liverpool's 1901 title-winning side. The teams arrived, with Liverpool reported to be sporting a changed jersey of white, with orange neck and wristbands. We were puzzled by the reference to orange here, and after checking with the club's museum curator and historian, we remain uncertain as to whether Liverpool ever sported such colours. Nevertheless, it's there in black and white, as it were. Perhaps this was a curious one-off, or maybe it was an error on the part of the reporter.

The game got off to a scrappy start, with Satterthwaite fluffing his lines in front of goal, perhaps to the delight of his former team-mates and supporters. Then it was the turn of Liverpool's Sam Raybould to miss his chance, with a wild shot that was easily cleared by the Arsenal keeper, Liverpool-born Jimmy Ashcroft. Liverpool full-backs Alf West and Billy Dunlop were kept busy, but dealt with the Londoners' attacks with ease. Then, Scottish wing-half Roddy McEachrane spearheaded another Arsenal attack, before sending a low shot, which Ned Doig saved brilliantly.

Liverpool were then presented with a golden opportunity to take the lead, as Bobby Robinson was gifted an open goal following Jack Cox's brilliant centre. He inexplicably miscued his shot, much to the delight of the home support. The game was end to end now, with Maurice Parry instrumental in keeping both Bobby Templeton and Jimmy Blair at bay, as the Londoners began to take control.

Liverpool almost found a breakthrough when, following some smart play down the wing, Jack Parkinson netted for the Reds, only for his goal to be instantly disallowed. As the half drew to a close, both teams had created chances; however, the battle had been in midfield, and the game's frantic nature had several players leaving the pitch in a lather of sweat.

Liverpool, unfortunately, endured a calamitous second half, despite going a goal up after Bobby Robinson, following a great centre from Cox, opened the scoring after just five minutes. The celebrations were short-lived, though, as Tim Coleman headed Arsenal's equaliser. Both teams then raised their game, before Blair fired the home team into the lead. The home crowd was jubilant. However, they were silenced when the visitors were awarded a penalty for handball. Raybould placed the ball on the spot and the fans got ready to witness a new penalty ruling in action. Goalkeepers were now required to remain on their line. As the scorer of 20 league goals the previous season, Raybould was expected to level the scores for Liverpool, but his strike was wild, missing the goal by several yards. With it went Liverpool's hopes, and the result was secured for Arsenal with former Red Charlie Satterthwaite scoring their third.

The result was compounded by an injury to star centre-forward Jack Parkinson, which saw him fracture his wrist. Following a tussle with one of the Arsenal backs, Parkinson fell awkwardly, and his outstretched right hand hit the ground. Reports detail the severity of the injury, describing how the hand was turned completely round. Parkinson was immediately transferred to the Woolwich Infirmary, where doctors administered chloroform and set the broken bones.

Following the game, Liverpool remained in the capital as they were to play a friendly in West London against the newly formed

Chelsea, who had been admitted into the Second Division, on the Monday. Some 5,000 spectators descended on the new ground. Woolwich Arsenal reserve players Charlie McGibbon and George Shalders featured for Liverpool, to cover the shortfall of players thanks to the bruising defeat to Arsenal. Liverpool's early probing was suitably fended off by Chelsea keeper Bill Foulke. A legendary figure in the game and Chelsea's captain, Foulke was a giant of a man, towering over his peers at 6ft 3in, with a weight of more than 20 stone. The game was dominated by Chelsea, as Foulke and his men comfortably defeated Liverpool 4-0. Though the game mattered little, Watson's men had endured a sobering start to the new campaign.

No sooner had the Liverpool party arrived home from the capital than they were preparing themselves for an evening of merrymaking. They were scheduled for an evening dinner and presentation night at the Hotel St George on the Tuesday. The club's new director, John Fare, had promised gold medals should the team return to First Division status, and he duly handed out the fine medals to the players. It would prove to be a busy week, as on Friday the club was handed the Second Division Championship Shield, at the Football League Management Committee meeting.

Liverpool went on to lose their next two league games, in what was turning into a nightmarish start to their First Division campaign. However, heavy defeats to Blackburn (3-1) and a particularly bruising away thrashing at Villa (5-0) failed to dampen the spirits of the Anfield faithful. Reporters were at Liverpool's Lime Street station to witness a huge crowd of Reds supporters board trains to the Midlands. When asked if the start to the season had made them 'downhearted', they greeted this with a resounding 'no!' They may have felt differently at full time, of course, but many of them would make the journey to Sunderland on Saturday, 16 September.

The Wearsiders had appointed a new manager in August. Bob Kyle, a native of Belfast and one of the great team builders of the era, had previously been secretary of Belfast Distillery. His appointment at Roker Park was aided by the recommendation of one of the driving forces behind the establishment of Liverpool FC, John McKenna. Prior to their departure, the club purchased James Bradley, Stoke City's left-sided centre-half. A fine tackler, capable of turning defence into attack, he was seen as a player who would seriously benefit Liverpool's cause. Bradley would be available for selection the following week.

Liverpool stayed at the Grand Hotel in Sunderland the evening before the game. Tom Watson, born and bred in the North East, had, of course, previously led Sunderland to three league title wins, and was on familiar territory. In good spirits, the team spent the evening at the Palace Theatre, before returning for a night's rest.

On the morning of the game, the players enjoyed a stroll through Roker, benefitting from the bracing sea breeze. Sunderland had won one and lost one so far this season and were fancied to take the two points on home soil, particularly given Liverpool's disastrous start to the season. Watson made two changes to the side that lost to Aston Villa, with Dunlop returning at full-back and George Latham replacing George Fleming at wing-half. Not only was Tom Watson back on old turf, but so too were three of his players, with Doig, Robinson and Hewitt all former Sunderland players.

The game was also announced as the benefit match for Jimmy Watson, Sunderland's distinguished Scottish full-back, and the good weather guaranteed a healthy crowd. As the sides took to the pitch, a special Roker welcome was reserved for Ned Doig. As the Liverpool players assembled, a tactical change was revealed, with Hewitt and Raybould changing places. This made Hewitt the central figure of the forward line. Liverpool captain Alex Raisbeck won the toss, electing to play from the South Stand end of the ground, and Sunderland got the game underway.

The opening exchanges were uneventful, with the midfield seeing most of the action. The odd foray into the opposition's penalty area came to nothing, until Sunderland forward George Holley sent a through ball to England forward George Bridgett, only for him to see his effort drift over the bar. Doig was called upon several times and at one point cleared three shots in quick succession. At the other end, Jack Cox's effort, which was saved by Tom Naisby, was trumped by the appearance of a terrier, who had made its way on to the pitch, before eventually being ejected by the local constabulary. Sunderland began to press, but Liverpool's defence held strong. Both sides saw efforts go begging, before an Arthur Goddard corner eventually found the assured foot of Sam Raybould, who tapped Liverpool in front from close range. However, just as in London, Liverpool's celebrations were short-lived. Sunderland levelled within minutes, with Bridgett's low shot towards the upright bouncing over the hands of the outstretched Doig and into the net. The teams left the pitch level at the interval.

The second half began with Doig being greeted by rapturous applause as he made his way to the goal at the north end of the ground. Both sides created clear chances during the opening exchanges, with Sunderland's Harry Buckle skimming the crossbar. Shortly after, Raybould netted a second for Liverpool. The goal was shrouded in controversy, however, with the Sunderland players, fans and press looking on, expecting a call for offside. However, the goal stood and Liverpool had earned their first two points of the season.

The teams left the pitch at full time, and one Sunderland supporter could barely contain himself, yelling, 'Oh, Teddy!' at the departing Doig. Liverpool's victory had been delivered in large part thanks to the heroics of the former Sunderland man.

The Lancashire Senior Cup provided a midweek interlude, as the competition's first round got underway. There was a growing feeling that these games were increasingly better suited to the so-called junior clubs of the region, with the bigger clubs less inclined to risk playing their star men. Tuesday afternoon saw Liverpool host Bury. Watson named a strong side, however, featuring the likes of Doig, Raisbeck and West. Despite this, it was Bury who progressed to the next round, after beating Liverpool 2-0.

Liverpool won their following game, at home to Birmingham, 2-0, thanks to goals from Bobby Robinson and Joe Hewitt. The result set up a huge encounter with neighbours Everton at Goodison Park. The Blues trailed the Reds by a single point, with both sides below midway on the table, in 14th and 15th respectively.

Back in 1905, the Merseyside derby stirred the Scouse imagination as much as it does today. Among the numerous press articles on football and the impending meeting of red and blue was a piece on the Everton keeper, Billy Scott. However, this was not a description of his preparations for the game, or his views on tactics. Instead, the *Liverpool Echo* spilled the beans on Billy's wedding, incognito, with Mary Carlisle, at St Anne's church, Aigburth. His team-mates had been probing him for a date for the impending nuptials, but the couple married with a limited number of guests, with no contemporaries in attendance. Billy and his new wife managed to fit in a few days' honeymoon in Blackpool. Here, they could enjoy the promenade and the views from the top of Blackpool Tower. And, for 6d, the newlyweds could sample the recently opened River Caves of the World ride, which the *Blackpool Herald & Fylde Advertiser* described as 'the most magnificent sight in Blackpool'.

Billy was back with his team-mates by Friday. Everton had organised a training camp at Hoylake, with the team returning to the Hotel St George for tea at 6pm. Then, the blue entourage made their way to the Shakespeare Theatre, where they enjoyed George Dance's musical play *A Chinese Honeymoon*.

Liverpool were training at Anfield, where the routine included sprinting on the famous turf. The *Liverpool Echo* reported that Billy Dunlop was nursing a leg injury and was based in Manchester at Allison's football shop, but he would be ready for Saturday.

Fine weather embraced the city on the morning of the match. Some 50,000 supporters made their way to Goodison, where the matchday band provided a musical backdrop to the build-up to kick-off, with the gates opening at 1.30pm. Among those in attendance were the Lord Mayor of Liverpool and city councillors. The crowd, bedecked with blue and red favours, some with rattles, created a great atmosphere. Hundreds of tons of ashes had been deposited on the banks adjacent to the pitch, enabling huge numbers of supporters to bear witness to the battle.

Everton were at full strength, while Liverpool, despite hopes that Dunlop would be fit, saw Murray step in at the last minute. As 3.30pm approached, the weather became overcast, with the teams taking to the pitch some ten minutes before kick-off. Liverpool headed out first, to a large cheer from the crowd. The visitors won the toss, forcing Everton to face the sun in the first half.

As battle commenced, Everton immediately went on the front foot. However, Liverpool charged back. The game became a ferocious battle, end to end, with Liverpool's Raisbeck and Everton's Balmer responsible for breaking up the play. Then Hewitt met a cross from Cox, only to see Billy Scott heroically palm away his effort for a corner. Eventually, Liverpool's pressure began to tell on the Everton defence, and when Arthur Goddard struck a sublime shot, it sailed straight through them and into the net. It was a brilliant strike, but it was instantly ruled out for offside.

Then, on 18 minutes, Everton took the lead after several skirmishes had severely tested the Liverpool defence. Jimmy Settle struck a low shot past Doig and the home support erupted in rapturous celebration, with cheering and rattles creating a deafening noise. Not to be cowed in the face of such impassioned Goodison support, Liverpool went on the front foot and managed to force Scott into two brilliant saves from Raybould and Hewitt. However, despite their efforts, the Blues extended their lead through Walter Abbott.

As the half wore on, both sides continued to fight themselves almost to a standstill, and just before half-time Liverpool found a lifeline. Cox whisked in a cross that Goddard trapped, spun round to face the goal, before centring for Hewitt, who tucked his shot away, much to the delight of the Red contingent in the stands.

The second period saw Liverpool start positively, but Everton soon grabbed a third through Harold Hardman just two minutes into the half. Things were about to get worse. With Liverpool desperately searching for a way back into the game, they were continually frustrated by Everton's back line. Then a powerful counter-attack saw Jack Sharp fly past Liverpool's David Murray before sliding the ball past the onrushing Doig. It was now 4-1 to Everton, yet Liverpool continued to push forward. This was a derby and, with local pride at stake, no quarter was given. However, they continued to be wasteful in front of goal. There was, though, time for one more moment of glorious derby controversy.

Though it meant nothing in terms of the eventual scoreline, Goddard unleashed a terrific shot that cannoned off Hewitt and deflected into the Everton net. Despite Everton's furious attempts at claiming offside, the goal stood. That would prove to be the Reds' final flourish and they eventually had to accept their medicine. A 4-2 defeat and the bragging rights belonged to the Blue half of the city.

As September gave way to October, Liverpool was lashed by rain and gale-force winds. Ships had been unable to dock due to the Mersey swell. It was against this backdrop that Watson's men would blow past the in-form Derby County on Saturday, 7 October. County had won all of their games thus far, and the Reds must have gone into the game with great trepidation.

Such was the interest in the fixture in Derby that a large number of workers at the Carriage and Wagon Department of the town's Midland Railway Works had applied for and been refused early leave from work to catch the Saturday excursion to Liverpool.

Anfield saw 20,000 brave the miserable weather, and they would be amply rewarded. Amid torrential rain, the ball seemed like it was coated in 'duck fat' and Derby struggled to cope with the conditions and the howling wind. Liverpool took full advantage and their attackers were now producing some great moves. Backheels from Raybould and precision crosses from Bradley enthralled the crowd, who were lapping this up, despite the horrendous weather. Then, against the run of play, the visitors broke towards Liverpool's goal and Billy Dunlop made a careless challenge on Ben Warren that so enraged the referee, Mr Robinson, that the infuriated Scot hauled Dunlop by the back of his neck to reprimand him. Warren took the subsequent free kick, which glanced off the head of West and curled into the corner of the net.

The goal temporarily took the wind out of Liverpool's sails. As they struggled to regain the initiative, a depressed and saturated fox terrier made its way on to the pitch and attempted to nip at the ankles of Derby's Jimmy Methven, before his team-mate, Steve Bloomer, stepped in, throwing the canine imposter into the crowd.

Liverpool began to retake control. Corner after corner came their way. Thanks to the wet conditions, County's players struggled to cope with the ball, which appeared to have taken on a life of its own. Shots from Raybould, Hewitt, Cox and Goddard peppered the visitors' goal. County's keeper Harry Maskrey proved equal to them all. However, he could do nothing to prevent the onrushing Cox, who breezed past Warren and Charlie Morris, before rounding Maskrey and nestling the ball in the back of the net, with five minutes to go before half-time.

The second half continued in the same vein as the first half, with attack and counter-attack, before Liverpool's James Bradley began to dazzle with his footwork. Then, following something of an onslaught on Doig's goal, the ball broke to Bradley, whose perfectly executed centre met the head of Robinson, and the ball landed in the back of the net.

Liverpool had now moved up a gear, as Cox once again set off on an explosive run, leaving Warren in his wake. His cross saw Maskrey scamper out to meet the ball, but he was distracted by Robinson, with the onrushing Goddard clattering in Liverpool's third. Now hungry for a fourth goal, Liverpool were once again denied by Maskrey, who pulled off a magnificent save from a Sam Raybould header.

The game edged towards its finale, as both sides turned defence into attack. Cox then capped a magnificent afternoon by scoring his second and Liverpool's fourth goal. Only Preston, Bury and now Liverpool had managed to breach Derby's defences. The win lifted Liverpool into 13th place, but there was no sign yet of a serious title challenge.

For Watson, the Reds' start to the season had been far from promising. He wasn't fooled by the victory over Derby County, and knew that much improvement was required. They had lost four of their opening seven games, shipping 17 goals in the process. While the most ardent of Liverpool supporters would have been given a lift by the mauling of Derby, that was about to be severely tested. The team faced a journey to Owlerton, the home of The Wednesday.

Wednesday were in second place in the table, one point behind Stoke City. If Tom was to prevent the season spiralling out of control, he surely had to coax a victory out of his team, or at least earn a point and stop the rot.

The party that set off for Yorkshire on Saturday morning contained some noticeable absentees. Jack Cox had suffered a sprain while sprinting on the Thursday, while Sam Raybould was suffering from a cold. To further add to Liverpool's woes, the *Liverpool Echo* reported that Alf West was 'hors de combat', a French expression that effectively meant out of action. Harry Griffiths made his first appearance as he stepped in for West, while John Carlin and James Garside replaced Cox and Raybould. The Wednesday saw the return of Harry Chapman, following several weeks of injury. Harry was the younger brother of the famed Herbert Chapman, and was a highly rated forward.

Liverpool made good time, eating en route and arriving at Owlerton for 2.30pm. Despite the cold and gloomy weather, plenty of fans had taken their place ready for the kick-off. Facing a strong wind, Liverpool made a lively start. However, they would soon find themselves in difficulty. Doig had saved well from a powerful hit from England international Harry Davis, but he failed to deal with the resultant goalmouth scramble, and Wednesday's Ruddlesden put the ball in the net.

Gradually, the home side took charge. Wednesday forward Jimmy Stewart hit the crossbar, and the 15,000-strong crowd surged forward as a melee in the Reds' goalmouth threatened to produce a second. Liverpool cleared, but it felt like only a matter of time before they went further behind, with Watson's men penned into their own half.

The inevitable happened when full-back Harry Burton fired a long, dipping shot at goal. Doig managed to fist away the effort, only for Stewart to catch the ball on the volley and launch it into the back of the net. The crowd surged again, roaring their approval, and Liverpool heads dropped.

Wednesday were well up for the fight now, and in the stands their supporters struggled on tiptoes to catch as much of the action as they could, willing their side to grab a third. Their wishes were granted when Doig again failed to hold on to a shot, instead electing to punch the ball to Chapman, who spun around and smashed in the home side's third.

This was turning into a rout and Liverpool had so far been barely able to muster an attack. But, when things seemed at their lowest, Watson's men dug in. Soon the chances came. First Hewitt drifted a shot wide, then Carlin hit a daisy-cutter that Lyall attempted to palm away, only for Bobby Robinson to claim the Reds' first with barely a minute to go before half-time. In the stands, flat-capped men, who had moments earlier been buoyant, now puffed hard on their cigarettes, their confidence dented ever so slightly. And that smaller contingent of Liverpool supporters sensed a glimmer of hope.

The second half saw the crowd swell further and the clouds above Owlerton were ominous. Harry Burton, The Wednesday full-back, sprained his wrist and play was paused for a period. The player elected to continue, but he was clearly struggling. Liverpool did their best to take advantage, and in the closing stages they forced Lyall into a series of saves. Then, with Burton having to go off, the Reds stepped it up, and six minutes later Hewitt reduced the deficit to a single goal. They continued to press for what would have been a memorable equaliser, but it wasn't to be. It was yet another defeat, but the manner of Liverpool's fightback gave Watson some positives to hold on to, particularly as they had managed it with some notable absentees.

The *Liverpool Echo* tended to agree, but pointed to 'Liverpool's procrastination, injuries and defensive lethargy' as markers for the defeat. This was not the result Watson wanted. Having defeated Derby County so convincingly a week earlier, he would have been looking for his team to build on that.

Watson had noted that his keeper, Ned Doig, was beginning to struggle. Doig had admirably held the role of Liverpool's custodian since arriving at Anfield from Sunderland in 1904. Helping Liverpool claim the Second Division title, he had previously won four First Division titles with Sunderland and five international caps with Scotland. Rightly considered one of the greatest goalkeepers of his era, now in his late 30s, time had finally caught up with the 'Prince of Goalkeepers'. Dogged by rheumatism, his performances were beginning to suffer. However, dropping him was still a big decision, let alone replacing him with a younger, untested deputy. Such was Doig's status in the game that a letter appeared in the *Arbroath Herald* on 19 October 1905, from R. E. Crammond of Newcastle-upon-Tyne, who was hoping to rally a large number of Arbroathians and followers of Doig to attend the Newcastle United game against Liverpool in November.

Watson was his own man, respected in the game, and possessed a huge personality. He was confident enough to make the big decisions. Doig would step aside, and in his place for the visit of Nottingham Forest would be a 23-year-old Sam Hardy.

'The Lacemen', as Forest were known at the time – a reference to the Nottingham lace industry – sat just two places above Liverpool, separated by a solitary point. West, Raybould and Cox were also welcome returns to the Liverpool side. Forest were at full strength and included the England goalkeeper Harry Linacre. Their defence included James Iremonger, the brother of Notts County keeper Albert.

As supporters made their way to the ground, a new direct entrance to the shilling stand opened, which was accessed via Orrell's field. Fine weather welcomed a crowd of around 15,000 as the teams took to the pitch. Liverpool started brightly and Cox had a shot saved brilliantly, following a great cross by Robinson. Then it was the turn of Goddard, with a magnificent effort that just missed the target. The Anfield crowd was now in great form, and the noise levels began to rise.

Then came a moment of brilliance from Hewitt, who weaved past George Wolfe and Walter Dudley, before striking Liverpool's opener after just five minutes. The roar of appreciation was as much in relief as it was joy. Forest were far from out of the game, however, despite a wave of attacks from the Reds. It didn't take long for the visitors to find their feet, and Tommy Niblo and Grenville Morris combined well, before Morris's effort skimmed the crossbar. Then Iremonger lifted in a free kick, which Morris leapt to head towards goal, only for Hardy to make an easy save.

Hardy was in fine form, and produced another save from Niblo's testing effort. The pattern of the game was beginning to settle into an end-to-end battle, when Maurice Parry sent a long, searching pass forward. Cox and Iremonger were immediately locked in a race for the ball, but it was the Liverpool man who reached it first, sweeping the leather into the path of Raybould, who headed past Linacre to make it 2-0. There was a huge roar, and the crowds of youngsters whose meagre spending power meant they were forced to gather outside the ground were desperate to know who had scored. Soon word reached them and a small game of football involving a ball of tightly packed newspaper, secured with string, broke out in the streets, with the tearaways attempting to emulate their heroes.

Liverpool continued to threaten, and as Iremonger and fellow full-back Walter Dudley passed between each other, Raybould darted in to win the ball, shooting between the two of them and sending the ball beyond a helpless Linacre for Liverpool's third. This sent the home crowd into a frenzy. On the pitch, Watson's men took heart and flew towards Linacre's goal. The pressure proved too much for Forest, and eventually Robinson netted Liverpool's fourth.

Memories of Sheffield were beginning to fade. This was the Liverpool that trounced Derby County, and the same spirit that saw their incomplete fightback against Wednesday was all too evident. They had given Watson some belief, a sign that they could mount a serious challenge.

For Linacre, the second half started in the same way that the first half had ended. The England keeper proved equal to every foray by the Liverpool forwards. The speed of Cox tormented the Forest defence, and his cross to Raybould seemed certain to result in a fifth. With the goal at his mercy, Raybould somehow conspired to shoot wide.

Liverpool were in complete control. Raisbeck and Bradley dominated the Forest halves and were integral in stifling their attackers. Nottingham-born Alf West produced a sterling performance, while Sam Hardy played as though he had been the Reds' keeper for years. Liverpool could and should have scored more. However, Forest somehow managed to grab a goal. Billy Dunlop upended Morris in the area, and George Henderson scored from the resultant penalty. The goal did little to dent Liverpool's pride, though. However, the home crowd had been so impressed by the performance of Forest's Linacre that it offered magnanimous applause for the England man at the final whistle. The tradition of Liverpool supporters showing respect for opposition goalkeepers will be familiar to those attending games today. It's interesting to note just how far that custom goes back.

The victory over Forest coupled with Liverpool's second-half performance against The Wednesday had changed the complexion of the season. Defence had been an issue thus far, and in particular the decline of Doig in goal. Injuries were easing, and as Watson's men entered the next phase of the campaign, there was reason to feel a sliver of optimism.

The introduction of Hardy proved pivotal, as the young keeper immediately earned the confidence of his team-mates and the crowd. His assured and almost routine handling of his area meant that the Reds' forwards could attack with more assuredness. Liverpool's next ten games took them to Christmas Day, and they won eight of them, drawing the other two. They lost the Boxing Day fixture, but the run took them to the top of the table, two points clear of Aston Villa. During the run, they scored 26 goals, conceding just eight. The turnaround was remarkable.

In among that run was an impressive 3-0 victory over George Ramsay's Villa, at Anfield on 2 December 1905. Billed as the 'fixture of the afternoon', such was the sense of anticipation that a crowd of nearly 25,000 people arrived at Anfield to see Liverpool take on one of the country's most attractive sides. The match would also double as a benefit game for Sam Raybould.

The Reds were at full strength for the first time since October, and coming into the contest on the back of five wins in six. Villa were missing Billy Brawn, Harry Hampton and Freddie Miles. However, they were in a similar vein of form, and had beaten Wolves 6-0 in their previous fixture.

Only three points separated the sides as the captains stood in the centre circle. Villa sat at the summit of the table, and Liverpool were in sixth, behind a tightly packed group of challengers. Their previous game, against Newcastle, had ended in a 3-2 victory, thanks to two penalties scored by Alf West. Raisbeck won the toss and Liverpool kicked off against the Villans, facing the Anfield Road end, with a faint wind at their backs.

The Reds' forwards took the game to the visitors and promptly had the Villa defenders bamboozled. They were soon ahead thanks to a fine strike by Jack Cox, following a brilliant cross from Goddard. The roar was deafening, and the crowd's enthusiasm drove the players on. *Athletic News* would later describe Liverpool's play as 'fast and exciting'. However, in a warning to Watson's men, Villa's Albert Hall struck the crossbar with a brilliant shot. But the Reds were not to be deterred and Goddard once again turned provider, sending the ball into the visitors' goalmouth for Hewitt to score. Then Robinson squandered an easy chance to make it 3-0.

Hardy, in the Liverpool goal, could barely have expected such an easy afternoon. He was only called into action once in the first half, saving a Howard Spencer effort comfortably. The teams went into the changing rooms with the score at 2-0, while supporters rushed out to grab a pint, served from a hatch at the Albert Hotel on Walton Breck Road.

George Murray must have read his players the footballing equivalent of the riot act, because they roared out of the traps in the second half. Hardy was forced into several saves, as the Villa threat seemed to be coming from the left wing. However, it didn't take long for the home team to get going, and from a corner Raisbeck headed in to make it 3-0. The fans, standing on a pile of rubble and slag that would one day become the Kop, leapt for joy. Liverpool were irresistible for long periods, until Maurice Parry handled in his own area. Villa were awarded a penalty at the Anfield Road end. Billy Garraty stepped up to take it, and Hardy's face was a study in concentration. Cool and calm, he didn't ruffle easily. As the crowd held its breath, Garraty struck the ball with force, but Sam was equal to it, saving the penalty comfortably to huge applause. Liverpool immediately rushed up the other end and put the Villa keeper under enormous pressure, but they would have to settle for three. The spoils and the points belonged to Watson and his men.

The arrival of December in Liverpool saw its city centre decked out in colour, with public Christmas trees on display. The city's major department stores boasted huge festive displays. Just two years later, the city's premier store, Blacklers, located on the corner of Elliot Street and Great Charlotte Street, would open its doors. Famed for its giant Father Christmas and extravagant displays, it would become a jewel in Liverpool's retail crown. Those who could afford it would be looking forward to a luxurious festive season, with young children's excitement reaching fever pitch. For the children of poorer families, there would be the hope of receiving an orange or a few sweets in their stockings.

As was the custom right up to the 1960s, official league football matches would be contested on both Christmas Day and Boxing Day. Liverpool welcomed Bolton Wanderers to Anfield on 25 December, and a healthy crowd of 25,000 made its way through the turnstiles for a 2pm kick-off. However, the Reds slumped to a two-goal deficit by half-time, thanks to goals from Bob Clifford (16) and Albert Shepherd (20). Whether Watson's men had indulged a little too heavily the evening before, or it was a case of complacency, the first half was certainly one to forget. Somehow, though, they lifted themselves for the second half, and goals from Joe Hewitt (60) and Arthur Goddard (74) restored parity. A point would have to suffice, and supporters would be sent home satisfied, to the pub and on to their Christmas dinner.

For the players, Boxing Day brought a trip to Stoke, and a 2-1 defeat. Aston Villa took four points from their games on the 25th and 27th, so gained ground on Liverpool, but they would then lose 1-0 to Blackburn Rovers on 30 December, which meant that a victory for Liverpool against Woolwich Arsenal at Anfield on the same day would see them into the New Year at the top of the table.

The win was delivered in some style, with goals from Goddard, Raybould and Raisbeck sealing a 3-0 win. A report in the joint Everton and Liverpool programme feels harsh, given the emphatic nature of the scoreline, suggesting a highly complacent display, with Liverpool's players seemingly going through the motions. In truth, there may have been an element of them trying to conserve their energy. The festive period had been packed, as is customary in England. The game against the Arsenal had been their fifth in two weeks, and they had the visit of Stoke to come on 1 January.

Interestingly, with Stoke playing in maroon, Liverpool elected to play in all white, despite being the home team. The game started late due to Billy Dunlop failing to make the kick-off. It appears to have been a feisty affair, with both Dunlop and a Stoke player having to leave the pitch to receive treatment at different times during the match. Dunlop returned but City's George Gallimore was less fortunate. Liverpool won the game 3-1. They were now three points clear of Aston Villa going into 1906.

The year began with a general election, which saw the Conservative Party lose 246 seats. This meant a Liberal victory, with leader Henry Campbell-Bannerman becoming Prime Minister. Meanwhile, members of the Labour Representation Committee in Parliament adopted the name the Parliamentary Labour Party for the first time.

In football, Manchester United, who had been Newton Heath until 1902, were on course to gain promotion from the Second Division. Meanwhile, Liverpool navigated January with three wins, a draw and one defeat by a single goal away to Birmingham.

February saw them dispatch Barnsley in the second round of the FA Cup before travelling to the Baseball Ground to face Derby County eight days later in the league. Watson and his men arrived to horrendous weather conditions, with the pitch something of a quagmire, yet they coped far better than their opponents, taking the lead inside five minutes. From that moment on, County were done for. Liverpool had trebled their lead within 20 minutes thanks to further strikes from Raybould and Robinson. Watching the game was a reporter for the *Derby Daily Telegraph*, who could only wax lyrical about Liverpool's brilliance, claiming that there wasn't a weakness anywhere throughout the team, and that they were 'a splendidly balanced side, and don't spoil their work through over elaboration. Their play on a treacherous surface was a revelation, their passing and shooting alike being brilliant.'

The home side did manage to rouse themselves in the second half, and managed to strike Liverpool's woodwork twice. However, their forwards found Hardy in excellent form. In truth, Liverpool were in complete control, and there was even time for Dunlop to see a goal ruled out in comical fashion. The Reds won a free kick, and the Liverpool man – and, for a moment, the referee – seemed to forget that he wasn't allowed to score directly from a free kick. As Dunlop stepped up to take the set piece, he blasted the ball over the keeper and into the net. The referee immediately pointed to the centre circle, before realising he had to disallow the goal.

All that remained was for Watson to take his men back to Merseyside and prepare for the next challenge. They were three points clear at the top of the league, with both Manchester City and Preston North End their nearest challengers, Aston Villa having faded away.

Liverpool navigated their way through the third and fourth rounds of the FA Cup without too much difficulty, and managed to maintain their place at the top of the league throughout February and March, despite losing 1-0 to challengers Manchester City at Anfield. They also suffered a 3-0 defeat on the road to Notts County as they prepared for the semi-final of the cup, against Everton. We will discuss this in detail in a later chapter.

Overall, February and March had brought eight wins and three defeats, and, by the time April came around, they were now four points clear of their closest challengers, Preston North End, thanks in no small part to a vital 2-1 victory at Deepdale, in which they had come from behind to win. Their goal average had also been helped thanks to a 6-1 drubbing of Middlesbrough at Anfield on 17 March 1906. They were now in the run-in and looking very comfortable.

The Reds had a rearranged fixture on 2 April against Bury at Gigg Lane. It was a top versus bottom battle, with Liverpool trying to secure the title as early as possible, while Bury – languishing in 18th place – desperately needed the points to avoid relegation. The match was watched by 10,000, with the league leaders virtually at full strength. Only Jack Cox was missing, James Garside taking his place. Meanwhile, Bury were missing several key players. It should have been a straightforward job for Watson's men. But football can be a fickle business.

Despite their weaknesses, Bury put up a brave fight, and in a game that was, at times, end to end, defences came out on top. The *Liverpool Daily Post* reported:

> End to end play kept the spectators upon the tiptoe of expectation, and the home supporters became rather anxious when it was seen that the Anfielders were much the cleverer team. In spite of the breeze they moved forward with clock like accuracy, and after Raybould had been dispossessed by Lindsay, Garside sent wide.

It would prove the story of the game, unfortunately, and the teams played out a goalless draw that did neither of them any favours. Hewitt did have the ball in the net on one occasion, but was correctly ruled offside. It was a frustrating afternoon for Watson, but, fortunately, Preston had also drawn 0-0 away to Sheffield United. Tom would now need to work out a battle plan for the visit of Newcastle on Monday, 9 April.

The visitors were far from full strength, and the game was played at a tremendous pace, with Newcastle giving Liverpool a difficult test in the opening exchanges of the first half. However, the Reds' quality started to tell, and a brace from Parkinson either side of half-time and a Sam Raybould strike in the 63rd minute sealed the vital two points for Liverpool, who were now edging closer to their second league title.

A report in the match programme, published after the game, looked forward to the Easter break and the visit of Everton on Good Friday. 'The Reds should beat the Blues,' it proclaimed, before warning, 'But it will be no gift.' Wise words.

Under a banner headline 'EXTRAORDINARY SCENES AT ANFIELD', the *Liverpool Courier* did its best to describe an incredible contest between Liverpool and Everton. A combination of factors, which included the bright sunshine and an Easter weekend, the proximity of the league title for the Reds, Everton on the cusp of an FA Cup Final and the extreme partisan nature of the fixture, almost guaranteed a record crowd at Anfield. In all, 33,000 passed through the turnstiles, with the crush so great that the club was forced to accommodate fans close to the playing area, with supporters lining all four sides of the pitch, close to the touchline. Fully one hour before kick-off, there was not a single space available inside the ground. The *Courier* spelled it out:

> At half past two the dense and swaying crowd at the Oakfield-road end broke down the railings and surged on to the field. A staff of constables, kept the spectators behind the touch line, but shortly afterwards a similar incident occurred, and further avalanches of spectators poured on to the green. All round the playing pitch enthusiastic supporters of either club swarmed around the touch line.
>
> Others climbed on the roofs of the stands while several partisans swarmed up the pillars supporting the roofs and perched themselves in forks of the ironwork. The ground is supposed to hold 28,000 people, but there were probably 35,000 present, while thousands remained outside unable to gain entrance.

Scenes like this had never been witnessed at Anfield before and, as well as the obvious risk to life, the game itself was in doubt. Eventually, the players arrived on the pitch, just before three o'clock, to a crescendo of cheers that made it hard for anyone to hear themselves think. Somehow the game got underway.

With neither side at full strength, the stage was set for an incredible battle. And so it proved to be, with both the Reds and Blues launching wave after wave of attacks in the bright sunshine, with neither able to break the deadlock. Thousands outside the ground were living off the sound emanating from within and desperately trying to get a handle on what was going on.

Midway through the first half, the incredible pressure in the stands proved too much and again the crowd broke through, with scores of supporters running on the pitch, and the game was stopped for several minutes. Eventually, though, order was restored and the match was restarted. There was no suggestion of trouble between the rival sets of fans; this was simply a case of the ground not being able to accommodate the sheer number of people who wanted to see the game.

The match continued at a frenetic pace, and Liverpool should have been awarded a penalty when Balmer shoved Hewitt into the back of the net, but the referee failed to spot the incident. After more goalmouth action at either end of the pitch, a third crowd invasion again halted play. Once more, the pitch was cleared and the game resumed, but half-time was fast approaching.

Everton launched an attack, and Jack Taylor hit a shot high and dipping. Hardy seemed to catch it, but then dropped the ball in front of Taylor, who had followed the ball into the box. The forward blasted the ball into the net, and the Blues were a goal up after 40 minutes. The scenes in the stands and along the side of the pitch were sheer chaos, as Blues' rapturous celebrations erupted alongside the now sullen Reds.

The second half was a mirror image of the first, with both sides going at it hell for leather. Then, in the 55th minute, Balmer was again guilty of being overly physical, barging into the back of Parkinson. He crashed to the ground in the full view of the referee, who immediately awarded a penalty. As West stepped up to take it, an eerie hush descended on the stands. The pressure must have felt immense, as the Liverpool player carried the hopes of every Red inside and outside the ground on his shoulders. However, he showed no nerves as he blasted the ball into the back of the goal. As the net rippled, an almighty roar filled the air. Those outside knew such a noise could only have greeted a Liverpool goal, and there were celebrations in the streets outside the stadium.

Both sides continued to battle away in search of a win but, in the end, a draw seemed a fair result following such a pulsating encounter. This was one for the ages and, as the final whistle sounded, the pitch was filled with supporters, who danced and celebrated as they sought out their heroes amid the throng. These were clearly unusual scenes, as the newspaper reports attested. The atmosphere had been simply breathtaking and no doubt would be discussed for weeks to come. An editorial in the *Liverpool Courier* called upon the Liverpool management to increase capacity at Anfield, with these words:

> The management of the Liverpool Football Club could not have had a greater object lesson as regrets the necessity for extending the accommodation of the Anfield-road enclosure than was afforded yesterday. Never in the history of the club have more people been on the ground at any match.
>
> Many of them could not see the game, but when doors are rushed police and officials are powerless. So great was the crush that barriers were smashed, and it was exceedingly fortunate, that no accident occurred. Still, the play was sadly interfered with by reason of the great

> attendance, and it was no wonder that the game, had to be stopped several times in order to keep the people from getting over the touch line.

This feels eerily and depressingly familiar to us. The description of a severe crush outside the ground before the game, which led to barriers collapsing, coupled with a stadium ill-equipped to deal with the size of the crowd will no doubt resonate with supporters today. Sadly, the reference to doors being rushed seems at odds with the overall description of the scenes outside the ground. To be fair, it's impossible to say whether this was editorial interpretation, or if the sentence is as a result of a briefing by police or the club's management. There's no reference to 'rushing' earlier in the actual match report. Instead, we're told that the pressure of the dense swaying crowd caused the barriers to collapse, with fans climbing pillars and on to the roof of the stand. This behaviour could have been more about escaping the crush than simply attempting to gain a better view. The claim that doors were 'rushed' appears, unsubstantiated, later in a comments piece.

While it's impossible for us to litigate the incidents, which occurred more than a century ago, with so little evidence to draw upon, we're struck by how familiar this feels to us today. We'll learn in a subsequent chapter about how the club responded to this and other incidents, but for now, suffice it to say that increasing capacity along with the number of entry and exit gates was top of their list of priorities.

There is no evidence of crowd violence in these reports, with Liverpool and Everton fans sitting alongside each other next to the pitch without any reported incidents. However, it's incredible that there were no serious injuries or deaths as a result of the incidents.

The draw had reduced Liverpool's lead to three points over Preston North End, who had played a game less. Despite Raybould being absent with a cold, Liverpool next beat Wolves 2-0 at Molineux on 14 April, the day after the Merseyside derby, to stretch their lead to five points, after Preston had suffered a 3-0 defeat away to Stoke. The Reds were now on 49 points, and had just two games remaining. They needed one more win to seal the championship. Preston needed to win their remaining three to be in with a chance of finishing on 50 points, and hope that Liverpool lost their remaining games.

With the league title so close, they could taste it, and around 1,000 Reds supporters travelled to Burnden Park on Easter Monday, 16 April, in hopes of seeing Tom Watson's Liverpool crowned champions against Bolton Wanderers. Sadly, Bolton raced into a first-half lead and scored again soon after the restart. Parkinson pulled one back for the Reds, but within a minute Bolton were 3-1 up. Liverpool battled valiantly, and in the 80th minute Parkinson scored again to make it 3-2. Try as they might, though, the Reds couldn't draw level, and in the stands those Liverpool supporters grew anxious that the ultimate glory may be snatched from their grasp at the final hurdle.

They needn't have worried. Because 142 miles away, Preston were beaten by two goals to nil. The news wouldn't have reached them immediately, however, and many wouldn't have found out that Liverpool were champions for hours.

Liverpool had lost four out of their opening six games, and yet still managed to storm their way to the championship. It was an incredible feat, and one worthy of an Anfield welcome fit for conquering heroes. Sadly, however, a torrential downpour before and throughout the final game against Sheffield United meant that the match was watched by only 10,000 supporters. The newly crowned champions won 3-1.

They finished the season on a record 51 points out of a possible 76. Only Villa, in 1900, had come close, with 50 out of a possible 68. Liverpool had also become the first club to win the Second Division and First Division in successive seasons, and Tom Watson had now claimed his fifth career league title.

The sense of joy and optimism around the club at the end of the 1905/06 campaign drips from the pages of newspaper reports and records of Liverpool FC's internal meetings. In addition, Watson's men went on to secure the Sheriff of London Charity Shield (otherwise known as the Dewar Shield) by beating Corinthians 5-1 at Craven Cottage, and they also won the Liverpool Senior Cup. This was a feat no other club had achieved. It should be noted that with no Football League Cup or European competition for teams to contest, such trophies would have felt more important to clubs and their supporters. It's noteworthy that the club references these achievements in club programmes. In addition, Liverpool had also progressed to the semi-final stage of the FA Cup during the season.

By any measure, this had been a hugely successful campaign. The Annual General Meeting of the club in June 1906 would find the members of the board and Tom Watson in ebullient mood. Little wonder with the announcement of a five per cent dividend for shareholders. Tom joked that the team had always had 'ups and downs' but that he hoped they were 'done with the latter', to great applause. He concluded that, from that point on, their motto should be 'Upwards'.

Liverpool were now building for the future. They had enjoyed a season of record crowds and unparalleled success. Such factors would allow them to complete terms between the club and William Houlding for the purchase of Anfield on 19 January 1906. They successfully concluded the deal on 24 May 1907, via a £10,000, 20-year mortgage from the Royal Liverpool Friendly Society. The club would satisfy this mortgage in full on 2 March 1921. Meanwhile, significant ground improvements were now being planned at pace. In many respects, they owed their ability to move forward in this way to Tom Watson. Without the progress he delivered on the pitch, the success achieved off it would have been impossible.

## Chapter Fifteen

# The men who brought home number two

THE TEAM that brought home the championship in 1906 contained five survivors from the squad that won the league in 1901: Bill Dunlop, Maurice Parry (a bit-part player in 1901, Maurice missed only two league games in 1906), Alex Raisbeck, Jack Cox and Sam Raybould. The captain, Raisbeck, played 36 league games, Dunlop made 31 league appearances, Cox played 28 times and Sam Raybould ran out 25 times in league fixtures.

The club's stated aim was to recruit players of established quality or youth who possessed considerable potential. However, Watson continued to deal with an enormous amount of squad churn in the seasons that followed the 1901 championship win. An astonishing 27 players left Liverpool FC between 1901 and 1905, including six men who were regulars during the campaign that brought the championship to Anfield: Charlie Satterthwaite, Tom and Tommy Robertson, Johnny Walker, Bill Perkins and Bill Goldie.

Meanwhile, the club also added 27 players in the same period. Of those, four would qualify for winners' medals in 1906, while eight of them played minor roles in the club's second First Division championship. Watson was creating a reserve team at Liverpool with the aim of supplying the first XI with replacements for injured players.

However, the huge number of players moving in and out of the club will have undoubtedly been difficult to manage. Many of them appear to have been recruited for the reserves, and went on to have limited impact. It's hard to escape the fact that the scale of such recruitment, with many of the players having a limited role, possibly contributed to Liverpool's inconsistency in the league between 1901 and 1905.

While such squad churn seems commonplace in the First Division during the period, the more successful teams seemed able to advance via gradual evolution, and saw much less upheaval. Tom's old club, Sunderland, for example, who won the league in 1902 and finished runners-up in 1904, saw just 12 players join the club between 1901 and 1905. Another club, The Wednesday, who won the title in 1903 and 1904, signed just three players during this time, a fraction of the business done by Liverpool.

That Tom and the Liverpool board presided over such changes in the early years of his reign makes his two First Division titles in 1901 and 1906, three FA Cup semi-final appearances, the runners-up position in 1899 and a successful promotion push from the Second Division in 1904/05, all in the first decade of his reign, somewhat remarkable. How much could have been achieved if he and the club had created a stable squad.

Nevertheless, Tom did build two championship-winning teams within ten years of arriving at Anfield. We've detailed the men who delivered his first in an earlier chapter. Below are a series of pen portraits of those who claimed his second.

## Arthur Goddard

*Watson's 'shining star' and hall-of-fame hero*

Of course, the joy of writing these books lies in the discovery of long-forgotten stories of players whose achievements on the football pitch have faded from the collective memory as the generations pass by. Equally, there's great pleasure in stumbling across the myriad peculiar words that once dripped from the pen of journalists and have now been consigned to the dustiest of history books. We recall our research for *The Untouchables: Anfield's Band of Brothers*, when we delighted in coming across the use of 'fiddle-faced' in a joint Liverpool and Everton matchday programme, which apparently means wearing a long, sad or gloomy facial expression. For this chapter, we're delighted to reintroduce the word 'refulgent', which was used to describe Arthur Goddard's performance in his debut for Glossop against Sheffield United, after his transfer from Stockport County in 1899. The word means to shine brightly or having radiance, which gives us an insight into his impact on the game.

Pitted against the legendary England international left-back, Ernest Needham, Goddard was expected to endure a stern test. However, to the surprise of many, he dazzled in his position of outside-right, providing an assist and a goal in the game. This is how the *Lancashire Evening Post* saw Goddard's debut, on 9 December 1899:

> It is generally agreed that he shone with something like refulgence, making the run and centre which produced goal No. 1 to his side, and also getting a brilliant single-handed equaliser on the post.

After Liverpool clinched the title in 1901, their fortunes dipped, and with ten games left of the 1901/02 campaign they had slumped to 14th place. Alarmed by their terrible form, the club forked out a record £460 fee to tempt Glossop to part company with the winger. Tom Watson handled the negotiations personally, with Goddard having his pick of 'four other prominent clubs', which included Nottingham Forest. However, it was Tom's overtures that proved to be the difference for Liverpool.

Arthur was born in Heaton Norris, in Manchester, on 14 June 1878. One of five children, his parents were Martha and James. His father was a 'Coal Dealer' and the family lived at 4 Parsonage Street. He married Annie McLaughlin on 31 July 1900 and, despite his footballing fame, his occupation on his marriage certificate is recorded as 'Packer'. However, Arthur described himself as 'Professional Footballer and Greengrocer' in the 1901 census, although curiously his wife is now named 'Mary'. This was clearly an error as she returns to being Annie by the 1911 census.

The Goddards set up home at 20 Breckfield Road North, Liverpool after he joined Watson at Anfield, where the couple lived with his sister, Barbara. The family experienced tragedy early in their marriage, with Annie giving birth to a child that subsequently died.

Though he would go on to be regarded as one of Liverpool's great players of the era, it seems that, at least as far as the authors of the joint Everton and Liverpool match programme were concerned, his early career at Liverpool was something of a disappointment. A short piece, dated 30 September 1905, suggests that Goddard had been seen as a significant capture, and was highly regarded in the game. However, according to this scribe, he had for two seasons failed to light up the game at Anfield, although it seems the 1905/06 campaign would prove a turning point:

> The outside right of Liverpool for two seasons has been somewhat disappointing. On Saturday, however, he came right back to his best form, and it is to be hoped that he will go on right through improving week by week. To my mind Arthur Goddard is one of the most gratifying forwards who ever played. He has a way of getting along the wing unsurpassed by any, while he can centre with most. His fatal tendency is to drop the ball on top of the net. If this is corrected he will be the equal of the best.

Arthur was an ever-present in the league during the title-winning 1905/06 season, featuring 38 times. He also made five appearances in the FA Cup, reaching the semi-final, only to taste defeat at the hands of the eventual winners, Everton. Goddard also played in the Sheriff of London Charity Shield, which Liverpool won 5-1 against the amateur side Corinthians at Craven Cottage.

That some felt Goddard had disappointed in the two seasons before Liverpool's second league championship is perhaps explained by the fact that he had set himself a very high bar early in his Liverpool career, scoring 11 goals in 33 league games during the 1902/03 season. This was a high return for a winger, and a feat he couldn't match until he surpassed it with 12 during the 1909/10 campaign, in which Liverpool finished runners-up to Aston Villa.

He would make 28 appearances during the club's promotion campaign, which saw them finish as champions of the Second Division in 1905. Arthur scored seven league goals in a season that saw Liverpool promoted back to the First Division at the first attempt.

Described a 'clever dribbler with excellent judgment and a great shot', Arthur was also famed for having a long stride, which saw him cover the ground quickly. Perhaps evidencing his improvement during Liverpool's championship-winning campaign, the *Liverpool Football Echo* had the following to say of him on 21 April 1906:

> Arthur Goddard has been the most consistent of the forward line. He has always been ready to go that last yard, whereas he previously seemed to ease up where he now bustles and hampers the defence. He is a graceful player is Goddard, and when one sees him trip along the touch-line could imagine him gliding on ice. He is an artistic footballer, and nothing but the ultra-excellence of the outside right of other clubs kept him from being recognised in the internationals.

*Thomas Hemy painting depicting Sunderland vs Aston Villa, 1895. Variously known as* A Corner Kick, The Last Minute – It's Now or Never *or* Sunderland v Aston Villa – Struggle for the Championship, *it is said to feature Tom Watson in his role as linesman holding a white flag in the background. Courtesy of Rob Mason and Sunderland Football Club.*

*Cartoon depicting David Hannah scoring for Liverpool. The game is unknown, but the picture is dated 6 November 1896, a matter of months after Tom Watson became Liverpool manager. Courtesy of Liverpool FC museum collection.*

*(Left) Tom Watson: Liverpool manager 1896–1915. Image colourised by George Chilvers courtesy of Liverpool Football Club.*

*(Right) Club captain and 'half of Tom Watson's team', Alec Raisbeck in his Scotland international shirt.*

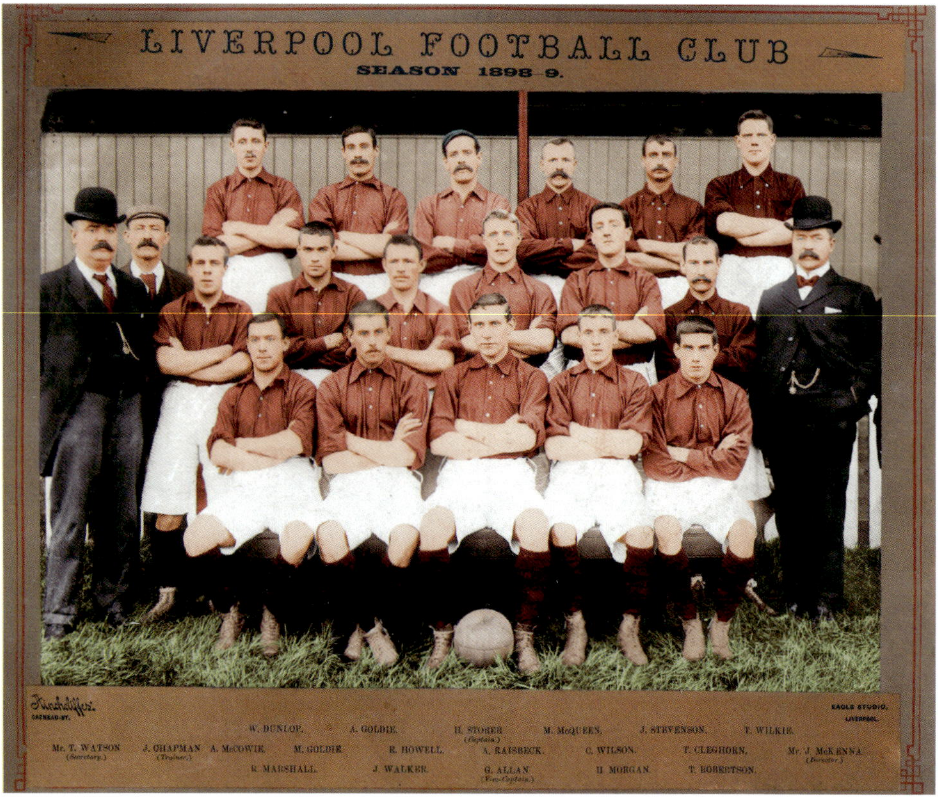

1898/99 squad Squad photo. Colourised by George Chilvers. Courtesy of Liverpool FC museum collection.

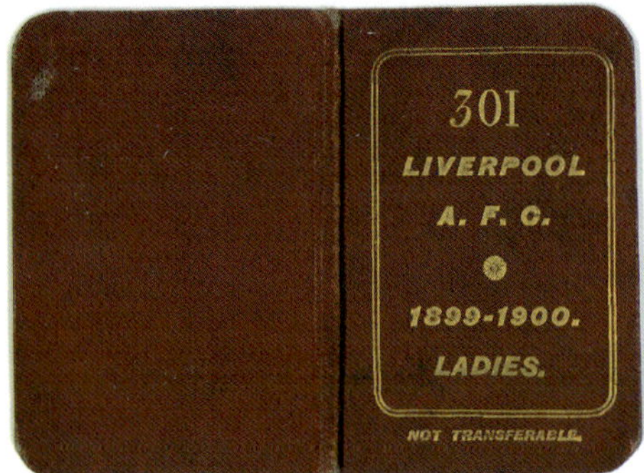


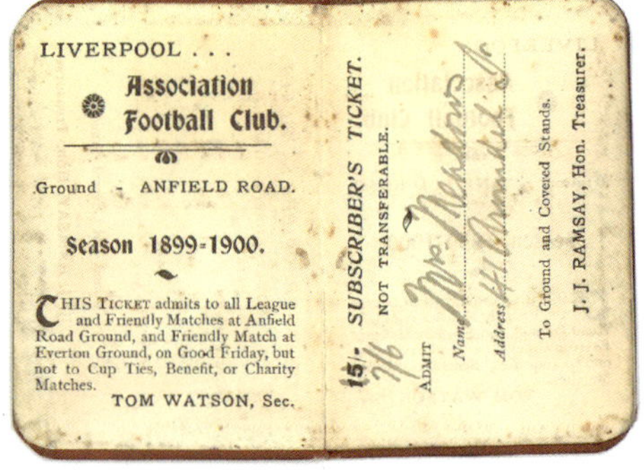

LIVERPOOL . . .

**Association Football Club.**

Ground - ANFIELD ROAD.

**Season 1899-1900.**

THIS TICKET admits to all League and Friendly Matches at Anfield Road Ground, and Friendly Match at Everton Ground, on Good Friday, but not to Cup Ties, Benefit, or Charity Matches.

TOM WATSON, Sec.

15/. SUBSCRIBER'S TICKET.

NOT TRANSFERABLE.

ADMIT

Name

Address

To Ground and Covered Stands.

J. J. RAMSAY, Hon. Treasurer.

LIVERPOOL FOOTBALL CLUB FIXTURES.

FIRST TEAM. 1899-1900.

| DATE. | NAME OF CLUB. | GOALS. F | GOALS. A | Pts. | | Where Played |
|---|---|---|---|---|---|---|
| 1899. | | | | | | |
| Sept. 2 | Stoke | 2 | 3 | - | L. | Away |
| " 4 | Glasgow Rangers | 2 | 2 | | F | Away |
| " 9 | Sunderland | 0 | 2 | - | L | Home |
| " 16 | West Bromwich | 0 | 2 | - | L | Away |
| " 23 | Everton | 1 | 2 | - | L | Home |
| " 25 | Queen's Park | [illegible] | [illegible] | | F | Away |
| " 30 | Blackburn Rovers | 0 | 2 | - | L | Away |
| Oct. 5 | Notts County | 1 | 3 | - | L. | Away |
| " 7 | Derby County | 0 | 2 | - | L | Home |
| " 14 | Bury | 1 | 2 | | L. | Away |
| " 21 | Notts County | 3 | 1 | 2 | L | Home |
| " 28 | Manchester City | 1 | 0 | 2 | L. | Away |
| Nov. 4 | Sheffield United | 2 | 2 | 1 | L | Home |
| " 11 | Newcastle United | 1 | 1 | 1 | L. | Away |
| " 18 | Aston Villa | 3 | 3 | 1 | L | Home |
| " 25 | W'hampton W. | 1 | 1 | 1 | L | Home |
| Dec. 2 | Burnley | 1 | [illegible] | - | L. | Away |
| " 9 | Preston N'h End | 1 | [illegible] | [illegible] | L | Home |
| " 16 | Notts Forest | 0 | 1 | | L. | Away |
| " 18 | 1st Round L. Cup | | | | | |
| " 23 | Glossop N'h End | 5 | [illegible] | | L | Home |
| " 25 | Derby County | [illegible] | [illegible] | | L. | Away |
| " 26 | Glasgow Rangers | [illegible] | [illegible] | | F | Home |
| " 30 | Stoke | 0 | 0 | | L | Home |

| DATE. | NAME OF CLUB. | GOALS. F | GOALS. A | Pts. | | Where Played |
|---|---|---|---|---|---|---|
| 1900 Jan 1 | | | | | | |
| " 6 | Sunderland | 0 | 1 | | L | Away |
| " 13 | West Bromwich | 2 | 0 | | L | Home |
| " 15 | 2nd Round L. Cup | | | | | |
| " 20 | Everton | 1 | 3 | | L | Away |
| " 27 | 1st Round E. Cup | 0 | 0 | - | A | STOKE |
| Feb. 3 | Blackburn Rovers | 3 | 1 | | L | Home |
| " 10 | 2nd Round E. Cup | 1 | 1 | | H | WBA |
| " [illegible] | [illegible] | 1 | 2 | [illegible] | [illegible] | [illegible] |
| " 24 | 3rd Round E. Cup | | | | | |
| Mar. 3 | Manchester City | 5 | 2 | | L | Home |
| " 5 | Semi-Final L. Cup | | | | | |
| " 10 | Sheffield United | 2 | 1 | | L | Away |
| " 17 | Newcastle United | 2 | 0 | | L | Home |
| " 17 | Final L. Cup | | | | | |
| " 24 | Aston Villa | 0 | 1 | | L | Away |
| " 24 | Semi-Final E. Cup | | | | | |
| " 31 | W'hampton W | 1 | 0 | | L. | Away |
| Apl. 7 | Burnley | 0 | 1 | | L | Home |
| " 13 | Everton | 1 | 3 | | F | Away |
| " 14 | Preston N'h End | 3 | 1 | | L. | Away |
| " 16 | Queen's Park | 4 | 2 | | F | Home |
| " 21 | Notts Forest | 1 | 0 | | L | Home |
| " 21 | Final E. Cup | | | | | |
| " 28 | Glossop N'h End | 2 | 0 | | L. | Away |
| " 30 | | | | | | |

1899/1900 Liverpool FC Ladies season ticket issued by Tom Watson. Note the owner has documented the scores for the season. Courtesy of Liverpool FC museum collection.

1899/1900 squad photo Squad Photo. Courtesy of Liverpool FC museum collection.

Liverpool squad prior to the 1899 FA Cup semi-final against Sheffield United. After drawing 2-2 and 4-4, Liverpool eventually crashed out after losing 0-1 in the second replay. Colourised by George Chilvers. Courtesy of Liverpool FC museum collection.

Aerial photograph of Anfield dated 1906 showing the former 'Oakfield Terrace' transformed into the Spion Kop, and Archibald Leitch's gable arch at the centre of the main stand. Courtesy of Liverpool FC museum collection.

1900/01 Liverpool FC First Division winners. Courtesy of Liverpool FC museum collection.

First Division championship trophy complete with ribbons. Courtesy of Liverpool FC museum collection.

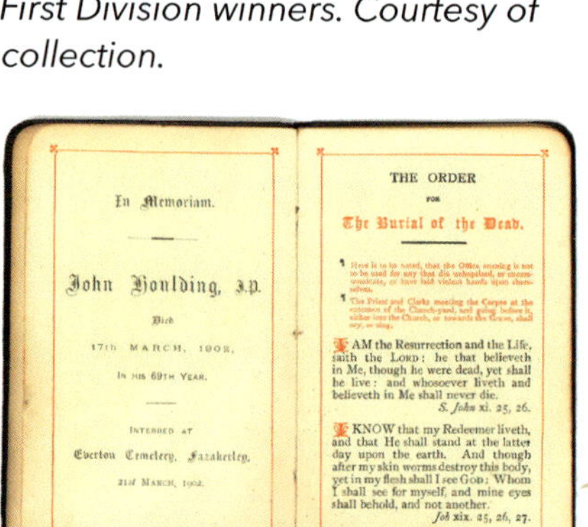

In Memoriam.

John Houlding, J.P.

Died

17th MARCH, 1902,

IN HIS 69TH YEAR.

INTERRED AT

Everton Cemetery, Fazakerley,

21st MARCH, 1902.

THE ORDER

FOR

The Burial of the Dead.

¶ Here it is to be noted, that the Office ensuing is not to be used for any that die unbaptized, or excommunicate, or have laid violent hands upon themselves.

¶ The Priest and Clerks meeting the Corpse at the entrance of the Church-yard, and going before it, either into the Church, or towards the Grave, shall say, or sing.

I AM the Resurrection and the Life, saith the LORD: he that believeth in Me, though he were dead, yet shall he live: and whosoever liveth and believeth in Me shall never die.

*S. John* xi. 25, 26.

I KNOW that my Redeemer liveth, and that He shall stand at the latter day upon the earth. And though after my skin worms destroy this body, yet in my flesh shall I see GOD: Whom I shall see for myself, and mine eyes shall behold, and not another.

*Job* xix. 25, 26, 27.

Tom Robertson's 1900/01 league winners' medal. Courtesy of Liverpool FC museum collection.

Order of service for the funeral of John Houlding, first President of Liverpool FC, who died in 1902. Tom Watson would have undoubtedly been at his funeral. Courtesy of Liverpool FC museum collection.

James Bradley's 1906 First Division winners' medal. Courtesy of Liverpool FC museum collection.

Sketch of John Houlding in his favourite spot at Anfield. Courtesy of Liverpool FC museum collection.

*Liverpool Football Club, 1906 Sheriff of London Charity Shield (Dewar Shield) winners. Image colourised by George Chilvers. Courtesy of Liverpool Football Club.*

*Liverpool FC 1906 champions reunion (date unknown). Courtesy of Liverpool FC museum collection.*

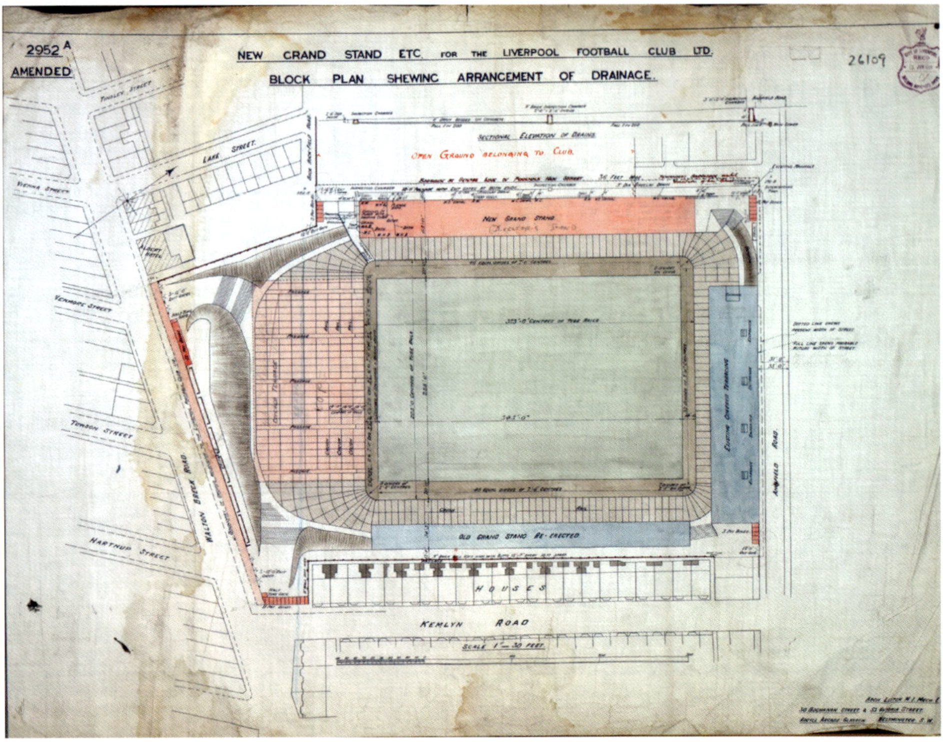

Original drawings by architect, Archibald Leitch, depicting plans for the redevelopment of Anfield in 1906. Courtesy of Liverpool FC museum collection.

Fragment of the 1907/08 squad photo. Courtesy of Liverpool FC museum collection.

1907/08 Liverpool FC squad pin badge, which would have been worn by an unknown supporter. Courtesy of Liverpool FC museum collection.

THE ONLY PROGRAMME PUBLISHED BY AUTHORITY OF THE EVERTON AND LIVERPOOL CLUBS

Vol. 3.—No. 33. [Copyright. Entered at Stationers' Hall.] SATURDAY, FEBRUARY 2, 1907. PRICE ONE PENNY.

**BEATY BROS.,**

THE CELEBRATED

**TAILORS.**

**THE PREMIER LIVERPOOL FIRM F**
**GOOD CLASS TAILORING**
AT RIGHT PRICES.

Two Great Specialities:

**Overcoats at**
**25/= & 30/=**

"THE BEST VALUE IN THE TRADE."

Only Addresses—
**28 & 30, CHURCH ST. & 37 TO 43, LONDON ROAD.**

**ROYAL HIPPODROME, TWICE NIGHTLY, AT 6-50 AND 9.**

*Cover of joint Everton and Liverpool matchday programme from the 1907/08 season. Courtesy of Liverpool FC museum collection.*

*1909/10 squad photo. Courtesy of Liverpool FC museum collection.*

*1910/11 squad photo. Colourised by George Chilvers. Courtesy of Liverpool FC museum collection.*

He would become a firm favourite with supporters during a career that spanned 12 years from 1902 to 1914, in which he played 414 times in all competitions, scoring a very creditable 77 goals. The following appraisal of his skills, written in the club match programme on 29 October 1910, suggests a player of considerable talent:

> By his gentlemanly demeanour on the field, and the genuinely-consistent character of his play since he became associated with the Anfielders, Goddard has deservedly become a great favourite in Liverpool, and he is a typical example of the highest class of footballer. His play is not of the vigorous order; quiet and unassuming, he awaits his opportunity, and then with the embodiment of grace and elegance, he glides down the wing with such ease, that he scarcely seems to be exerting himself. But when we see the half-back and full-back gradually left in the rear, then we tumble to the fact that Goddard is travelling.

Arthur spent a year at Cardiff City after leaving Liverpool and before the First World War put a stop to the Football League in 1915. He appeared 49 times as a wartime guest player, and by all accounts he remained a very popular player on Merseyside. In September 1915, the *Liverpool Echo* reported:

> A well-preserved, gentlemanly player, with a graceful style, Goddard is able to keep time with present day football without straining himself, and, in truth, I think his play will be all the better suited by the friendly game, because he has not to worry about trips and backs, as in former years.

Goddard would have been around 37 years of age when those words were written. He eventually hung up his boots for good in 1919, as reported in the *Liverpool Echo* of 20 August 1919:

> And now I learn from first-hand information that Arthur Goddard has finished his football career.
>
> Goddard was ever truly popular with crowds and opponents. He never remembered fouls that were perpetrated upon him, and he was always clean in his game. His innings was a long one and an honourable one, and although he was not fashionable when selections for big matches were made, there was no doubt about his class being international.
>
> Grace abounded in his every movement, and his centres from the right wing were a study of strength and direction. If anything he courted the corner flags a trifle too much, but that is an arguable matter.

Arthur Goddard remained in Liverpool until his death on 27 May 1956, at the age of 77. He's known to have lived at 5 Conyers Street, which was demolished as part of a slum-clearance programme in the 1960s. The place where his house once stood is now known as Jason Street. After football, and in later life, he was employed as a 'Social Club Steward'. He's buried in the same Anfield Cemetery as his boss, Tom Watson. In addition to his First and Second Division winners' medals, Arthur also won the Sheriff of London Charity Shield and two Liverpool Senior Cups, in 1905 and 1906.

## Robert Smith Robinson

*Watson's goalscoring champion*

Robert Smith Robinson is referred to as 'Robbie' by the National Football Archive, while other sources variously refer to him as 'Bobby' and even 'Whitie', possibly due to his fair hair. Here, we have chosen to refer to him as Robert, the name on his birth certificate.

Signed by Tom Watson in what was a double raid on his former club, Robinson was joined by Joe Hewitt at Anfield in 1904. The *Manchester Courier* reported the deal:

> Mr. Tom Watson, the secretary for the Liverpool Club, visited Sunderland and signed on two of the Wearside forwards, Robert Robinson and Joe Hewitt. Robinson is a local lad, and this was his second season with Sunderland. Lately he has figured at right half and among the forwards in the A-team. Hewitt belongs to Chester, and was his third Sunderland season.

He was born on 22 October 1879 in Sunderland to parents Thomas and Margaret. The family lived at 39 Victor Street, Monkwearmouth Shore, along with Robert's sister, also called Margaret. Robert's father, Thomas, worked as an engine fitter, most likely at the local shipyard.

By 1891, Robert was one of five children and the family had moved to Ellerslie Terrace, next to Sunderland's Newcastle Road stadium. Interestingly, the club owned several properties in that road, although Robert wouldn't join Sunderland until 1902. He played football for several local clubs, including South Hylton and Sunderland Royal Rovers, before spending two seasons with the Newcastle Road club from 1902 to 1904. At this time he was still living with his family, now at 4 Blackett Terrace, Sunderland. Looking at the 1901 census, his occupation is difficult to decipher, and he's either a 'Machine' or 'Marine Engine Worker'. His father is clearly recorded as a 'Marine Engine Builder', however, and perhaps the pair were working together.

Robert played 24 times for Sunderland, scoring seven times over two seasons. This was enough to convince Watson to pay £500 for the player, and he arrived at Anfield on 11 February 1904, and made his debut alongside Joe Hewitt two days later in a goalless draw with Stoke in front of a home crowd of 10,000. Liverpool were languishing in 18th place and the season would end in relegation despite the acquisition of the pair.

Robert lived at 23 Edith Road, Anfield during the early years of his Liverpool career, and by 1911 he had become married to Mary, and the couple now had five children. He appears to have settled quickly into life on Merseyside and was a hugely popular figure.

Robinson played nine times as Liverpool battled to get out of trouble, and managed a highly creditable five goals. Though his signing and goals came too late to save Watson's men from the drop in 1904, his 24 strikes in 32 league appearances during the 1904/05 Second Division campaign would prove pivotal in the club's quest for promotion. The personal highlight of that campaign were his four goals scored in a 4-0 rout of Leicester Fosse at Anfield on 1 October 1904.

Robert was equally in his element in the top tier, and he recorded ten goals in 34 league games as he and Tom Watson's men secured their second league title in five years. However, he appears to have struggled with his weight, which looks to have prompted a move to half-back. According to lfchistory.net, the club resorted to 'extreme' measures to get his weight down, including being 'made to sit in a small "hot room" in furnace-like conditions and sprinted, ball-punched, skipped, and lifted dumbbells'.

However, despite these issues, and perhaps aided by the move to the back line, he made 271 appearances for Liverpool between 1904 and 1912. Ernest Edwards, writing in the *Liverpool Echo* in January 1913, suggests that there was much optimism surrounding

Robinson's efforts to resume his playing career, and hints at the player's undoubted popularity:

> I am delighted to inform this legion of friends that 'Bobby' Robinson, the Liverpool half back, has not finished with football, and under the careful attention of Dr. Ferguson, a director of the club, he is making such progress towards health and strength that there is every hope and chance of his playing football; in fact he is training again. As I said yesterday, there is no more loyal member of the Liverpool club, and the supporters appreciate all his good work, and will welcome him back.

It wasn't to be, however, and Robert would make no further appearances for Liverpool after 6 April 1912, a 2-1 home defeat to Aston Villa. The National Football Archive suggests a move to Tranmere later that year. However, he does not appear to have played any games for the Wirral club.

Robert remained in Liverpool for the rest of his life. At the time of his death, on 16 October 1950, at the age of 71, Robinson was living at 175 Stanley Park Avenue. He's buried in Anfield Cemetery, section 9, grave 26. A Second and First Division champion, Robert played a significant role in Watson's success at Liverpool.

## Joe Hewitt

### *Watson's brilliant centre-forward and an Anfield stalwart*

As we've already stated, Robert Robinson's Sunderland teammate, Joe Hewitt, joined Liverpool at the same time. He had made 39 appearances for the Newcastle Road club, scoring nine times. Watson and Liverpool were clearly looking to boost their firepower as they battled the drop in 1904.

Born on 3 May 1881 in Chester to parents Joseph, a 'Stationary Engine Driver', and Emma, one of three children, Joe would go on to make 164 appearances for Liverpool, scoring 74 times.

According to the 1901 census, Joe was still living with his family in Chester, and their address is recorded as 100 Westminster Road, Hoole, Chester. There he played for numerous local youth teams, St Pauls and amateurs, Chester Locos, and Newtown Rangers, where he won the Chester League in 1901. Joe then moved to Sunderland at the age of 20. His new team became First Division champions in 1902, with Joe making five appearances and scoring once, from the inside-left position.

Watson persuaded the Liverpool board of directors to pay £500 for Joe and fellow Sunderland team-mate Robert Robinson. He made his debut, alongside Robinson, on 13 February 1904. His first goal for his new club came in the 3-0 Anfield victory over Sheffield United, in front of a crowd of 20,000, on 12 March 1904. That would prove to be his only goal of the campaign, in which he played ten league games. The 1904/05 campaign would prove to be a disappointing one for Hewitt, at least on a personal level. Although Liverpool earned promotion, Joe only featured nine times, scoring just once.

In a joint Everton and Liverpool matchday programme dated 7 October 1905, Hewitt, who according to historian Kjell Hanssen, had earned the nickname 'Punch', is praised for his ability to play in several positions, including inside-left, inside-right and left half-back during his youth football days and as a league player. Somewhat prophetically, the sketch declares:

> At present he is proving a useful rover in the Anfield ranks, and deserves every credit for his efforts to fill the vacancy unfortunately created by the injury to Parkinson. Such a deserving, unassuming, and unselfish footballer should become a prominent personality in the game.

Joe's breakthrough came after Tom Watson moved him to the centre-forward position, and his Liverpool career took off. He made 37 league appearances en route to the First Division title, scoring an astonishing 24 league goals. Sadly, however, Hewitt failed to build on his breakthrough campaign, and a series of injuries kept him out of the team, with Raybould reclaiming his place. However, with Raybould moving on in 1907, Joe was given another opportunity, which saw him feature in 75 games in all competitions between 1907 and 1909, netting an impressive 34 times.

In *The Untouchables: Anfield's Band of Brothers*, we detail a story that appeared in the *Dundee Courier*, in which Joe was involved in a horrific incident in 1907. Awoken by screams from his next-door neighbour, Sarah Ann Sweeney, who lived at 12 Finchley Road, Anfield, Hewitt was confronted by the sight of the poor woman engulfed in flames. He tried unsuccessfully to save her. Although he managed to douse the flames, she, sadly, died as a result of her injuries. The Liverpool Coroner recorded a verdict of accidental death.

Joe played his last game for Liverpool two years later, in 1909. However, after brief spells at Bolton Wanderers, and then Reading in the Southern League, he returned to Liverpool, where he spent the rest of his life. His final club was South Liverpool FC.

Hewitt became a member of Liverpool's coaching staff after his retirement as a player in 1912, and would be part of the backroom team when Liverpool won back-to-back league titles in the 1920s. He later served the club as a steward and as a press-box attendant for almost 60 years.

According to the 1911 census for England, Joe was living at 294 Breck Road and, as well as being recorded as a 'Professional Footballer', he also ran a sweet shop, assisted by his wife, Alice. The couple had one son, Joseph. Joe Hewitt died on 12 November 1971 in Sefton Grange Nursing Home. He was 90 years of age. Reporting on his death, the *Liverpool Echo* had the following to say:

> Joe Hewitt, one of the great old-timers associated with the Liverpool club, has died, aged 90. He joined the club from Sunderland in 1904 and was with the Anfield club for 60 years as player and coach, with other duties in his later years.
>
> Up to seven years ago he worked behind the scenes and had a special duty on match days as Press box attendant. When he had to call it a day in 1964, Liverpool gave him a pension and latterly he had been living in an old people's home in Croxteth. [...] He was a very popular figure at Anfield throughout his 60 years there and always had an anecdote about some of the great figures in the game to keep his audience amused.

In a 1955 *Liverpool Echo* Merseyside derby feature looking at Liverpool's 'old timers', Joe gives an interview in which he recalls the 1906 FA Cup semi-final against Everton, a game Liverpool lost 2-0. In it, he confidently talks about how he was asked by Watson to play outside-left, due to the absence of Raybould and Cox, to which he answered, 'You are my master.' Hewitt, now 74, claimed that he 'had the game of his life', and bemoaned the fact that if Liverpool's forwards had put away the chances he created they could have won the game.

Clearly a man with enormous self-belief, he also stated that had Liverpool signed him and Robert Robinson a fortnight earlier, they could have avoided relegation in 1904. Who are we to argue?

Joe was also a huge fan favourite, as recalled by 78-year-old Liverpool supporter, and denizen of the old Kemlyn Road, Charles Wannop of Childwall. In an interview given for the *Anfield Review* in the 1970s, Charles recalled Hewitt's impact on the team and the supporters, when he replaced Jack Parkinson as centre-forward:

> Parkinson was a sprinter, a real goer – but when Joe Hewitt replaced him at centre-forward the fans found a scoring

> hero. People used to stand outside the ground – suppose they couldn't afford to pay – and when they heard a roar they'd shout, 'who scored' The answer always seemed to be, Joe Hewitt.

He was a league champion with Liverpool in 1906, and his goals would prove pivotal for Tom Watson's team. History shows he became an adopted citizen of his chosen city, a fan favourite, and continued to serve Liverpool Football Club well after his playing career had ended.

## 'Silent Sam' Hardy

### *Watson's 'jolly good goalie'*

On 30 May 1912, one of Liverpool Football Club's greatest goalkeepers stood on the precipice of leaving the club. That man was Sam Hardy, who was now transfer-listed. At a fiery Annual General Meeting of the club's shareholders and directors, questions were being asked.

Sam had lived in Chesterfield throughout his Liverpool career, and despite requests to move to Liverpool to complete his training duties, the player had steadfastly refused, leading to a stand-off. The story eventually made it into the pages of the *Liverpool Echo*, and the Anfield board decided it was time for a parting of the ways. The keeper was listed for transfer along with Jim Harrop and John Macdonald. Hardy had been accused of 'breaking discipline'.

Hardy was born in Newbold, Derbyshire on 26 August 1882. The son of a miner, he grew up in the area close to the ground of Chesterfield FC, where he would spend three seasons from 1902 to 1905. Sam followed his father into the pit, but football was his passion, and his first team was Newbold White Star, which he joined in 1901. In 1905, the *Liverpool Daily Post* reported on Tom Watson's capture of the talented keeper:

> Liverpool has been for some time on the look-out for a really reliable goalkeeper to act as deputy to Ned Doig, and have now been successful. The new man is Sam Hardy, who is a native of Chesterfield, and is considered by competent judges to be out of his proper sphere when figuring in Second Division matches. There has been competition for his services. Hardy has the youth on his side, being only twenty-two years old. He stands 5ft. 10in., and weighs 12st., and is of sound physique.

Liverpool paid £340 for his services. They had initially agreed to pay £300 and provide a money-spinning friendly match. However, when the game couldn't be arranged, Liverpool added £40 by way of compensation. The signing may have been seen as a gamble, given that Hardy had conceded six goals against Liverpool while he was in goal for Chesterfield during a Second Division match on 7 January 1905. Liverpool won the game 6-1, but Watson believed they could have scored 20 if it hadn't been for Sam.

Initially signed as deputy to Doig, Hardy grew into one of the finest proponents of his art, and would replace the former Sunderland man, who was suffering from rheumatoid arthritis. He made 35 appearances during the title-winning season of 1905/06, with five of those in the FA Cup.

Sam's debut came on 21 October 1905 in a 4-1 victory over Nottingham Forest at Anfield. Though he enjoyed a relatively quiet game, his performance stood out, as this report in the club programme makes clear:

> Hardy had not a great deal to do, but he shaped like a workman. Two of his saves were masterpieces and he has only to reproduce the same form under pressure to obtain the confidence of all. Even now it is no light measure to

> understudy Doig, and Hardy was more than an understudy – he was the prince himself.

Sam was so impressive as a goalkeeper that Charlie Buchan, co-founder of the Football Writers' Association, said the following of his abilities:

> Hardy, I consider the finest goalkeeper I played against. By uncanny anticipation and wonderful positional sense he seemed to act like a magnet to the ball. I never saw him dive full length to make a save. He advanced a yard or two and so narrowed the shooting angle that forwards usually sent the ball straight at him.

Liverpool had started the 1905/06 season badly. With Doig between the sticks, they lost five of their opening eight games, conceding an astonishing 20 goals. The run included a chastening 5-0 defeat on the road at Aston Villa, and a 4-2 reverse away to Everton. Watson had seen enough and promoted Hardy to the first team. He never looked back.

Liverpool went on an astonishing run, which included victories over the previous season's champions, Newcastle United, 3-2, and the current holders of first place, Aston Villa 3-0. Hardy saved a penalty against the Midlanders. The joint Everton and Liverpool programme was full of praise:

> Judging from the cool, yet effective, methods which he adopts in clearing his goal, we feel pretty well assured in prognosticating a successful future for this young player. He is fearless in stopping a rush, and remarkably agile in covering the goal space, and is equally at home with both high and low shots. When his first gruelling afternoon

> comes, we trust Hardy will show himself a master of his craft.

Liverpool sailed to their second league title, finishing four points clear of Preston North End. And, as much as the Reds' strikers would earn the plaudits for firing the goals that won the games, so too should Hardy receive high praise for his performance as Liverpool's last line of defence.

Hardy had won over an army of admirers in his first season at Anfield, and one ten-year-old boy, Walter Dutton, was moved to poetry by his devotion to the goalkeeper. The *Liverpool Football Echo* published his limerick in April 1906:

> I know a good goalie called Hardy
> And when the ball comes he's not tardy
> He belongs to the 'Pool
> And he's been to school
> Has that jolly good goalie called Hardy

In the same issue of the paper, a T. Ellis writes:

> While walking through one of our parks the other day I met a youngster about the age of three walking along by his father's side. 'Eh, daddy,' said he, 'there's Hardy.' 'Where and what Hardy?' asked the parent. 'There he is, daddy – him as keeps goal for the Reds.' The father looked and I looked in the direction indicated by the youngster's pointed finger, and there stood, between two piles of coats and caps, a ragged barefoot lad, about ten, engaged might and main in resisting the earnest attempts of other lads to force a penny soft India rubber ball between the said piles of coats and caps. This is true.

Sam had elevated the art of keeping goal, and he was as much a hero figure at Anfield as any forward player. Known as 'Silent Sam', and partial to a cigarette, Hardy was far from flashy. In a 'Soccer Special' issue of *Shoot* magazine, published in 1981, a writer describes how Hardy had no time for the spectacular, and saw goalkeeping as a serious business.

Sam made a total of 240 appearances for Liverpool, keeping 63 clean sheets. He was afforded a benefit match against Woolwich Arsenal, at Anfield, on 17 April 1911. With the *Liverpool Echo* advertising the league match as a benefit for Liverpool's custodian, 20,000 turned out to cheer on Sam, who captained the team for the game. It finished 1-1.

At this point, Sam was married and still living in Brockwell, in Chesterfield. Despite his performances and value to the team, his living arrangements were becoming a problem for the directors of the club, who were insisting he moved to Liverpool. The disagreement would prove pivotal and Hardy was transfer-listed as a result.

At the age of 30, he was replaced by Scotsman Ken Campbell, who was ten years younger. It was also felt that Hardy was no longer at the peak of his powers, a factor that perhaps made it easier for the club to part company with him, despite his popularity. The *Liverpool Echo* had the following to say of his declining skills: 'The change has been beneficial for the club, for whereas Hardy was beginning to show signs of inability to get to a shot with that electric speed that made him famous.'

Ken Campbell, the man who replaced Hardy, while talking to *Weekly News* on 21 May 1921, recalled Hardy as a splendid fellow, and reflected on the pair's first meeting, and Sam's greeting to him: '"Glad to meet you, young 'un", he said: hope you like Liverpool, and I wish you all success.'

Campbell would credit Sam as playing a huge part in his own development, and claimed that watching Hardy during his career at Anfield had caused him to change his style of goalkeeping, giving him a greater understanding of the importance of positional sense and narrowing the angles available to the centre-forward.

Hardy had been a firm proponent of goalkeepers holding position in their own goal area. For much of the early years of the game, a keeper was able to handle the ball anywhere on the pitch. When that rule was changed, limiting handling to the 18-yard box, Sam felt more able to adapt as a result.

He played his final game for Liverpool in a match against Aston Villa on 6 April 1912. The game finished 2-1 to Villa, who would pay £1,000 for his services just a few weeks later. It represented great business for the club. However, Hardy would go on to achieve FA Cup glory in his first season with Villa, as his new team ran out 1-0 winners over Sunderland.

He reached the semi-final of the cup the following season, but suffered heartache, conceding two goals and crashing out at the penultimate hurdle. Liverpool made the final but sadly, lost 1-0 to Burnley. Sam would go on to win another FA Cup winners' medal in 1920, however. He registered 183 appearance for the Midlands club and would go on to play for Nottingham Forest until 1925, before becoming a scout and secretary for them.

Sam joined the Navy during the First World War, enlisting as Ordinary Seaman L9639 on 30 October 1916, and was subsequently posted to HM Naval Base Devonport in Plymouth for training. On 28 July 1917, he was appointed to the 'A' Class destroyer HMS *Opossum*, serving in home waters for the duration of the war. Hardy narrowly escaped injury when the *Opossum*'s bridge was badly damaged by enemy fire in the English Channel. On 1 March 1918, he returned to HMNB Devonport, where he would remain until 8 May 1918, when he was discharged. Sam was awarded the Silver War Badge on 27 April 1918 for his services.

Debates will rage forever over who was Liverpool's greatest goalkeeper. In such cases, recency bias plays a huge part in deciding such matters. However, a Liverpool fan of 76 years, one Bob Evans, writing in the *Liverpool Annual 1983*, argued: 'I liked Ray Clemence but he wasn't as good a goalkeeper as Sam Hardy.'

As a prominent figure in the Professional Footballers' Association, Sam's views were often sought on the game, and he was never afraid to oblige. Commenting on the treatment of footballers as commodities in 1909, he had the following to say in the *Dundee Courier*:

> To footballers the question of the hour is the prospective abolition of the wage limit and where we shall find ourselves once that barrier is lifted.
>
> After reading many of the authorities on this subject one is inclined to think, like Lord Rosebery on the Budget, that it will be the end of all things. In my view it is absurd to imagine that we players lack the virtue of commonsense or that we are incapable of discriminating between what is good for the game and good for ourselves.
>
> It is club managers and officials that are going about placing a greater commercial value upon us day by day, and their very own actions are making us think seriously not so much about our usefulness as men but as to our commercial value to that section of the community we entertain. It is not the players who will debase the game by being able to sell their abilities in the best market, but the Directors, who are placing a greater value upon us.

On 21 October 1921, Hardy took over as licensee of the Gardeners Arms pub in Chesterfield. He would remain in the area for many years. In 1939 he was living at 195 Sherwood

Street, Alfreton, Derbyshire. His occupation was now 'Billiard Hall Proprietor'.

He died at his home, 4 West View Road, Chesterfield, on 24 October 1966, and was cremated at Chesterfield Crematorium, his ashes scattered in the plot 'Heath 24'. He was 84 years of age. Sam bequeathed £4,384 to his wife, Maria.

He had lived a long and distinguished life as a family man, a professional footballer, achieving success at the top of the sport for both Liverpool and Aston Villa, and in the business world too. He had sought to advocate for fellow professionals at the Professional Footballers' Association, and had served his country at sea during wartime. That's quite a legacy.

## Maurice Parry

*Watson's Celtic warrior*

Maurice Parry must rank as one of the most colourful characters in Tom Watson's charge. A fiery right-half with a tendency to get 'overenthusiastic at times' he quickly gained a reputation with referees, who subsequently failed to give him the benefit of the doubt – his reputation went before him, shall we say. Nevertheless, Parry would become a key figure in the team that won the league title in 1906. He featured in 36 league games during the campaign, and five in the FA Cup. Parry also featured in 30 league games as the club fought its way out of the Second Division. In all, he made 221 appearances, scoring four times. He would also enjoy a career in coaching and management after the First World War, during which he served extensively overseas.

Born on 26 October 1877, in Trefonen, in England, he lived with his father, Samuel, a 'Manager Skinner' in the leather trade, and his mother Sarah. Maurice was educated at a high school in Oswestry, where he played football largely as a half-back, and after leaving school he joined the Old Boys' Club of that town.

Prior to moving to Liverpool in 1900, Maurice played for numerous clubs, including Newtown, Long Eaton Rangers, Nottingham Forest, Oswestry United, Leicester Fosse, Loughborough Town (on loan) and Brighton United. However, he would describe himself as something of a reluctant professional and, at least in the early days of his career, he didn't envisage a life in football.

In 1901, we pick him up in number 27 Arkles Road, in the shadow of Anfield. The address belonged to a Maria Jones, and Maurice described himself in census records as a professional footballer. He was now a Welsh international, and his neighbours were fellow Liverpool players Billy Dunlop and John 'Sailor' Hunter, who were boarding at number 29.

Maurice remained at Anfield until 1909. As we know, he had featured during the 1901 league championship campaign, though he didn't play enough games to earn a medal. He would subsequently win medals for being part of the Second Division and First Division winning seasons.

As well as playing primarily as a right-half, we note from this excerpt from a match report in *Cricket and Football Field*, 29 February 1908, that he did on occasion play at centre-half:

> Maurice Parry was one of Liverpool's few representatives who succeeded in rising to the occasion at Newcastle; not only in his endeavours to cope with a clever and tricky wing, but also in battling with the elements. It was Maurice at his best. By the way we note Parry is selected as centre half for Wales in her coming International. This is a position he has once or twice filled for Liverpool.

The game referred to was a 3-1 defeat to Newcastle United at St James' Park. Maurice would have been 30 years old at this point, and coming to the end of his Liverpool career. In a 1909 portrait of the player, penned in a matchday programme, we get a sense of his appearance and also his interests outside football:

> Parry is finely proportioned for a footballer, standing 5ft. 11in. and weighing 12st. 10lbs. In adding to being a capable performer in the football field, Parry is a skilful musician, and on the piano or organ is equally at home.
>
> During recent weeks the right half back has been displaying his finest form, and in this respect has fully earned his right to be recognised as the most consistent back in the team. Few left wings can take the measure of Parry.

Of course, by now Maurice was 31 years old. He was still making regular appearances for Liverpool, running out 20 times in the league during the 1908/09 season. However, this was to prove his last season at the club and he would follow his old team-mate Alex Raisbeck to Partick Thistle. From there he signed on at Wrexham in November 1910, according to a short snippet in the *Lichfield Mercury*.

Now into his early 30s, Parry spent some time in South Africa, where he learned to be a coach, before returning to England before the war. He enlisted in the 7th (Merioneth and Montgomery) Battalion of the Royal Welch Fusiliers, where he became a sergeant. He was then commissioned in 1915, becoming a second lieutenant, according to the *Wellington Journal & Shrewsbury News* of 19 June 1915. On 13 October 1915, the following letter concerning Maurice's war activities appeared in the *Liverpool Echo*, addressed to Ernest 'Bee' Edwards:

> We have not heard much in later months of our old friend, Maurice Parry, Welsh international, Scottish player, and well-known Liverpool player. Today, from the boys of a boat which has had some 'crummy' experiences, I get news of Maurice as follows:

> 'Dear Bee. – I thought you would be interested to know that Mr. Maurice Parry landed from this ship on Saturday, September 18, at Lemnos, which is the advanced base of the M.E.F. He is, as you are no doubt aware, a second lieutenant in the South Wales Borderers. Of course, he was a person of no small importance in the eyes of our crew, who are all Liverpool men. He was the life and soul of the party, and it was always he who started the music and singing. In an impromptu concert held on the last night the cry was always "Parry."'

An incredibly popular soldier, Maurice suffered two separate gas attacks, suffering inhalation injuries, in the Dardanelles. He was hospitalised for three months, before rejoining his regiment in Luxor, Egypt, in 1921.

The Thistle Archive, an online portal containing historical documents, records and articles related to the history of Partick Thistle FC, contains some interesting information about Maurice's work after the war. It's claimed that he presented himself as five years younger in order to join the Auxiliary Division of the Royal Irish Constabulary but, in March 1921, just three months after joining, perhaps the call of football had once again proved irresistible to Parry. He took up the post of manager at Rotherham County, later Rotherham United, towards the end of 1921, where he remained for two years.

While he may have been finished with Rotherham, he certainly hadn't given up on the game or coaching. Maurice would go on to work with Barcelona, Köln, Eintracht Frankfurt and also in the Channel Islands. And his journey would lead him back to Anfield.

In August 1932, we find an announcement in the *Liverpool Echo,* again from the legendary 'Bee', that Parry was to assume the role of coach, under the control of secretary George Patterson, and trainer Charlie Wilson. Parry's tactical nuance was hoped to benefit the team. He officially started in his new role on 22 August 1932, and a further article in the *Liverpool Evening Express* on 27 August suggests that the Liverpool reserve team, which had been below par for some time, would benefit from Maurice Parry's guidance.

Sadly, the following year, the club decided not to renew his position, which had involved encouraging the young players. He had introduced a goal-shooting space at the approach to the grandstand, and had received good feedback from the players. However, having started well, the reserve side's fortunes in the Central League plummeted and they eventually finished in the bottom three, with Oldham Reserves and Stockport Reserves finishing below them. There is some sympathy, though, for Maurice from 'Bee', who argues that Parry had made the most of limited talent and 'could hardly be expected to be a miracle worker'.

Ernest 'Bee' Edwards clearly admired Parry greatly, and claimed he was nicknamed 'Daddy Long Legs' due to his height. The pair had enjoyed a great relationship spanning 30 years, and 'Bee' had been instrumental in securing Maurice's appointment as coach in the Channel Islands, claiming, in March 1935, that he had received separate letters from the chairman, secretary and president of the association, praising Parry's excellent manner and the value of his football talks.

However, the shadow of war had followed Maurice in the decades after he returned home. With his lungs so badly damaged by gas, he developed bronchitis, which prevented him travelling abroad and often confined him to bed. He would never marry, and died at the age of 57 in Bootle in 1935.

## Alf West

*Watson's cool and classy full-back*

Born in Radford, Nottingham, to parents Levi and Mary, on 15 December 1881, Alf West would grow up to be one of Liverpool's finest full-backs. His father worked in the lace industry, and Alf would follow him, becoming an apprentice lace machine builder by the age of 20.

Alf played for several clubs prior to joining Liverpool in 1903 for a fee of £500. These included Nottingham Jardines Athletic, Radford Congregational, Ilkeston Town and Barnsley.

West was known for his calmness under pressure, eschewing aggression and force for skill and perfectly timed challenges. Alf made 25 appearance in the league and FA Cup in his first season, and, although his capture plugged leaks in the Liverpool defence – they lost their first five games of the campaign, conceding 14 goals – he couldn't save the team from relegation.

A sketch of Alf, published in the matchday programme in 1905, refers to an 'unfortunate accident' that kept him out of the team until Christmas 1904, as Liverpool battled their way to promotion. While out shooting, his trainer, William Norman, accidentally discharged his weapon, shooting Alf in the chest. Though critically ill, he miraculously recovered, much to the relief of Mr Norman. The gunshot had missed his heart and lungs.

Amazingly, he made 16 appearances for Liverpool towards the end of the 1904/05 campaign, seeing his team crowned champions of the Second Division. His style as a defender was no doubt enhanced by his natural pace. Alf was a keen sprinter over 80 to 120 yards, and had competed in several finals, winning the 120-yard handicap in Barnsley in 1904. He had spent a lot of time working on building up his speed as he recovered from his injuries.

The 1905/06 title-winning season saw him establish himself as a regular player and a key man in Watson's back line. He missed just one game during the campaign.

West got injured against Middlesbrough four games into the 1906/07 season, and this, combined with a terrible family tragedy, meant he would miss the rest of the season. Sadly, Alf's wife, Lilly, who he had married just a year earlier, passed away in October 1906. The couple had a daughter, Lillian, who was just 11 months old.

He made 36 appearances in the league and cup during the following campaign, but his career at Liverpool began to wane. He left for Reading in 1909, but returned to Anfield in 1910, where he featured in a further four games for the club. Alf eventually ended up at Notts County, where he spent four seasons before the war intervened.

West enlisted at Kingsway, London on 2 February 1915, and requested to join the famed Football Battalion, 851 Middlesex Regiment 17th (service) Battalion. Just 18 months later, Alf was wounded in action, due to a trench fall, injuring his knee, and requiring surgery. A 1916 report in the *Liverpool Echo* suggests that he spent time in Paisley recovering, and that surgeons had presented him with the knee cartilage they had removed, as a souvenir.

After his injury, Alf was transferred to the Labour Corps and is listed as Private (447888). He remained in the military for some years, and three years later he spent a further 12 days in hospital, with his medical records indicating that he had become one of many who contracted influenza during the 1919 pandemic. On 18 April 1919, Alf was transferred to Class 'Z', reserved list.

By 1921, Alf was back in Nottingham, living with his parents and siblings. He was working in Nottingham's lace trade as a 'Brass Bobbin Finisher'. His daughter, Lillian, was also living with the family and working in the lace trade.

By the age of 58, Alf had changed jobs and was now working as a 'Fitters Labourer', which he did until his death in 1944, at the age of 62. He is buried in an unmarked grave in Northern Cemetery, Bulwell, Nottingham. The *Nottingham Evening Post* reported the death of Alf West on 28 June 1944:

> Mr. Alfred West, who died at Garfield-road, Radford, yesterday, was a full back for the Notts County, Liverpool

> and Barnsley clubs. Prior to joining the Meadow-lane staff during the summer of 1911, when he was 28, this Nottingham born player had been associated for six seasons with Liverpool, and was an accomplished full back, who had also seen service with Ilkeston and Barnsley.
>
> In his first two seasons with the County he was ever-present (38 League games), holding his place on merit, and proving a great favourite, converting four penalties. He missed only two of the 38 League games in 1913-14, and was still with the County on the outbreak of the 1914-18 war. He earned a good reputation as a golfer.

Alf played 141 times for Liverpool, scoring six times. He won both the First and Second Division championships. After suffering much personal tragedy, he fought bravely on both the battlefields of Europe and the playing fields of England.

## James 'Jimmy' Bradley

*Watson's clever tackler*

James Bradley signed for Liverpool in September 1905. There's some dispute and confusion as to his date of birth, with the 1903 edition of *Men Famous in Football* claiming he was born in Goldenhill in 1881. This date is repeated on Wikipedia, and on lfchistory.net. However, PlayUpLiverpool's Kjell Hanssen uses an article in *Athletic News*, dated 1905, which gives his date of birth as 25 June 1877. We have identified from the 1939 census that his birth date is recorded as 20 September 1876, while his military records indicate that he was born on 12 May 1878, which does line up with his funeral notice in 1961, which states he was 83 at the time of his death.

Such confusion, however, is typical of records at the time. Census records are sometimes not completed by the person in question, and even contemporaneous newspaper articles contain inaccuracies and contradictions. Fortunately, we have been able to cross-check our findings with birth certificates. In this case, Liverpool's official archivist, Jonny Stokkeland, came to our rescue, confirming that James's date of birth was 20 September 1877.

James's family lived at 18 New Building, Goldenhill, Staffordshire, England. His parents, Peter, an iron worker, and Mary, were born in County Mayo in Northern Ireland. James moved around Staffordshire as a boy, and at 13 he was working as a potter in Stoke.

Bradley developed a keen interest in football and played for local team Goldenhill Wanderers between 1897 and 1898, before moving to Stoke, where he played for seven years and made 199 appearances. It was there that he began to attract the attention of Tom Watson at Liverpool. He would spend six years at Anfield, during which time he lived at 130 Dacy Road, Anfield with his wife, Catherine, and their four sons.

He had originally wanted to sign for Plymouth Argyle, but due to the fact that the FA refused to sanction the move, he became available again and Liverpool swooped. James, or Jimmy, made his debut for Liverpool in a 2-0 win over Birmingham on 23 September 1905, at Anfield. *Athletic News*, dated 6 November 1905, described the attributes that persuaded Liverpool to sign him:

> He is the sort of player to operate behind speedy artists like John Cox and Sam Raybould, and the fine form shown by the Liverpool left-wing this season is due to the admirable nursing which the Staffordshire man adopts. He possesses the happy knack of drawing the opposition, and giving his forwards every opportunity. Seldom is it that he places awkwardly to the men in front of him; a deft touch along the turf is his manner of sending the ball forward. Needless to state the excellent quality of his football has already installed him a favourite with the Liverpool public.

James was a tough character, and not afraid to 'mix it up' when necessary. He had famously become embroiled in a fight with Liverpool player Fred Buck, while he was at Stoke, in 1903. Both players were dismissed. Buck received a six-week ban, while Bradley got 14 days. Fortunately, Buck had left Liverpool in 1904, thereby avoiding any potential awkwardness.

Playing predominantly on left wing, Bradley featured 186 times for Liverpool, and scored eight goals. He featured 32 times in the league and five times in the FA Cup, as the Reds won the league title in the 1905/06 season, his first at the club. He continued to be a mainstay of the side until the 1909/10 season, playing 30 or more league games for five seasons, including one appearance in goal (he kept a clean sheet in a 3-0 win over Bolton Wanderers). However, in the 1910/11 campaign, James fell out of favour and only featured four times before moving on. A biography of the player in a Liverpool match programme dated 2 February 1908 references him playing at half-back. It had the following to say of his qualities:

> Bradley possesses a splendid idea of the requirements of a successful half back, and the forwards in front of him cannot complain of the accurate attention. He believes in keeping the ball on the turf, and his clever tackling is only equalled by the skilful manner in which he places to his front rank.

Curiously, in his 'life story', as told to *Athletic News* in 1915, Alex Raisbeck refers to James as a 'centre forward'. He also relates an amusing anecdote about a man who travelled around the country impersonating Bradley's brother and gaining employment on the strength of his association with the player. We reproduce the story here, though readers should note that it contains cultural references that some may find offensive today:

> Really it is marvellous the tricks some folks will try. I remember when I was at Anfield of an individual who travelled all over the country presenting himself as a brother of James Bradley, our centre forward.
>
> On the strength of this he was signed on by quite a number of country clubs to whom he had offered his services, always, of course, for a consideration. It was rather an ingenious way of raising the wind. No sooner had he signed one 'professional' form than he folded his tent like the Arabs, and silently stole away, only to make his appearance at some other quaint hostelry, where he immediately revealed his identity, and commenced to trade upon Bradley's fame as a centre forward. But the bold youth went on signing forms galore, until truth triumphed and he signed one too many.

James did have a brother, Martin, who also played football. He was an inside-right, played 28 games for Grimsby Town and two for The Wednesday between the years 1907 and 1911.

James was playing for his old club Stoke before the outbreak of war, and was registered with the club for the 1914/15 season. He enlisted for military service with the Royal Garrison Artillery on 24 June 1916. He became a gunner and was called up for active service in 1917. His army records describe him as being sober, reliable and 'fairly' intelligent. However, he is docked three days' army pay in 1918 for overstaying his leave.

Bradley's active service would see him serve in Alexandria, Egypt towards the end of the First World War in 1918. He thankfully survived his deployment and returned home to England after the cessation of hostilities, and the 1921 census records that he was back living in Goldenhill and employed on a casual daily basis at Birchenwood Colliery, Kidsgrove. James now had six children, and two of them (James and Michael) were employed as miners at the same colliery.

By 1939, he had found employment as a general labourer for the Goldenhill Corporation. By this time, he would have been around 62. James passed away on 17 September 1961. He was 83 years old.

James Bradley had served Stoke and Liverpool with distinction, winning a league championship, the Liverpool Senior Cup and the Sheriff of London 'Dewar Shield' in 1906. Clearly a family man, he also saw active duty during the First World War.

## The nearly men

It's important also to recognise the contributions of the following players who, though they didn't appear as regularly as others, no doubt made their own contribution. We honour them by recording their appearances here:

John Carlin – 14 league, 2 FA Cup
Jack Parkinson – 9 league, 1 FA Cup
Ned, or Ted, Doig – 8 league
Tom Chorlton – 6 league
George Latham – 5 league, 1 FA Cup
James Garside – 4 league
David Murray – 3 league
George Fleming – 3 league
James Gorman – 1 league
Harry Griffiths – 1 league

All men who played five or more times during this campaign received a winners' medal.

## Chapter Sixteen

# Watson and the rise of the 'Spion Kop'

IN THE summer of 1906, Liverpool FC were basking in the glory of their second First Division championship, and the directors even commissioned a special commemorative flag to celebrate the achievement. Meanwhile, Britain was in the grip of a heatwave, with one area in South Yorkshire recording temperatures of 35.6°C.

At Anfield, Tom Watson and various members of the Liverpool board of directors were showing off their plans for ground improvements to local journalists. A dinner had been provided for the gentlemen of the press and 'prominent supporters of the Liverpool Club' at the Bee Hotel, St John's Lane. Present was Scottish architect Archibald Leitch, who gave a speech on his proposed works, which included improvements to the playing surface, now described as an 'emerald green expanse', that would facilitate the playing of 'scientific football'.

An unnamed reporter at the *Birkenhead News*, who almost missed the lunch, was on hand to capture the details of the speeches and subsequent tour for posterity. The club had previously been reluctant to carry out major works due to the significant costs involved. However, as we learned earlier, the capacity and facilities at the stadium had led to dangerous situations developing, such as those experienced in the Merseyside derby. There was also a significant risk of fire associated with the collection of newspapers under the wooden stands, which made for perfect kindling as cigarettes and spent matches were dropped from the terraces.

Now, with the club having enjoyed back-to-back league championships in both the Second and First Divisions of English football, the board of directors was ready to improve both the size and facilities at the ground. Plans were afoot to increase capacity to 60,000 and vastly increase the number of entry and exit gates, with the aim of being able to fill or empty the stadium in as little as five minutes. While it's doubtful that this has ever been achieved, clearly the club had factored safety and crowd comfort into their plans.

A later report, on 25 August 1906 in the *Lancashire Evening News*, clarifies that the expansion to 60,000 would be staged, with the capacity for the 1906/07 season beginning with spaces for 40,000. Further increases were to come later.

The pitch had been raised up to afford supporters a better view of the game, and 'much filling in had been required' to level the surface, which Leitch said was 'off-level to the extent of 5' 6"'. And, to give the grass the best opportunity to flourish, the players' practice sessions had been moved to the Tower Athletic Grounds, New Brighton. However, the crowning glory of the planned improvements would surely be the creation of a giant new stand on Walton Breck Road, a huge embankment that would house 20,000 spectators, providing uninterrupted views of the game. It would replace the huge heap of rubble on which supporters previously stood to watch games. Little did Liverpool's directors, and Leitch, who had been involved with stadium design at Ibrox, Chelsea and Fulham, realise, but they had just given birth to something magical in the world of football.

The new stand would be constructed from cinder and brick. The sports editor of the *Liverpool Daily Post and Echo*, Ernest 'Bee' Edwards, gazed upon the completed structure and immediately declared that it put him in mind of the Spion Kop, the scene of a famous battle during the Boer War, where many men from Liverpool had perished.

The Kop was not afforded a roof until 1928, so supporters watched games from its steps in all weathers. At its height, it's believed that the Kop could play host to more than 30,000 supporters.

The first game to take place in front of the mighty stand was a Football League opener against Stoke City on 1 September 1906. According to the local press, the city of Liverpool was sweltering under record temperatures. Shock was expressed at the fact the game wasn't postponed, but the heat didn't deter the first-ever Kopites from turning out in their droves, though the gate fell well short of the planned 60,000 capacity.

With no roof above their heads, supporters would have been exposed to the burning sun and, packed together, they would have struggled in conditions that must have been unbearable. The *Liverpool Echo* gives a sense of the conditions, with a headline that declared:

LIVERPOOL
V
STOKE
LEAGUE DIVISION 1
TROPICAL HEAT
HEWITT SCORES FIRST GOAL
FOR LIVERPOOL
CROWD ESTIMATED AT 30,000

The Reds won 1-0, thanks to a 20th-minute goal scored by Joe Hewitt, who became the first player to score in the shadow of the now world-famous Spion Kop. Some match reports suggest that the crowd at kick-off stood at 25,000. However, thousands continued to pour in as the game progressed. It must have been a fearsome sight.

The numbers climbing on to the Kop ebbed and receded as the season unfolded, but, on 29 September 1906, 40,000 crammed into the stadium to see Liverpool take on Everton. Sadly, despite going a goal up in the first half through Jack Parkinson, Everton's Sandy Young hit two in the second half to take the spoils.

Anfield remained unchanged until a roof was added to the Kop in 1928, with Leitch's improvements serving the club well for many years. To those used to the old stand, the addition of cover must have seemed like luxury. The noise, amplified under that tin roof, created an incredible sound.

Unfortunately, Liverpool failed to live up to the ambition on display in the summer, and never rose above mid-table throughout the season. They finished in a disappointing 15th place on 33 points, after losing 18 of their 38 games. Watson had moved on James Garside to Accrington Stanley and brought in five new players, although none made a significant impact. The following season saw some improvement with Liverpool finishing eighth, and Watson conducting more surgery on the squad.

It was a case of five out and five in, with one notable sale involving Sam Raybould, as we've discussed previously. In terms of additions, Watson paid good money for two players, Jimmy Harrop who arrived from Rotheram Town for £250, and Ronald Orr, who joined from Newcastle United for £350. Both men arrived in 1908. Harrop was viewed as a potential replacement for captain Alex Raisbeck, who would leave the club in 1909. Regarded as being good in the air, he earned the nickname 'Heads up Harrop'. On 16 January 1910, the *Sunday Chronicle* had the following to say of Jimmy:

> Who would ever have thought that the legitimate successor to Alex Raisbeck could be found at the first attempt? James Harrop has followed the great Scot with such felicitous feet

> and such harmonious heading that he is unquestionably building a lasting reputation.

Jimmy endured a difficult spell in his early seasons, with the team performing inconsistently, slumping to 17th in 1908/09. However, he would be a key player as Liverpool fought Villa for the title in 1909/10, finishing second. He would leave along with Sam Hardy to join Aston Villa in 1912.

Another highlight for Harrop was his involvement in the famous 6-5 victory over Newcastle United, at Anfield, on 4 December 1909. Harrop featured in that game alongside Sam Hardy, Tom Chorlton, Tom Rogers, Bobby Robinson, James Bradley, Arthur Goddard, Jimmy Stewart, Jack Parkinson, Ronald Orr and John McDonald. The city was still reeling from a terrible disaster in Liverpool Bay, which took place the day before. The *Ellan Vannin* had sunk on its way back from the Isle of Man, with the loss of all on board. Many of the victims of the tragedy are buried in St James' Cemetery, which lies in the shadow of Liverpool's Anglican Cathedral. In all, 15 passengers and 21 crew were lost.

Young supporter Frank Ryan, who was just 11 years old, was at the game. He wrote to Liverpool FC's matchday programme in 1972 to tell them of his experiences of following the club in the early years of the 20th century. He tells of scrambling beneath the Kemlyn Road stand looking for cigarette packets that might contain a clean football card. Occasionally he would find a shiny silver coin that had fallen through the cracks. However, his fondest memory is sitting on his dad's shoulders as Goddard scored the winner against Newcastle in that historic 6-5 encounter, completing a monumental comeback.

Another fan, Charles Wannop, of Childwall, describes how he was in a sweepstake and had Liverpool to win. At half-time, the Reds were 5-2 down and he thought he had seen the last of his bet. Instead, he would leave Anfield clutching his two shillings with pride.

1911/12 squad photo. Colourised by George Chilvers. Courtesy of Liverpool FC. Museum collection.

Chelsea versus Liverpool, 9 September 1912, Stamford Bridge. Liverpool won the game 2-1 thanks to goals by Arthur Goddard and Tom Gracie. Angus Douglas scored Chelsea's goal. Image colourised by George Chilvers. Courtesy of Liverpool FC. Museum collection.

1912/13 Liverpool FC member's ticket, issued by Tom Watson. We can see the member lived at 20 Endbourne Road, Aintree, Liverpool. Note also the common practice of recording match results in the ticket. Courtesy of Liverpool FC museum collection.

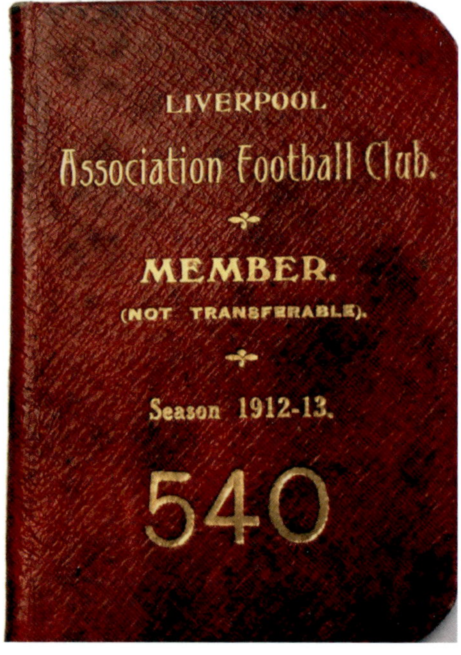


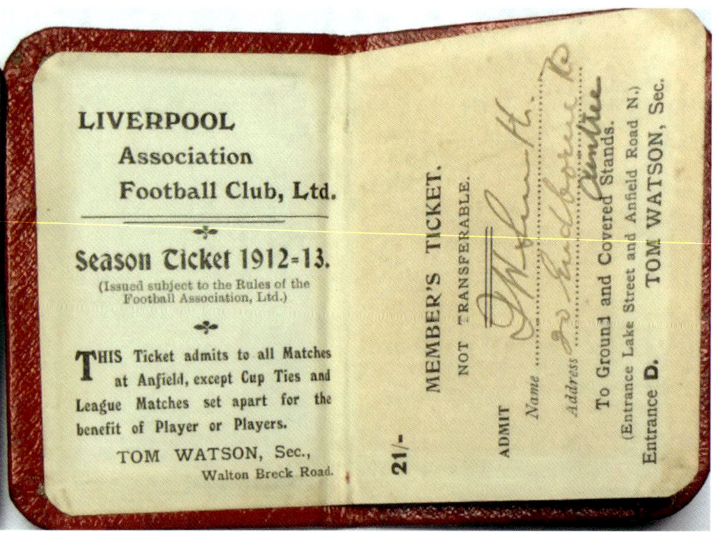


LIVERPOOL FOOTBALL CLUB FIXTURES.

*FIRST TEAM.* *1912-1913.* *FIRST TEAM.*

| DATE | NAME OF CLUB. | GOALS. F | GOALS. A | GOALS. Pts. | | Where Played |
|---|---|---|---|---|---|---|
| 1912. | | | | | | |
| Sept. 4 | Oldham Athletic | | | | L | Home |
| ,, 7 | Woolwich Arsenal | | | | L | Home |
| ,, 9 | Chelsea | | | | L | Away |
| ,, 14 | Bradford City | | | | L | Away |
| ,, 21 | Manchester City | | | | L | Home |
| ,, 28 | W. Brom. Albion | | | | L | Away |
| Oct. 5 | Everton | | | | L | Home |
| ,, 12 | Sheffield Wed. | | | | L | Away |
| ,, 14 | Sheffield United | | | | L | Away |
| ,, 19 | Blackburn Rovers | | | | L | Home |
| ,, 26 | Derby County | | | | L | Away |
| Nov. 2 | Tottenham H'spur | | | | L | Home |
| ,, 9 | Middlesbrough | | | | L | Away |
| ,, 16 | Notts County | | | | L | Home |
| ,, 23 | Manchester U. | | | | L | Away |
| ,, 30 | Aston Villa | | | | L | Home |
| Dec. 7 | Sunderland | | | | L | Away |
| ,, 14 | Bolton Wanderers | | | | L | Away |
| ,, 21 | Sheffield U. | | | | L | Home |
| 25 | Oldham Athletic | | | | L | Away |
| ,, 26 | Newcastle United | | | | L | Home |
| ,, 28 | Woolwich Arsenal | | | | L | Away |

| DATE. | NAME OF CLUB. | GOALS. F | GOALS. A | GOALS. Pts. | | Where Played |
|---|---|---|---|---|---|---|
| 1913. | | | | | | |
| Jan 1 | Newcastle United | | | | L | Away |
| ,, 4 | Bradford City | | | | L | Home |
| ,, 11 | E.C. Tie | | | | | Home |
| ,, 18 | Manchester City | | | | L | Away |
| ,, 25 | W. Brom. Albion | | | | | Home |
| Feb. 1 | E.C. Tie | | | | | |
| ,, 8 | Everton | | | | L | Away |
| ,, 15 | Sheffield Wed. | | | | L | Home |
| ,, 22 | Blackburn R. E.C. | | | | L | Away |
| Mar. 1 | Derby County | | | | L | Home |
| ,, 8 | Tottenham H. E.C. | | | | L | Away |
| ,, 15 | Middlesbrough | | | | L | Home |
| ,, 21 | | | | | | |
| ,, 22 | Notts County | | | | L | Away |
| ,, 24 | Chelsea | | | | L | Home |
| ,, 29 | Manchester U. E.C. | | | | L | Home |
| Apl. 5 | Aston Villa | | | | L | Away |
| ,, 12 | Sunderland | | | | L | Home |
| ,, 19 | Bolton Wan. E.C. | | | | L | Home |

**English Cup.**—Competition Proper Jan. 11th, Feb. 1st and 22nd, Mar. 8th and 29th, April 19th.

*FA Cup second round clash between Woolwich Arsenal and Liverpool at the Manor Ground on 1 February 1913. Liverpool won the game 4-1 thanks to a hat-trick from Arthur Metcalf, and one goal from Bill Lacey. Charlie Lewis scored Arsenal's consolation goal. Image colourised by George Chilvers. Courtesy of Liverpool FC. Museum collection.*

*Liverpool versus Sunderland, 12 April 1913, at Anfield. Liverpool lost 2-5. Both of the Reds' goals were scored by Arthur Metcalf. A Charlie Buchan hat-trick and two goals from James Richardson ensured a miserable day for Tom Watson's Reds. Image colourised by George Chilvers. Courtesy of Liverpool FC. Museum collection.*

*Liverpool versus Gillingham, 31 January 1914, at Anfield. Liverpool, on their way to the final for the first time in their history, won this game 2-0 thanks to goals from Bill Lacey and Bob Ferguson. Image colourised by George Chilvers. Courtesy of Liverpool FC. Museum collection.*

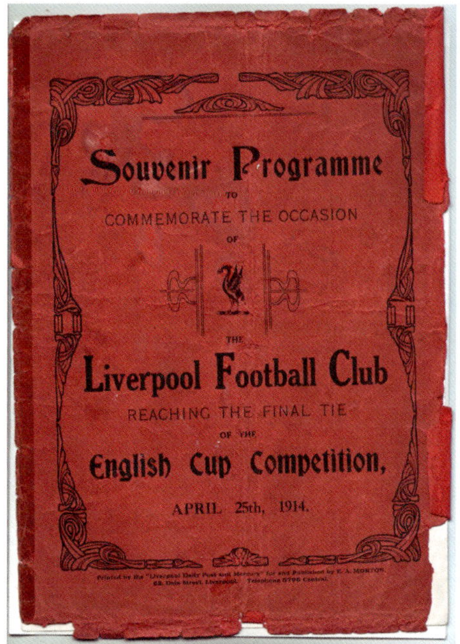

Souvenir Programme
TO
COMMEMORATE THE OCCASION
OF
THE
Liverpool Football Club
REACHING THE FINAL TIE
OF THE
English Cup Competition,
APRIL 25th, 1914.

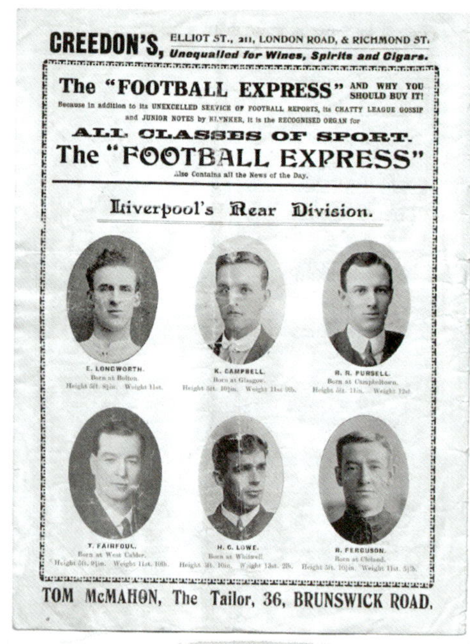

CREEDON'S, ELLIOT ST., 211, LONDON ROAD, & RICHMOND ST.
Unequalled for Wines, Spirits and Cigars.

The "FOOTBALL EXPRESS" AND WHY YOU SHOULD BUY IT!
Because in addition to its UNEXCELLED SERVICE OF FOOTBALL REPORTS, its CHATTY LEAGUE GOSSIP and JUNIOR NOTES by KLYNKER, it is the RECOGNISED ORGAN for
ALL CLASSES OF SPORT.
The "FOOTBALL EXPRESS"
Also Contains all the News of the Day.

Liverpool's Rear Division.

E. LONGWORTH.
Born at Bolton.

K. CAMPBELL.
Born at Glasgow.

R. R. PURSELL.
Born at Campbeltown.

T. FAIRFOUL.
Born at West Calder.

H. C. LOWE.
Born at Whitwell.

R. FERGUSON.
Born at Cleland.

TOM McMAHON, The Tailor, 36, BRUNSWICK ROAD.

*Cover and inside page of 1914 FA Cup Final official Liverpool FC souvenir. Courtesy of Liverpool FC. Museum collection.*

*Liverpool versus Burnley, FA Cup Final, 25 April 1914 at Crystal Palace. Liverpool lost the game 0-1 thanks to a goal from former Everton player Bertie Freeman. Image colourised by George Chilvers. Courtesy of Liverpool FC. Museum collection.*

THE FOOTBALL ASSOCIATION

Patron:

HIS MAJESTY THE KING.

President:

THE RIGHT HON. LORD KINNAIRD.

The Football Association Challenge Cup Competition

FINAL TIE

BURNLEY

*v.*

LIVERPOOL

Played at the

CRYSTAL PALACE

Saturday, 25th APRIL, 1914

*Cover of Official 1914 FA Cup Final programme. Courtesy of Liverpool FC. Museum collection.*

## BURNLEY

~~**DAWSON**~~ Sewell
Goal

**BAMFORD** Right Back — **TAYLOR** Left Back

**HALLEY** Right Half — ***BOYLE** Centre Half — ***WATSON** Left Half

| NESBITT | LINDLEY | *FREEMAN | HODGSON | *MOSSCROP |
|---|---|---|---|---|
| Outside Right | Inside Right | Centre | Inside Left | Outside Left |

**O**

| NICHOLL | †LACEY | MILLER | METCALF | SHELDON |
|---|---|---|---|---|
| Outside Left | Inside Left | Centre | Inside Right | Outside Right |

**FERGUSON** Left Half — **LOWE** Centre Half — **FAIRFOULL** Right Half

**PURSELL** Right Back — **LONGWORTH** Left Back

**CAMPBELL**
Goal

## LIVERPOOL

---

**BURNLEY will play in Claret and Light Blue Shirts and White Knickerbockers, and LIVERPOOL in Scarlet Jerseys and White Knickerbockers.**

---

*Referee:* H. S. BAMLETT (Durham).

*Linesmen:* J. TALKS (Lincolnshire).
R. O. ROGERS (London).

**Should the match result in a draw after 90 minutes has been played, spectators are earnestly requested to keep their seats, as an extra half-hour will be played.**

*** English International. † Irish International.**

*Inside page of Official 1914 FA Cup Final programme. Courtesy of Liverpool FC. Museum collection.*

*Medal awarded to William Connell, trainer, following the 1914 FA Cup Final. Courtesy of Liverpool FC. Museum collection.*

*Liverpool squad on a pre-season tour of Scandinavia. Photo taken in Stockholm on 22 May 1914. Image colourised by George Chilvers. Courtesy of Liverpool FC. Museum collection.*

*Cigarette cards depicting Liverpool player Billy Dunlop. Courtesy of Adrian Killen and Liverpool FC. Museum collection.*

*Cigarette card depicting Liverpool player James Gorman. Courtesy of Adrian Killen and Liverpool FC. Museum collections.*

*Cigarette card depicting Liverpool player Arthur Goddard. Courtesy of Adrian Killen and Liverpool FC. Museum collections.*

*Cigarette card depicting Liverpool player Joe Hewitt. Courtesy of Adrian Killen and Liverpool FC. Museum collections.*

*Cigarette card depicting Liverpool player Charlie Wilson. Courtesy of Adrian Killen and Liverpool FC. Museum collections.*

Reading these accounts, we can almost feel the atmosphere inside the ground as Liverpool surged forward, and hear the roar that greeted each goal. The *Liverpool Echo* spoke of the Reds' 'pluck' and their 'wonderful rally in the second half'. It was, they reported, an 'amazing game'. The match report continued:

> The seemingly impossible happened when McDonald, Parkinson and Orr, with almost superhuman energy, swept all before them, Orr equalising under very great difficulty. The excitement of the crowd was intense and the noise almost deafening at times. Would you believe it. Robinson's forward pass, crossed to Goddard, and lo and behold, the Reds were ahead.

As stated in the above report, the man who levelled for Liverpool in that incredible game was 5ft 5in Scottish forward Ronald Orr. In doing so he had broken the hearts of his former team-mates. Orr had joined Liverpool along with Harrop a year earlier in 1908. He would go on to play 112 times for the Reds, scoring 39 goals, including a goal on his debut against Aston Villa.

In the 1908/09 season, his 20 goals in 33 league games helped to stave off the spectre of relegation, with the Reds finishing in 16th place. His heroics against Bury – who were level on points with Liverpool going into the penultimate game of the season – gave his team a glimmer of hope. His two goals in that game secured a 2-2 draw and a vital point. They now needed at least a point from their final game against the newly crowned champions, Newcastle.

Liverpool thankfully went one better than that, winning the game 1-0, thanks to an 87th-minute goal by, yes, you guessed it, Ronald Orr. Sadly, Orr struggled to recapture his early successes at Anfield, and an injury during the Merseyside derby in 1911 curtailed his appearances further. He left for Raith Rovers in Scotland in December that same year.

Typically, the Reds followed up a campaign scrapping at the bottom of the league with one spent battling away near its summit. In truth, they were becoming synonymous with such ups and downs, and their directors would even joke about it in front of the press. As the club entertained local journalists at a hotel in the city prior to showing off ground improvements at Anfield, a Mr J. J. Bentley – a director at the club – joked to great laughter that 'Liverpool have a reputation for doing things thoroughly. They were either at the top or the bottom.'

Given that they had escaped relegation the season before, his words could not have been more prophetic. They would indeed follow up that campaign by finishing runners-up in 1909/10. However, in truth, they had never been in contention for the title, and their efforts during the run-in were even billed as a 'battle for second place'.

It's interesting to consider the impact of Liverpool's inconsistency on the attitude and behaviour of supporters. Their modern-day counterparts may well be driven to distraction by such yo-yoing between the lower and upper echelons of the league. Yet, it seems that Tom Watson had banked considerable capital with his two league wins, and there's little evidence in the archives and records of any significant discontent among those who turned out to watch the team.

While Liverpool never looked in danger of repeating the travails of the previous campaign, neither did they seriously threaten to win the championship at any stage of the 1909/10 season. One highlight was a rare victory at Goodison Park on 2 October 1909, in which Liverpool twice came from behind to win 3-2 in front of a crowd of 45,000. The winning goal was scored by Jack Parkinson in the 85th minute, but Everton refused to lie down. Under enormous pressure, as the Blues pressed for an equaliser, Liverpool resorted to time-wasting, kicking the ball into touch in an effort to preserve the lead and the points. This offended some; however, a reporter for the *Liverpool Courier* refused to criticise them for their tactics, as this was only their fifth win over Everton in 27 attempts.

The Reds laboured through December, and January, hovering around sixth in the table. A 1-0 defeat to their neighbours, Everton, at home on 12 February 1910 did little to warm Liverpudlian hearts. However, the visit to the newly opened Old Trafford a week later did much for civic pride. Although the footballing rivalry between the two sides was yet to develop by 1910, there was a healthy competitive spirit between the cities based on commerce and trade.

The game between the two sides was the first to be contested at United's new ground, the largest in the country with a capacity of 80,000. Tom Watson and his men were about to wreck the party. Liverpool won 4-3, and a brace apiece from Arthur Goddard and Jimmy Stewart sealed the victory and lifted the Reds temporarily into fourth place.

Throughout the remainder of the campaign, Liverpool began a steady climb up the table, arriving at the run-in, amazingly, still in with a shot at second place. The summit of the league table was heavily congested going into the final six games – six teams sat on 39 points, just one point off second-placed Notts County. Aston Villa, however, sat on top with an unassailable seven-point lead. Watson's men were eighth after losing back-to-back games against Sunderland and Preston North End. The Preston setback was perhaps mitigated by the absence of Hardy and Parkinson, both on international duty with England, who were playing Scotland at Hampden Park on the same day.

Watson's next opponents were second placed Notts County, at Anfield, with a chance to put those setbacks behind them and climb the table. It was Parkinson, absent against Preston, who showed Liverpool just what they had missed when he settled a tense encounter with the winning goal in the 80th minute of the game. The result saw the Reds climb to third, level on points with Blackburn Rovers, and eight points behind Villa. The battle was indeed on for second-place respectability.

Liverpool then travelled to St James' Park, where they thumped Newcastle 3-1, with a brace from Goddard and one from Jimmy Stewart. Then what followed was a Jack Parkinson masterclass at Anfield, as Nottingham Forest arrived as lambs to the slaughter. With Halley's Comet clearly visible overhead, the Reds ran out 7-3 winners, and Parkinson scored four of their goals. The game was played in the evening, with a kick-off time of 7.10pm, and floodlighting being many years away may explain the low turnout of only 5,000 spectators. This was indeed something of an anomaly, with 15,000 turning out for the previous home fixture and a season average of around 24,000.

The result against Forest took Liverpool clear of Blackburn Rovers in the fight for second place. What followed for them, though, was a long journey to Middlesbrough in miserable weather, and a disappointing 2-2 draw ensued. Watson's men were leading 2-1, when a handball by McConnell gifted the North East club a penalty, which they duly scored. Despite that, Liverpool remained in second place. To guarantee their position they would need to beat the newly crowned champions, Aston Villa, at Anfield in the final game of the season.

The visit of the champions was eagerly anticipated. On the face of it, there was little at stake for either side. However, Villa were hoping to set a points record for the season and Watson was keen to cement second place. In truth, there was a great rivalry between the two clubs stretching back more than a decade, and a personal one between Villa's George Ramsay and Tom Watson. This resulted in a bumper crowd of 30,000, which contained many supporters who had travelled from the Midlands to see their team.

Reports suggest that both teams received a generous reception, with the home crowd eager to show their appreciation for the champions as well as their own team. Liverpool suffered a blow in the first half of the game when goalkeeper Sam Hardy sustained a dislocated wrist. The 'Spion Koppers' were in a gloomy mood when he failed to come out after half-time. The incident reduced Liverpool to ten men, and meant that Arthur Goddard took Hardy's place in goal. The murmurings of the crowd turned to a huge roar of appreciation as Goddard ran towards the goal, resplendent in white. Amazingly, Liverpool not only kept a clean sheet but, thanks to goals from Ronald Orr and Jack Parkinson, they ran out 2-0 winners. The goals were scored in the 50th and 55th minutes, meaning Goddard had to defend the lead for 35 minutes, a task he was more than equal to.

Second place had been secured, and Liverpool closed a decade of contrasting fortunes. They had proven to be frustratingly inconsistent. However, Watson had led the club to two First and Second Division titles, and reached three FA Cup semi-finals. That was more than enough to earn him the trust and patience of the board and the club's army of supporters.

Tom had continued to operate a revolving-door policy when it came to recruitment in the years between 1906 and 1910. Among the many players he brought in during this period was an absolute gem, Donald McKinlay. A tough Scottish defender, McKinlay played in numerous positions across the back line, and went on to captain the club. Liverpool signed him from Newton Villa in 1910. He would lead Liverpool to back-to-back league titles for the first time in their history in 1922 and 1923, before leaving the club in 1927 after an incredible 17 years. For a more detailed account of Donald's time at Anfield, see *The Untouchables: Anfield's Band of Brothers*.

As Liverpool entered the next decade, they would encounter similar challenges, filled with highs and lows. Throughout this time,

Tom set about building his third great team, and a club fit for the future. He would tragically be denied the fruits of his labours, which continued until his untimely death. However, his toil would not be in vain. As we'll see, his efforts would lay the foundations for the success of others in the years to come.

## Chapter Seventeen

# Tom's adventures in the FA Cup

ALTHOUGH TOM was a five-times league champion with two football clubs, the FA Cup – viewed by many in the game as the more prestigious trophy – had alluded him. Liverpool had clearly enjoyed great success under Watson, but their near misses in the cup had frustrated him greatly. In records of speeches given after both his league title wins and at board meetings, there are references to his and the club's directors' desire to bring the Association Cup to Anfield.

Liverpool had come close in 1896/97, when Aston Villa had proved an insurmountable obstacle, winning the game 3-0. And, in 1899, they were dumped out by Sheffield United, this time by a single goal.

The issue was perhaps felt more acutely among Liverpool's players and supporters because Everton had won the cup in 1906. And although the Reds could point to their championship medals won that same season, the fact that they exited the FA Cup again at the semi-final stage, this time to their Blue neighbours, would have cut deeply. At the time, the game would prove to be the most eagerly anticipated encounter between the two rivals ever witnessed.

The game was contested on 30 March 1906 at Villa Park – 'Aston Park' as it was called in newspaper reports – in front of some 50,000 supporters. The *Liverpool Courier* estimated that some 10,000 of those were from Merseyside, though this seems like an underestimate. In bright sunshine, roughly 20 trainloads of supporters of both teams, decked out in their colours and wearing favours such as rosettes and scarves, ran from Lime Street to the Midlands. In addition, special trains were laid on in different parts of the country to carry 'neutrals' to the game. On their arrival in Birmingham, those supporters would find the weather mild, with cloudy skies, and the players would find the turf to be in perfect condition.

It would be around 20 years before radios were commonplace in the homes of working-class families; therefore, those left behind on Merseyside would have waited anxiously for news of the result, which some would not learn until the return of their loved ones from the game.

Everton's management had picked the team the night before, and were reported to be at full strength. However, Liverpool, it was said, were forced into a more 'experimental' line-up due to the absence of Jack Cox, who had picked up an injury at Preston the previous weekend. Raybould was not risked, due to an old injury sustained weeks earlier. In his place, Hewitt would play, with John Carlin supporting him. Jack Parkinson would play centre-forward and, on the right wing, he would be supported by Arthur Goddard and Bobby Robinson.

Everton were said to have had the better of the opening exchanges, with Sam Hardy the busier of the keepers. Liverpool's forwards were wasteful, with Robinson guilty of wasting a gilt-edged chance to put his team ahead, but 'over-excitement' saw him squander it. Another tame effort from Parkinson was punched away by the Blues' keeper, Billy Scott – brother of future Liverpool keeper Elisha Scott.

With the game goalless at half-time, Liverpool would bemoan their tendency to dally in front of goal, passing when they should have shot. Play was poor in the second half, with Liverpool continuing to be sloppy, before disaster struck 15 to 20 minutes into the half. Everton went one goal up, and here's how Liverpool's goalkeeper, Sam Hardy, described the goal in a *Liverpool Football Echo* article, published in 1955: 'Everton's first goal came [...] from our left-back Billy Dunlop. I shouted to him to leave the ball, which was coming steadily towards me. But instead he sliced it right past me and into the net.'

According to the *Liverpool Courier*, Everton scored a second shortly after, when Harold Hardman headed in a cross from the right wing. The ball struck the foot of the post and deflected into the net. Now 2-0 down, Liverpool sparked into action, but it was too little, too late. They forced a series of corners, but Scott and the Blues' defence repelled them all, and Everton soon regained control. Hardy remembered the second goal slightly differently almost 50 years later, and would have the following to say: 'We were trying hard for an equaliser and most of the team, including the defence were upfield, Everton launched a surprise attack, and with only me to beat outside left Harold Hardman, then, I believe playing as an amateur, had no difficulty in netting the ball from five or six yards out.'

Hardman's recollections also differ, unsurprisingly, given the passage of time, from the contemporaneous reports. He recalled the game in the same *Liverpool Football Echo* feature in 1955: 'The semi-final of 1906, when we defeated Liverpool by two goals to nothing at Villa Park, is one of the happiest moments of my career. I well remember the game because it brought me one of the goals. A free kick was taken on the right wing, I think it was Harry Makepeace who took it, but I remember the ball came over and dropped at my feet. Without hesitation I shot first time and found the net.'

Everton seemed to have grabbed a third, only for Young to see the goal disallowed for an obvious offside. The game finished 2-0, with the Blues worthy winners and Watson's men seeing their hopes of winning the FA Cup evaporate at the penultimate hurdle for the third time. The pain experienced by the Red half of the city would be exacerbated by the welcome afforded to Everton's conquering heroes. Here's how the *Liverpool Courier* reported it:

> There was a great scene in Lime-street when the victorious Everton team arrived on Saturday's night. During the whole evening crowds had gathered in and about the station and the Lime-street and large numbers of police were kept busily engaged in keeping a clear roadway for the passage of the trams and wheeled traffic. Many thousands of people were present and much cheering was indulged in. About eleven o'clock the station was thronged, and when the train arrived from Birmingham, bringing the Everton team and directors ringing cheers and shouts went up from the crowd. The greatest enthusiasm prevailed, the players and officials having great difficulty in working through the excited throng.

The Liverpool team disembarked one stop early, at Edge Hill. Could there be a more depressingly fitting metaphor than that.

Liverpool finally reached the FA Cup Final in 1914, after disposing of Aston Villa 2-0 in the semi-final at White Hart Lane. They would face Burnley at Crystal Palace in the final. This would be the last time the conclusion of the Association Cup would be played there, and the first time a reigning monarch attended the game. George V was patron of the Football Association and was said to have delighted crowds at the match.

Tom Watson's 1913/14 FA Cup campaign got underway against Barnsley at Anfield on 3 January 1914. Liverpool were somewhat lucky to come away from the game with a draw. Having gone a goal up in the first half, they were run ragged in the second. Barnsley levelled in the 70th minute and hit the bar with virtually the last kick of the game. However, Tom Watson's men would pull themselves together two weeks later at Oakwell, where they won the game 1-0 thanks to an 89th-minute winner from Bill Lacey.

Liverpool dispatched Gillingham in the next round, 2-0, but needed a replay to see off West Ham. After drawing the first game 1-1, they thrashed the Hammers 5-1 at Anfield. In what was described as a 'slaughter', over 40,000 watched Liverpool brush the Londoners aside with consummate ease. There then followed a 2-1 victory over QPR at Anfield, in which the visitors missed a penalty, to set up another semi-final, this time with Aston Villa, at White Hart Lane.

The press had Liverpool as clear outsiders to reach the final. Villa were the form side, and many felt they would stroll through the tie. This was something that clearly riled Tom Watson. Before the game, he assembled his players in a hotel for lunch and, as they finished, he rose to his feet to deliver one of the greatest battle cries the team had ever heard. The Reds' former goalkeeper Ken Campbell recalled the events later in an article for the *Weekly News* in 1921.

In it he describes Watson's harsh words for the gentlemen of Fleet Street, and by all accounts 'Owd Tom' had turned red in the face, such was his anger. As he finished his speech, Campbell recalls that he thumped the table, causing crockery to jump all over the place, before declaring: 'Never mind boys, I want you to turn out today and show them up. Show them there are more players than Aston Villa in the semi-final.'

His words seemed to have the desired effect and the Reds ran out 2-0 winners. For the first time in their history, they had reached the final of the FA Cup. Some described Liverpool's run to the final as lucky, a claim that angered Watson and players such as Ephraim Longworth, who told the *Sport Angus* on 12 September 1914:

> It was against Aston Villa, however, that we recorded our greatest triumph – that we won against the greatest odds.

> There is no need for me to recall the details; they will be well remembered. The amazing form of the Aston Villa side for the few months previous was discussed on every hand. They were the favourites. It was merely a question of how many goals we should lose by. The odds were against us, but we won against the odds. How did we do it?
>
> In the first place, the side who hope to win against odds must be fit as fiddles – every man trained up to a nicety to last the whole of the game, and every man ready and willing to put forth that bit of extra effort necessary if a better team is to be beaten. And it is no good trying to win against odds if your men go on the field with the fear of defeat in their hearts.

Liverpool would contest the FA Cup Final on 12 April 1914. Their achievement in reaching the final electrified the city, placing them within touching distance of elite status in English football. Were they to win it, it would exorcise Watson's ghosts, after he had come so close on six previous occasions, three of them with Sunderland, only to see his teams go out at the semi-final stage.

We now know what an emotional character Watson was, and can speculate on the turmoil of hope, expectation and anxiety that must have gripped him in the run-up to the final. For the club's supporters, however, there seems to have been excitement and joy bordering on delirium as they prepared to make their way to the capital. Reaching the final and seeing their team play before the king would have undoubtedly captured the imagination of everyone with a Red heart on Merseyside. The *Liverpool Echo* captured the excitement under the headline 'A ROYAL DAY: MERRY SCENES AT THE STATION'. The paper reported that more than 20,000 Liverpudlians made the trip to Crystal Palace by train and coach. So large were the crowds that 'one of the biggest trains on record' was pressed into service, carrying 1,200 fans. This may have been the first train ever referred to as a 'football special'.

In addition to this, 18½ coaches transported what was described as 'the population of a village from Liverpool to London in one swoop'. However, conditions on the trains were said to be crammed and uncomfortable, though passengers made up for this by plastering the carriages with red and white ribbons and rosettes and placing portraits of the team and their heroes – cut out from the local papers – in the windows. Specially produced *Liverpool Echo* badges, bearing football battle cries, were worn on nearly every hat and in buttonholes. There were also suggestions that supporters, just as they do today, would hide away refreshments of a liquid variety in their pockets, ensuring a merry day would be had by all, whatever the score.

Inside the carriages, those supporters were reported to have sung songs about their opponents, and the *Liverpool Mercury* may have captured one of the earliest recorded Liverpool songs. Though the tune is unknown, it went like this:

The Burnley men came like wolves on the fold
And their faces gleamed like the Klondyke gold
To the football field they all wended their way
To see their old foes at football to play
But nins and slack, when they got on the fluid
And saw their opponents, they knew they's to yield
For they rushed them and pushed them until all were sore
And beat them all hollow, as they'd oft done before.

Sadly, those merry supporters would have their hopes dashed. Liverpool lost the final 1-0, but events that took place a mere 48 hours before saw the players earn the wrath of their manager and may have affected morale in the camp.

In 1965, over 50 years after this historic occasion, and after another near miss in 1950 when Arsenal denied the Reds their first taste of victory in the competition, Liverpool would secure their first-ever FA Cup. The *Liverpool Echo* reported that five surviving members of the 1914 team had been invited to watch the final against Leeds United. All but Ephraim Longworth, who was too ill to travel, would witness Shankly's Liverpool lift the trophy that had eluded them over half a century earlier.

However, it's the headline and opening paragraph of that article that catches the eye most. Under the words, 'When Liverpool did a Chelsea at Epping', the local paper goes on to reveal remarkable details of a bust-up that took place in the Liverpool team hotel just days before the 1914 FA Cup Final. The players and club management had been staying in the Forest Hotel in Epping. In the early hours of the morning, a couple of days from the final, team trainer Bill Connell was awoken from his sleep by a loud noise coming from the billiard room below. The paper picks up the story:

> Down in the Forest [Epping] something stirred, and it wasn't the note of a bird, but of several players returning, via a window in the billiard room, in the small hours of the morning.
>
> They were not given railway tickets and sent home, like Chelsea. They were not even admonished as they re-entered the hotel after their midnight marauding. They were allowed to sleep in peace.

However, if the players thought they had got away with their nocturnal adventures, they would be in for a rude awakening. Manager Tom Watson would serve up the sternest of rebukes for breakfast, leaving none of them in any doubt of how he felt about matters. This meant so much to Tom, and the thought that his players were giving the occasion anything less than their utmost concentration had infuriated him.

'Manager Tom Watson, one of the greatest the club ever had,' the *Echo* continued, 'tore such a large strip off them they would far rather be sent Anfieldwards to escape such a verbal lashing.'

Secrecy around the events was maintained for five decades, and supporters who attended the match never heard of what happened before the game. The behaviour of the players was certainly not unusual for the time, and purveyors of the modern game will have similar stories to tell, but it's interesting – if perhaps unsurprising – to note that managers and trainers as far back as 1914 understood the value of discipline and focus as much as their latter-day counterparts, and it's a testament to their professionalism.

A special matchday programme was printed to commemorate the occasion. According to Dr Rob Gower, an avid collector and expert on programmes of the period, speaking to lfchistory.net, the document was just four pages in length, with black print on white paper. The front page contained the match details, while the inside cover lists the programme of music that was to be played by the Band of His Majesty's Irish Guards and the Band of 1st Battalion King's (Liverpool) Regiment. This included: 'Carmen', 'Land of Hope and Glory' and 'When the Midnight Choo-Choo', among others.

Page three listed the results of all the previous finals and where they had been staged. The back page listed the team line-ups and colours. Liverpool played in scarlet jerseys and white knickerbockers, which, the *Liverpool Courier* reported, were brand new for the occasion. The officials were also listed, as well as a note reminding spectators to keep their places if the match ended in a draw after 90 minutes, as extra time would have to be played.

Any Kopite who bought a copy would have obtained quite the heirloom for their descendants. One four-page issue recently sold for £4,560 at auction. 'Ring tickets' for the game cost 2/6, which in today's money would be just over £7. Naturally, just as it does today, the *Liverpool Echo* published a cup final special. By way of summarising the club's history to date, it had the following to say:

> The career of the Liverpool Football Club has been a very chequered one, and they have gained a name for inconsistency in their play. Such a thing cannot be levelled at the management at any time, as through thick and thin, success and failure, the policy of those responsible for the club's welfare has always been a forward one. In recent years the ground at Anfield road has been remodelled, new stands and offices have been made, and everything possible that could go towards making the players' quarters worthy of a first-class club has been done. Spectators have been well looked after; three sides of the ground have covered accommodation whilst at the Oakfield-road end is the noted Spion Kop, which is unrivalled in England. On its slopes a big crowd can find comfortable standing-room and get an excellent view of the game.

The paper also previewed the Liverpool team, describing each player in turn, including their characteristics and measurements. We have reproduced it here, below:

> Ken Campbell – goalkeeper, came to Liverpool from Cambuslang Rovers in May, 1911. Recognised as one of the best custodians of the present day. A native of Glasgow. Weighs 11st. and is 5ft. 10in. in height.
>
> Ephraim Longworth – right full back, joined Liverpool from Leyton in 1910. A sound defender, who is rarely off form,

and has strong international claims. Born at Halliwell, near Bolton. Weighs 11st.; height 5ft. 8½in.

Robert Pursell – left full-back, played as an amateur with Queens Park, Glasgow. Played as a forward, half back and full back for them at various times. He signed a professional form as a full back for Anfielders three seasons ago. He is a first rate sprinter. Born at Campbelltown [*sic*]. Weight, 12st. height 5ft. 11in.

Thomas Fairfoul – right half back. Previously with Third Lanark and Kilmarnock and played as a forward for these clubs. Has played for the Scottish League against Irish League. This is his first season at Anfield. Fairfoul was born at West Calder and weighs 11st. 10lb. and is 5ft. and 9½in. in height. Fairfoul is a very capable golfer.

Harry Lowe – centre half back, captain of the team. Born at Whitwell, in Derbyshire. He first made his name with Gainsborough Trinity. Left half back is his usual position, but he occasionally figured in the centre. Lowe's display against Liverpool in a cup-tie brought him to the notice of his present club, and he signed for them in the summer of 1911. He first played as a wing half-back, but when Harrop left he was moved to centre half position, and he has played many fine games as pivot. Lowe is a well-built player. Scales 13st. 2lb, and is 5ft. 10in. in height.

Robert Ferguson – left half-back, came to the fore with Third Lanark. He is a consistently good player who knows well how to break up opposing attacks, and is not slow in shooting at the goal when the opportunity occurs. Came to Anfield as a centre half-back, but has played really on the wing. Ferguson is a native of Cleland, in Lanarkshire, and as a lad worked in the mines. He stands 5ft. 10½in. and weighs 12st. 5lb.

Jackie Sheldon – outside right. It was only last November that Sheldon was secured by his present club from Manchester United, with whom he had figured as deputy for the famous Meredith. Was accounted a capture and has certainly proved his worth. He is a tricky player and can centre splendidly, and has considerable speed. Sheldon was born at Clay Cross, near Manchester. His height is 5ft. 7in. [unreadable] and he weighs 10st.

Arthur Metcalfe [*sic*] – inside right. A native of Sunderland. Was with Newcastle United before coming to Liverpool in 1912. He is a tricky forward who knows where the goal is. Metcalfe is a good cricketer, being a particularly smart wicketkeeper. Height 5ft. 6in. Weight 11st.

Tom Miller – centre forward. Came to Anfield from Hamilton Academicals in 1911. Until this season generally played inside right or inside left. Has a rare burst of speed and a good shot and knows how to hustle the defenders. Miller was born at Motherwell. He is 5ft. 8$^{1}$½in. height and weighs 11st. 5lb.

William Lacey – inside left. Irish international. Was born at Wexford. Came to the fore with Shelbourne and was secured from them by Everton. In March, 1912, he was transferred across the park to Liverpool and proved an invaluable player. Lacey is a clever dribbler, a good shot and an opportunist. A

> born footballer who never seems to give in. He works hard right up to the final whistle. Can play in practically every position on the field. Weighs 11st. 9 lb. Height 5ft. 8½in.
>
> Jimmy Nicholl – outside left. Transferred from Middlesbrough to Liverpool last January. He is a smart winger, centres well and shoots strongly, makes for the goal at first instance. Nicholl is a Port Glasgow man and played with several Scottish clubs before heading south. He is 5ft. 8in. in height.

Liverpool's captain, Harry Lowe, listed above, was fully expected to play in the final. However, the *Liverpool Echo* could not have forecast that he would suffer an injury that would ultimately keep him out of the game. He was replaced by 23-year-old Donald McKinlay. He, along with Ephraim Longworth and Bill Lacey, would feature in the game and also go on to be part of the famous team of 'Untouchables' who won back-to-back league titles in the 1920s.

The game was to kick off at 3.30pm, and there were already several hundred people in the ground at noon. Around Crystal Palace stadium the streets were densely packed, with some journalists estimating a crowd of 100,000 to be in the area. Many were there for the match, of course, and the official attendance was recorded as 72,778. However, undoubtedly the presence of the king meant many more turning out to catch a glimpse of him.

Naturally, that meant the police presence would be huge, and one *Liverpool Echo* reporter, Ernest 'Bee' Edwards, reflecting on the cause of the huge turnout from the London constabulary, remarkably declared in his column, in capital letters, 'BLAME THE SUFFRAGETTES'. Of course, such a police presence was inevitable where the monarch was concerned, especially in proximity to such a huge crowd.

Liverpool's opponents would field a former Everton player, Bert Freeman. Perhaps conscious of the potential for their former player to dent the Reds' ambitions, one Blue penned a poem to his city rivals, entitled 'Which?', a reference to a dream he had in which he awoke before he realised who had scored the winning goal in the game. We'll leave it to you to decide whether his 'blessings' are genuine or written with a hint of irony:

WHICH?

The Cup's to be won. There's work to be done
So Reds take your place at the Palace
Tho' still I'm a Blue, I leave it to you
I'll wear the red scarf without malice
For last night I dreamed I stood – so it seemed
'Mongst the crowd that stood surging and swaying
But right through the game I heard but one name
'That's Freeman' – the people were saying
My poor heart was torn, with the thought that was bourne
If the Reds win the coveted trophy –
After all his fine game (Bert was crème de la crème)
He'll still want the cup for his coffee
Then a hush on the crowd, seemed to fall like a shroud
Then a yell – that vast throng surely roared
Then peace to my soul, as the crowd thundered goal!
But – I woke fore I knew – what side had scored.

On the day of the final, the weather was described as sunny but overcast. Burnley, who had trained in Lytham and travelled to London the evening before, were staying in a nearby hotel. Of course, we know Liverpool had boarded at the Forest Hotel in Epping. On the morning of the game, the players, Tom Watson and his coaching staff travelled to the ground in taxis, with supporters and friends waving them off.

The players would be presented to the king, who had granted a personal audience to the captains of each side. He also posed for a photograph with them, as did the Duke of Lancaster, who, it was noted, was wearing a red rose on his coat.

The Liverpool goalkeeper recalled the day seven years later, in an article entitled 'My Five Minutes with the King', published 18 June 1921. Ken Campbell explains how the team had been aware of the challenge that lay ahead of them, but they were nonetheless confident that they would 'take a lot of beating'. He also recalled how the loss of captain Harry Lowe would prove extremely costly:

> Our hopes got a wee bit shattered by an unfortunate incident, and I do not hesitate to say that it had a deal to do with what happened to us at the Palace.
>
> We played Middlesbrough in a League match the week previous to the final, and owing to our having a somewhat weak team out – Lacey, Sheldon, Longworth, and myself of the cup-tie team were not playing – we went down 4-0.
>
> That in itself would have been a bit of a shock, but what really did tell was a regrettable accident to Harry Lowe, our centre-half, who had his knee injured in this game. Once more the uncertainties of football demonstrated.
>
> Never shall I forget the anxiety of the following week. We went down to Chingford again for special training on the Monday after the Middlesbrough match.
>
> Would Harry be fit? That was the question of the hour. You know how little things like that upset one, and we were strung up to the highest pitch.
>
> Harry was sent to a specialist in London, and he gave great hopes of being able to play. Our spirits rose again. We trained hard and earnestly, and felt that, after all, things were not to be so bad. Harry attended the specialist

every day, and on the Saturday he went to have his knee strapped up.

He came back to Chingford about lunchtime, and we all went on to the green in front of the hotel to see him try his leg.

I remember it all so well. Little Jacky Sheldon threw the ball to Harry's bad leg, and called – 'Kick it back to me, Harry.' Poor Harry made an attempt, and then drew back !! 'It's no use, boys,' he said, and the tears were in his eyes. And I am not ashamed to say that most of the boys felt like that.

It's clear to us, after reading Ken Campbell's words, how much of a psychological impact the loss of Lowe had on the rest of the team. It also speaks to the togetherness among the lads, and sense of family. However, it would mean that, at least in their heads, they felt they were at a disadvantage before they had even kicked a ball, and such things can prove pivotal as much then as they do now.

Did the Liverpool players believe they were already beaten? Consider these words from Campbell:

The tragedy of it! To be robbed of the services of our pivot on the eye of such an important event – one on which we had set our hearts so much – was a real tragedy to us.

After going through the rounds and reaching within touch of a footballer's highest ambition, it was a severe blow, and I know it upset all the boys. However, there was nothing for it but to put a stout heart to a 'sley brae'.

There would be further anxiety when the players arrived at Crystal Palace. Of the five taxis that took the men to the stadium, only four had actually arrived. The players joked among themselves that they had been kidnapped, but Tom Watson was beside himself with worry. In desperation, at three o'clock, the manager went to the entrance gates to see if his men had arrived. In just 20 minutes they were meant to be in their kits and presented to the king. To his enormous relief, he found them, struggling to make their way into the ground past a huge crowd. They had been trying to get past the commissionaire for quite a long time, but that official was adamant that all the players had already gone in. The poor man was used to chancers turning up at his entrance, pretending to be players. Watson, though relieved, was exasperated by all of this, and is said to have torn a strip off the poor commissionaire. Nevertheless, he would need the assistance of Mr F. J. Wall, the English Football Association secretary, to persuade the man to allow the players to enter the stadium.

To say that Tom and his men were ill-prepared for the final seems something of an understatement. Ill-discipline, an injured captain and distracted by pre-match drama, it really couldn't have been any worse. The only silver lining for the players was the late arrival of the king, which meant they would all be ready for inspection before kick-off.

The officials for the game were: referee Mr. H. S. Bamlett (Gateshead); linesmen, Messrs Talks (Lincoln) and Rogers (London). Both teams lined up in a two-three-five formation, as was common for the period.

Ken Campbell remembers that he had little to do in the first half, while – he claims – Burnley's Ronnie Sewell was a 'very busy man'. Again, after missing a series of chances, including a Tom Fairfoul shot that hit the crossbar, the Liverpool men began to believe that luck had deserted them and it wasn't to be their day.

Half-time brought lemons and tea, and their spirits were revived, as was their belief that they still had a chance. Those hopes would soon be dashed as Bert Freeman, the subject of a prophetic Evertonian dream, would unleash a lightning shot that sailed past the helpless Campbell and into the net 14 minutes into the second half. A huge roar greeted his strike, and it must have broken Tom Watson's heart.

'It was really a remarkable goal. I have never seen it equalled. The ball was almost breast high, and how Freeman got his foot on it and the force behind it I know not,' said the Liverpool keeper.

The goal would be enough to win the game. The Reds had caused a few moments of anxiety among the Burnley players towards the end of the game with their shooting, but to no avail. As a result, the Liverpool players cut disconsolate figures as they stood alongside their counterparts, waiting for their runners-up medals, as the king made the presentations.

However, they would soon recover from their despair. On the Sunday night after the game, they were entertained with a concert at the hotel. While the players may have taken their defeat like 'sportsmen', one Liverpool fan is reported to have muttered grumpily to Ernest 'Bee' Edwards of the *Liverpool Echo* that 'Freeman did nothing but score the goal'. Edwards had caught up with Freeman on the pitch as he attempted to make his way through a huge crowd, with his father on his arm. Naturally, the player was delighted, but he was full of praise for the Liverpool players, saying: 'I think we were just a trifle the better side. The ground was awfully awkward. If you fell down you got a jarring, and it was hard to keep up on the hard going.' He gestured to the palm of his hand. 'Here look at this, on the palm of my hand. It looks nothing more than a scratch yet I tell you it is most painful.'

His complaints about the pitch were shared by journalists as well as Liverpool's players. Nonetheless, it had been Burnley who had adapted to conditions better, and they deserved their win.

In an interesting side note to the occasion, the *Daily Express* reported on the experiences of a blind man who had gone to the game. A Mr W. Meredith, blind from birth, had become well known at football grounds in the north, and was well familiar with the details of the sport. He had been brought to the final by the National Institute for the Blind to record his impressions of the match for posterity. The *Express* claimed: 'At the Crystal Palace, relying chiefly on sounds, he followed the ramification of the play with an amazing confidence, and was frequently able, in the most disconcerting fashion, to name the player in possession of the ball and describe what he was going to do with it.'

According to the paper, Mr Meredith commented on the performances of both sets of players. We have reproduced his reflections below:

> I liked Liverpool's outside right, Sheldon, very much. He is a great forward. But I think he spoils many a good effort by holding the ball too long, instead of sending it to the centre. I was not favourably impressed by the play of Miller, Liverpool's centre, as in many instances he was very slow. I have known Miller at his best, and he was a long way short of it to-day.
>
> Of the half-backs, I liked Fairfoul best. Ferguson and McKinlay, although working so persistently, did not come up to my expectation. Pursell performed well at left back, but Longworth was my favourite; he kicked and tackled like a Trojan, and saved his goal time after time when it was in great danger.
>
> Kenneth Campbell is a great goalkeeper. The ball had only just been kicked-off when Mosscrop, receiving from the half-backs, ran along the wing, centred accurately, and someone, whether Freeman or Lindley I know not, shot in. Where Campbell came from I am at a loss to know, but he saved miraculously. Perhaps one other instance of his excellent goalkeeping will surface. Once in the second half

> the Burnley forwards were in line in full cry for goal. A hot bombardment took place, and three shots were directed at goal. Campbell was equal to the occasion, and saved wonderfully in each case.
>
> The Burnley side struck me as a very robust one; they played vigorous football, and swung the ball about in fine fashion.
>
> Taking everything into consideration, I cannot say it was a great game. I may hear someone say the best team won, but had a draw been the result should not have been surprised, as I consider the play veered pretty evenly.

As the dust settled on the encounter, the editor of the *Liverpool Echo* received a letter from the directors of Burnley FC, which it reported on 5 May 1914:

> To Mr. T. Watson, Liverpool F.C.
>
> I am instructed by my board of directors to forward to you and your club a letter of appreciation and thanks for the sportsmanlike manner in which you met us after our victory in London, and the handsome manner you received us in Liverpool on Wednesday.
>
> Both days will live long in the minds of our officials and players, and perhaps you will be pleased to learn that your actions were the chief topic of conversation among our party on their return to Burnley.
>
> We feel and sincerely hope that an everlasting friendship has been made between the two clubs which reflects great credit on you, and failing my club retaining the trophy next year, our earnest wish is that you will prove successful.
>
> Yours truly,
>
> J. Haworth, Sec.

Though nobody could know at the time, this would be Tom Watson's last chance of FA Cup glory. Just as was the case with Bob Paisley many decades later, the trophy would prove agonisingly elusive to him. However, it was not for the want of effort, desire and passion. Nor should his career be judged negatively due to the absence of the Association Cup.

No modern Liverpool supporter would judge Paisley, with his six English First Division league titles but no FA Cup, a failure. Nor should Tom be considered as such. Tom won an astonishing five league titles, and was the first of his order to lift a league championship at two different clubs, and he belongs among the pantheon of football's greatest managers.

## Chapter Eighteen

# Watson lays the foundations for 'The Untouchables', the team of the 1920s

THE YEAR of 1910 would prove to be another momentous one for both the city of Liverpool and the country. On the city's waterfront, a new 'skyscraper' was under construction. Commenced in 1909, and modelled on a building in Chicago, the Liver Building would be completed in 1911, and would form one of a set of buildings alongside the Cunard Building and the Port of Liverpool Building, known locally as the 'Three Graces'.

The year would also see two general elections, amid demands for Irish home rule, industrial conflict, and with the Suffragette campaign in full swing. The nation would also be gripped by the notorious Dr Crippen case, with the infamous killer hanged for the murder of his wife. He had been arrested on the SS *Montrose*, becoming the first criminal apprehended as a result of the use of wireless telegraphy. The police had sent a message to the captain of the ship, asking him not to set sail until Crippen was arrested.

And in the middle of all of this came the end of the Edwardian era, signalled by the death of Edward VII, which ushered in the reign of King George V. We were now entering the Georgian age.

Tom Watson was now living at 246 Anfield Road, Liverpool, along with his wife Kate and children Ralph, Ethel and Winifred. The family had experienced deep personal sorrow, as census records for 1911 indicate that Tom's wife had given birth to and lost a child. Tom appears to have carried on, though the pain felt by the whole family must have been enormous. The team also struggled through the final five league campaigns with him as their manager. The 1914 FA Cup Final aside, Liverpool had become a shadow of the team that conquered the league in 1901 and 1906.

From 1911–1915, they finished 13th, 17th, 12th, 16th and 13th respectively. It's perhaps remarkable, given the team's league performances, that the board of directors maintained their unwavering trust in Watson. It's a testament to his personality, character and his achievements in the game that they didn't look elsewhere in order to launch a new era at the club. Tom had suffered a slump previously between 1901 and 1905, only to build the next great team and win the title in 1906. Again, after this championship win, Liverpool had gone into decline, before finishing as runners-up in 1910.

The club could certainly have afforded to replace him, if they so desired. A report of the 1912 Annual General Meeting, a somewhat fiery gathering that took place at the Liverpool Law Rooms, suggests that the club was in rude health financially, with record revenues and shareholders awarded a five per cent dividend.

Another factor in Tom's favour, perhaps, was a desire to see the club follow the approach of 1905/06, when they had achieved great success with relatively little outlay. There were now complaints that the club was not 'economising' sufficiently, and that they should return to the old ways. In this context, a change of manager and a resulting reshaping of the squad and backroom team may have proved unpopular with shareholders.

Finally, the proceedings of the 1914 Annual General Meeting reveal the extent to which Liverpool's gate receipts were filling the coffers as a result of the club's popularity. All of these factors – a popular manager with a history of success, a board of directors cautious about spending too much money and healthy financial performance – meant Tom remained safely ensconced in his position.

The Reds' subsequent run in the hugely prestigious FA Cup in the 1913/14 season would also have assured the directors – for whom the 'English Cup' had become something of a holy grail – that their trust was well placed. And, although he would never get to see the fruits of his labours, Tom was in the process of constructing the next great championship-winning team.

So integral was the manager to the club that their telegraph address throughout his reign was 'Watson, Liverpool'. It was only changed, to 'Goalkeeper', when a message about the signing of a player was sent to the wrong Mr Watson, who promptly took it to 'Bee' at the *Liverpool Echo*, thereby unceremoniously breaking the story before Liverpool could.

Tom was also in the throes of rebuilding the playing squad and equipping it for future success. As we've discussed, several men who would go on to win back-to-back league championships in 1922 and 1923 were brought to Liverpool under Tom Watson's leadership. These were Ephraim Longworth, Don McKinlay, Walter Wadsworth, Bill Lacey and Elisha Scott. The star striker of the 1920s team, Harry Chambers, would join the club after knocking on Tom's door in 1915. After a successful trial, he became Watson's last signing. Together, these six men formed the spine of one of the greatest teams Liverpool had ever seen.

Tragically, for Watson and Liverpool, these players would have their careers interrupted by the outbreak of the First World War. It would be left to the likes of Dave Ashworth and Matt McQueen – Reds managers in 1922 and 1923 respectively – to reap the benefits of Tom's work after his heartbreaking death in 1915.

There would be some cheer during the period, however, with Liverpool winning the Liverpool Senior Cup in 1913 and 1915. They also shared the trophy with Everton in 1912. Although these competitions were clearly not seen as being as important as official league fixtures, as evidenced by attendances, and certainly not as highly prized as the FA Cup, they certainly had value and there was local pride at stake.

The 1912/13 Liverpool Senior Cup Final was contested on Wednesday, 30 April 1913 at Anfield, with 6,000 supporters present. Liverpool ran out 3-1 winners after going a goal behind within two minutes. Everton remained by far the more successful team in the competition, with 16 wins, but Liverpool's eighth would no doubt have given Reds in the city great satisfaction.

They won their ninth Liverpool Senior Cup in the 1914/15 season. Following a 1-1 draw with Tranmere Rovers at Goodison Park, in which Fred Pagnam scored for the Reds, Liverpool went on to win the replay, fought out at Anfield on 10 April 2015. A penalty by Wilfred Bartrop brought the cup to the Reds.

Prior to the 1914/15 season, Tom led his players on a pre-season tour of Scandinavia. He was in fine health and, along with Liverpool player Tom Fairfoul, the Liverpool manager corresponded with Ernest 'Bee' Edwards at the *Liverpool Echo*, providing details of how the expedition was going. He included a photograph of the Liverpool party enjoying themselves, and on it he had written, 'Everyone has enjoyed himself. Home on Thursday at 2:15 p.m.'

Tom entered his final campaign as Liverpool manager at Anfield on Wednesday, 2 September 1914. War had already broken out in Europe and many had complained that it was inappropriate to play football under such circumstances. The season, however, would be played to a conclusion before the league was suspended in 1915.

Liverpool won their opening game 4-3, thanks to goals from Jackie Sheldon, Bill Lacey, Jimmy Nicholl and Arthur Metcalf. In the run-up to the game, the *Liverpool Echo* carried a photograph of supporters on the Spion Kop, under the headline 'THE SPION KOP ARMY'. A caption read: 'There is room for some of them in the ranks.' This was an early example of Lord Derby's recruitment drive, targeting football supporters.

On 12 February, an appeal appeared in Ernest 'Bee' Edwards's 'Notes' in the *Liverpool Echo* for supporters to donate footballs or money to send to the 'Tommies' in the trenches. In the same column, he chastised the fans for remaining silent during the playing of the national anthem. Of course, we do know that soldiers had footballs on the battlefield, and in one famous incident actually played football with their opposite numbers in the German trenches on Christmas Day during a truce in 1914. Interestingly, in a letter Tom Watson wrote to *The Times* in November 1914, he makes reference to the club sending 18 footballs to 'supporters of our club who wear the Kings uniform'. There's no way to confirm this, but it's intriguing to consider the possibility that one of those balls may have been used in that historic game of football.

Football clubs appeared to be under enormous pressure to assist the war effort. In his letter, Watson spells out the lengths the club was going to in this regard. He points out that players were being drilled by a retired army officer two days a week, that they had welcomed army bands on matchdays, and collections had been undertaken from players, staff, directors and supporters totalling more than £550. In addition, the players were donating 12½ per cent of their wages to the local war fund, and the club was providing free places at matches to soldiers, sailors and Belgian refugees.

Away from the war, though this would be a season of disappointment for Liverpool, there was one highlight for Reds supporters. After a 5-0 drubbing at the hands of the Blues at Anfield on 3 October 1914, Liverpool exacted a degree of revenge over Everton on their home turf on 6 February 1915, beating the Toffees 3-1 in front of 30,000 supporters at Goodison Park. *Liverpool Daily Post and Mercury* reported that the game was one of the best contested between the two teams, stating: 'So far as the game was concerned

*Cigarette cards depicting Liverpool player Alex Raisbeck. Courtesy of Adrian Killen and Liverpool FC. Museum collections.*

BIRMINGHAM AND DISTRICT LEAGUE FIXTURES.

*The Matches are played on the Ground of the Club first named.*

**September.**

1 Stoke v. Aston Villa
1 Birmingham v. Shrewsbury
1 Brierley Hill A v. Dudley
1 West Brom A v. Burslem PV
1 Crewe A v. Stourbridge
1 Coventry C v. Stafford R
1 Halesowen v. Wrexham
1 Kidderminster Harriers v. Wolverhampton Wanderers
1 Worcester C v. Walsall
8 Aston Villa v. Brierley Hill A
8 Burslem P V v. Birmingham
8 W'hampton W v. Coventry
8 Dudley v. Crewe Alexandra
8 Shrewsbury T v. Halesowen
8 Wrexham v. Kidderminster
8 Stafford R v. Worcester City
8 Walsall v. Stoke
8 Stourbridge v. West Brom A
10 BrierleyHill A v. Stourbridge
15 Crewe A v. Aston Villa
15 Birmingham v. Stourbridge
15 Brierley Hil A v. Walsall
15 Halesowen v. Burslem P V
15 Worcester C v. Coventry
15 West Brom A v. Dudley
15 Kid'rminster v. Shrewsbury
15 Stoke v. Stafford Rangers
15 Wrexham v. W'hampton W
22 Aston V v. West Brom A
22 Dudley v. Birmingham
22 Stafford R v. Brierley Hill A
22 Burslem P V v. K'minster H
22 Coventry City v. Stoke
22 Walsall v. Crewe Alexandra
22 Stourbridge v. Halesowen
22 Shrewsbury T v. Wrexham
22 W'hampton W v. Worcester
24 Brierley H A v. K'minster H
29 Birmingham v. Aston Villa
29 Brierley Hill A v. Coventry C
29 Wrexham v. Burslem P V
29 Crewe A v. Stafford R
29 Halesowen v. Dudley
29 K'minster H v. Stourbridge
29 Shrewsbury T v. W'hampton
29 Stoke v. Worcester City
29 West Brom A v. Walsall

**October.**

6 Aston Villa v. Halesowen
6 Walsall v. Birmingham
6 Worcester C v. Brierley H A
6 Burslem P V v. Shrewsbury
6 Coventry C v. Crewe A
6 Wolverhampton W v. Stoke
6 Stourbridge v. Wrexham
13 Kidderminster H v. Aston V
13 Birmingham v. Stafford R
13 Brierley Hill A v. Stoke
13 Burslem P V v. W'hampton
13 W Brom A v. Coventry C
13 Crewe Alex v. Worcester C
13 Wrexham v. Dudley
13 Halesowen v. Walsall
13 Shrewsbury T v. Stourbridge
20 Aston Villa v. Wrexham
20 Coventry C v. Birmingham
20 W'hamptonW v. Brierley HA
20 Stourbridge v. Burslem P V
20 Stoke v. Crewe Alexandra
20 Dudley v. Shrewsbury Town
20 Stafford R v. Halesowen
20 Worcester C v. West Brom A
27 Shrewsbury T v. Aston Villa
27 Birmingham v. Worcester C
27 Crewe Alex v. Brierley H A
27 Burslem Port Vale v. Dudley
27 Halesowen v. Coventry City
27 K'minster H v. Stafford R
27 West Brom A v. Stoke
27 Stourbridge v. W'hampton
27 Wrexham v. Walsall

**For FOOTBALL RESULTS see the EVENING CHRONICLE.**

*Cartoon depicting Alex Raisbeck in conversation with Jock Taylor over a game of cards. Source unknown. Courtesy of Liverpool FC. Museum collection.*

*Cartoon depicting Sam Raybould in training for the new season. Courtesy of Liverpool FC. Museum collection.*

*Cartoon depicting a Liver bird seemingly delighted after Liverpool snatched a point from Everton. Courtesy of Liverpool FC. Museum collection.*

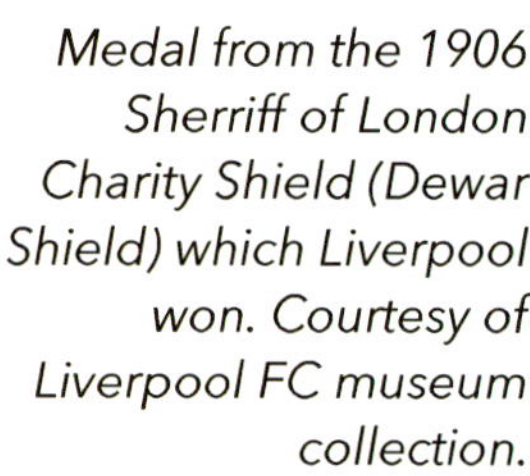

*Medal from the 1906 Sherriff of London Charity Shield (Dewar Shield) which Liverpool won. Courtesy of Liverpool FC museum collection.*

*Gavin Abrams, great nephew of Johnny Walker, holding his great uncle's 1901 championship medal, and displaying the front and rear of the medal. Courtesy of Gavin Abrams.*

*Jack Parkinson's 1899/1900 Second Division champions' medal. Courtesy of Liverpool FC museum collection.*

*Bill Goldie's 1900/01 championship winners' medal. Courtesy of Liverpool FC museum collection.*

*Alec Raisbeck's Scotland shirt, and international caps 1909/10. Courtesy of Liverpool FC museum collection.*

*Tom Watson's 1905/06 championship winners' medal. Courtesy of Liverpool FC museum collection.*

*Commemorative stone laid at Anfield in honour of Tom Watson. The stone is situated at the corner of the Sir Kenny Dalglish Stand and the Anfield Road Stand and looks across to the Shankly Gates, with Stanley Park behind it.*

it will certainly rank as one of the best ever played between them. It was keenly fought, full of incident, and, what is most important, free from the slightest suggestion of foul play.' The claim that the game was one of the best seems something of an exaggeration. Nevertheless, with Everton riding high and on course to win the league, Liverpool supporters would doubtless have left feeling very happy indeed.

Everton, however, would go on to win the league and to some degree they would have Liverpool to thank for it. On the final day of the campaign, 24 April 1915, Tom Watson's men travelled to Boundary Park to play Oldham Athletic, who were in second place in the table, level on points with Everton, who led the way on goal average. Liverpool, languishing in 13th and well clear of relegation, had little to play for. With Everton playing Chelsea on the Monday, Oldham desperately needed a win to stay in the race for the league championship. If they were to beat lowly Liverpool and Everton failed to win their game against the Londoners, Oldham would be champions.

Just 5,000 turned out to see the game, which Liverpool won 2-0, handing the title to their neighbours before they had even kicked a ball. Fred Pagnam scored both goals. Everton's players and officials were present at the FA Cup Final between Sheffield United and Chelsea at the time, and would have heard of the result as they watched the Yorkshire club win the cup. The *Liverpool Echo* reported:

> Naturally they showed the greatest delight when they heard the good news from Oldham. However, all the players were of one mind; they were anxious that goal-average should not be their margin over Oldham, and tonight, when the Cup finalists Chelsea, play at Walton, Everton will be all out for a solid victory over their conquerors in the Cup.

In the end, Everton drew 2-2 with Chelsea, winning the league by a single point. For Tom, though, there were bigger issues to worry about. Earlier, on Good Friday, his team had become caught up in a match-fixing scandal. The boss wasn't involved but, as a man of character with a great reputation in the game, it would have been something that deeply concerned him.

The affair involved a game against Manchester United at Old Trafford on 2 April 1915. The war the propagandists had forecast back in August 1914 would be over by Christmas was now eight months old. The eventual suspension of league football seemed an inevitability to many, as casualties were beginning to pile up on the battlefields of Europe. A large number of players had already left to fight, and those left behind may have thought their careers would end once the season was over. It was a time of great uncertainty and worry for many young men.

As United and Liverpool lined up to face each other, bookmakers had laid odds of United winning 2-0, which turned out to be the actual result of the game. Even before a ball had been kicked, stories began to emerge that players from both teams had been seen drinking together in a local pub before the game. Rumours were rife that the men were planning to fix the game in United's favour. An Old Trafford crowd of 12,000 watched in amazement as many of Liverpool's players seemed to be going through the motions, while United emerged 2-0 winners.

However, the odd behaviour of the players had not escaped the attention of match officials and journalists covering the game. In the first half, United were 1-0 up through George Anderson, when they were gifted the chance to extend their lead from the spot, after Bob Purcell had deliberately handled in the penalty area. Patrick O'Connell, United captain and centre-half, stepped up to take the penalty. He smashed the ball well wide, almost hitting the corner flag. However, it was his reaction as he walked towards the centre circle that caused outrage. He was seen to be laughing and it was suggested that he didn't care that he had missed, because he knew that United could get another goal at any time in the game. Liverpool had appeared lifeless and had offered little resistance.

Not all players were in on the fix, though, and there were reports of angry exchanges in the dressing rooms at half-time. The Liverpool team featured a young Elisha Scott, and two men who would captain Liverpool Football Club, Don McKinlay and Ephraim Longworth. All three were cleared of involvement and it's hard to imagine they would have looked favourably on such behaviour.

In the second half, United extended their lead thanks again to George Anderson, who was also said to be not in on the scandal. With the score at 2-0, it looked as if several players would be laughing all the way to the bank. However, Fred Pagnam had other ideas. The Reds' striker, who knew of the plot, was determined to wreck it. And he almost scored. Late in the game he rattled the crossbar with a fierce shot, much to the conspirators' anger. His own team-mates were seen angrily remonstrating with him, clearly worried that he could have cost them dearly. The game finished 2-0 as planned, and evidence soon emerged that large bets had been placed on that exact scoreline.

An FA investigation found that seven players from both teams were involved. United's Sandy Turnbull, Enoch West and Arthur Whalley were found guilty. For Liverpool, Jackie Sheldon, Thomas Fairfoul, Bob Purcell and Tom Miller were also found guilty. All received lifetime bans. The clubs, however, escaped punishment. The FA accepted that the players had acted alone. Soon the football league competition was suspended, and several of the players went off to fight on the Western Front.

By 1919, all but Enoch West had their bans lifted, largely in recognition of their military service. Turnbull was posthumously reinstated, as he had been killed in battle. West was aged 59 before the FA lifted his ban in 1945.

The scandal also allowed United to escape the drop to the Second Division at Chelsea's expense. However, the league was expanded for the 1919/20 season to allow them to re-join.

The decision to suspend the football league fixtures was taken just three days from the final game between Everton and Chelsea, on 28 April 1915. Plans were made to divide the league into regional tournaments. Liverpool were to enter the Lancashire Section Principal Tournament. It would have fallen to Tom Watson to begin getting the club ready for games and recruiting players from those who had not enlisted or been called up. He had an amateur game at South Liverpool a week before his death, and was also planning a trip to the United States on football business. Tom was certainly not planning to retire from the game, and all the evidence points a man gearing up to lead the club through wartime and beyond.

A month after the end of the season, Liverpudlians would learn that all was not well with Tom as they turned the pages of their *Liverpool Echo* on 5 May 1915. They were confronted with the following piece of news:

> I deeply regret to learn that Mr. Tom Watson has been suddenly taken ill, and his condition is somewhat serious. No football 'head' is so popular as Mr. Tom Watson. 'Owd Tom' is the call everywhere he goes, and the news of his illness will surprise and shock his numerous friends.
>
> Last week he was at a match and it is feared he caught a chill. At any rate, pleurisy led to this temperature jumping up. Later an improvement was seen, but last night's report of Doctor-director James Ferguson was not as encouraging as we should have liked. However, we trust that Mr. Watson

> will speedily pick up and be out and about again at his favourite summer game – bowls.

Sadly, hopes of a recovery would be dashed. Tom's condition worsened, he succumbed to pneumonia and passed away at his home, which was now on Priory Road, Anfield, the following day. He was 56 years of age. The *Liverpool Echo* reported the news the next day, under the headline 'OWD TOM DIES AT HIS HOME':

> We regret to announce the death of Mr. Tom Watson, the popular secretary of the Liverpool Football Club, which occurred at his residency, Priory-road, Anfield, this afternoon.
>
> Mr. Tom Watson – or 'Owd Tom', as he was familiarly and affectionately known throughout the whole football world – was perhaps the most popular figure in the Association code of professional football.
>
> A player himself, he became secretary of the Sunderland club – the district in which he was born.
>
> Thanks to his knowledge not only of the game, but of those who played it, he raised the famous North-Eastern club rapidly into the first flight.
>
> It was talked of in the same breath as Blackburn Rovers and Preston North End, and so far did its fame extend that it came to be called 'the team of all the talents'.

The footballing world reacted with great shock and disbelief. The *Evening Express* printed the following tribute on 6 May 1915:

> We regret to announce the death of Mr. Tom Watson, secretary of the Liverpool Football Club, which occurred at his residence, Priory-road, Liverpool, early this afternoon.

> Mr. Watson was present at the match between South Liverpool and Liverpool last Thursday, and was in town on Friday, but later he was taken ill, suffering from pleurisy.
>
> He was at once attended to by Dr James Ferguson but his condition became very serious and despite all attention he would succumb as stated. Mr. Watson was one of the best known football secretaries in the country and was a most popular figure in England and Scotland, a favourite with everybody, player and official alike who were greatly attached to him […]

The minutes of a meeting of the Anfield board in 1915 reveal that the directors passed a resolution to cover Tom's outstanding expenses, amounting to £30, and that a letter should be written to the chairman of every First and Second Division club inviting them to Tom's funeral.

The words, handwritten in an old ledger, barely do justice to the personal sadness and sense of huge loss felt by all those connected with the club. The reign of one of Liverpool's greatest managers – he's still the longest-serving manager in the club's history – had come to an end, suddenly and unexpectedly. The world was now a very different place, and there were many trials ahead for the people of Liverpool, England and Europe. The shock and sense of disorientation would have been palpable. No doubt these men set about dealing with the practicalities as soon as possible as, in truth, there was little else they could do.

The city of Liverpool and the team that bore its name would eventually rise from the ashes of war, and it's thanks to the diligent efforts of Tom Watson that the club and its team of players and staff would emerge stronger and better equipped for the future. They would go on to even greater honours, thanks in no small part to the men he recruited and the standards he set before his passing.

In a managerial reign that spanned almost two decades, from 24 August 1896 to 6 May 1915, and spanning 742 games, four major honours – two First Division championships, one Second Division title and the Sheriff of London Charity Shield – and the club's first appearance in an FA Cup Final, Tom had established the name of Liverpool Football Club as a major force in English football. He had changed the mentality of the club and cemented a belief in 'scientific football'. He had helped to drive stadium improvements at Anfield, and enhancements to the playing surface. Liverpool were now no longer overly reliant on recruitment from Scotland, and boasted a significant reserve of players recruited locally and from all four corners of the British Isles.

As we gaze back through the years and contemplate the greatest managers in the history of this football club, we find that we are heavily blessed. Shankly, Paisley, Fagan, Dalglish, Houllier, Benítez, Klopp and now Slot trip from the tongue so easily. They have each filled the club's coffers with enough silverware to inspire envy in all but a tiny fraction of Europe's footballing elite. However, this club's success didn't start with any of those great men; it started with Tom Watson, and his impact and the changes he made were every bit as revolutionary and pivotal as theirs.

He is, quite simply, the greatest Liverpool manager that most Reds have never heard of.

## Chapter Nineteen

# Farewell 'Owd Tom'

IT'S A warm sunny afternoon in Liverpool in 1915. The May sun beats down on Anfield Cemetery as a crowd of hundreds of mourners gather at a cool spot shaded by trees. On the ground, over a hundred wreaths are laid, left there by the public, charitable organisations and the world of football. They include tributes from both Liverpool and Everton football clubs. They are all left there for a man who seemingly had no enemies, who was admired by all who knew him, and whose coffin will be carried to its final resting place by the players he led to countless victories.

This was, of course, the funeral of Tom Watson, Liverpool's longest-serving manager. The *Liverpool Echo* captured the event in sombre tones on 11 May 1915. Its article listed literally dozens of dignitaries and organisations who were present, and it's clear that there would have been a huge number of Liverpool supporters there too. These opening paragraphs give a glimpse of both the popularity of the man and the affection he invoked in others, and, of course, the enormous sense of admiration many in the game held for him:

> A cool corner of Anfield Cemetery had been chosen. The sun's rays shaded his last resting place. 'Tom' was buried there. The day was beauteously fine, and the setting of the

> last act was all peaceful. The whole sportsworld seemed to be represented. The late manager of the Liverpool Football Club had no enemies and the far-stretching reach of his works – charity being placed No. 1 – was in a measure shown by the representative gathering which attended to pay its last tribute to an esteemed man.
>
> The body was borne to its resting-place by old and famed players of the club: Raisbeck, Maurice Parry (in his regimentals), Charles Wilson, Goddard, Ted Doig, Bobbie Robinson, and Trainers Fleming and Connell. The following players of the past season were present: – J. Hewitt, T. Fairfoul, K. Campbell, A. Metcalf, D. McKinlay, J. Parkinson, J. Sheldon, R. Terriss, J. Scott, H. Lowe, E. Longworth, E. Scott, P. Bratley, M. McQueen, W. Connell, G. Patterson, and R. Riley.

This was a who's who of Liverpool players, men who had laboured under Watson's management and earned the rewards he had mapped out for them. There were many eulogies, memorials and tributes paid to Tom Watson in the years after his death, and all of them reveal a little more of his personality, of who he was and what made him tick. Then, as is so often the case, he has faded from the collective consciousness, supplanted by more modern heroes whose achievements would cast shade over most.

This is understandable, but feels unfair to us. We hope this book has gone some way to redressing that injustice as we see it. By way of driving home the point, we invite you to consider the following memories and stories of Tom, shared by the people who worked with him and held him dear in the years after his death. This passage from a notice in the *Liverpool Echo* speaks not just to his popularity and influence, but also to how he changed the perception and trajectory of Liverpool Football Club:

Leaving the Wearside seventeen years ago [*sic*], Mr. Watson came to Liverpool in order to take up the management of the Liverpool Club.

The Anfielders at that time were not in too safe a position, but under the aegis of the prince of football managers it achieved a wholly satisfactory position. All who take any interest in the game know the exceptionally interesting history of the Liverpool club for the past seventeen years. In that period it has had its ups and downs, but underlying all was a fine sense of sportsmanship that has overcome most difficulties, both financial and otherwise.

It was a popular saying that one never knew where Liverpool would be at the close of the season, for the club had a curious habit of finishing either close to the top or near to the bottom of the League competition. The Anfielders, thanks in a large measure to Mr. Watson's prescience, carried off the First League championship, the Second League championship, and the Lancashire League championship.

It was never their privilege to win the English Cup, but they achieved the next thing to it by being the runners-up for that national trophy. During the summer season Mr. Watson was in the habit of spending his holiday abroad, and it is not too much to say that he had a distinct influence in popularising the game on the Continent. His illness came suddenly, and the fatal result will be heard with regret.

He was present at a match last week, and it seems that he then complained of feeling cold. This, unfortunately, developed, but his friends did not regard the attack as serious, and the expectation was that Mr. Watson would soon be taking his usual prominent part in the football world. It is a rather pathetic fact that Mr. Watson had just

> recently arranged to visit America this summer, where no doubt he would have further spread the popularity of the game.
>
> Apart from his great interest in football, Mr. Watson was an ardent bowler, and was chairman of the local bowling association.

Of course, local journalistic legend Ernest 'Bee' Edwards also penned his own tribute to the great man, on 7 May 1915. It's quite revealing, and casts Tom as a well-travelled wit and raconteur, an expert at team management and well connected in the football world:

> It was impossible to tell the public during the week how bad Mr. Tom Watson was. He read the paper assiduously, and when he saw a paragraph in this Notebook he pointed it out to his son.
>
> Poor 'Owd' Tom! There was no hope from the start. He could not resist pneumonia and pleurisy. His constitution was not too strong, and the end robs us of one of the features of the game. He was to football what Bunny was to 'the movies,' and he had a heart of gold.
>
> Time and space will not allow a memoir to-day, but to-morrow's 'Football Echo' will contain it, and will show one of W.H. Dorrity's best cartoons of Tom. All round the country one hears expressions of deepest sorrow at the sudden death of our friend, and the funeral on Monday at Anfield will show in some measure in what respect Tom was held. Bluff, hearty, jovial, fond of a joke, could tell one in spasms, and was always prepared to listen to one.
>
> Tom was a favourite all over the country. He hobnobbed with notabilities in his time and only last March when we were travelling to Glasgow for the inter-League match, he

> kept us intent for an hour or more with tales of Russia and with his meetings with Royalty there.
>
> Someone tried to 'pull his leg,' but Tom neatly turned the joke on his assailant. Summarised, I should say that he had signed more cheap and good players than any secretary in the world. He had a faculty not so much for finding a player in the rough, but for tapping sources that led to players coming to Anfield.
>
> I never knew a man who could tap so many parts of the country. His correspondence was abnormal. You could not mention a club's district without he could reply: 'Aye, I'll write So-and-So. He's sure to know.'
>
> He had great ideas about keeping a team together, and once in the long ago he had fears that a team would run riot prior to a big cup-tie. He kept them together very cutely.
>
> Billy Dunlop being the instrument by which he kept the players together. Dunlop was a very fair musician, and Tom timed Dunlop's appearance in the clubroom to a nicety, and the players passed time away pleasantly and forgot all about the passing of the hour. Last season at Chingford Town asked the writer to give them some music, and we eventually had a nightly concert, Tom being M.C. and demanding and giving songs ad lib.
>
> His very best was 'Bricks and Mortar,' but latterly he was loth to sing it. A regular church attendant, [...] his charity extended to all parts. I've heard him say harsh things to a woman who merited chastisement, and then he proceeded to go out of his way to help her in a practical manner.

This, from the *Evening Express*, 6 May 1915, supports the above, and illustrates that Watson's appeal and gravitas spread way beyond the confines of Merseyside football:

> His geniality has been known to secure players for his club where others have failed simply because the players could not refuse him. He made host of friends and in happy smile will be sadly missing from many sporting circles.
>
> Mr. Watson had spent his lifetime in the interest of football and it may be said that he was one of the pioneers of the professional game. A native of the Tyne district he was appointed secretary of the Newcastle West End Club in 1886 when there were no league, and no £1,000 transfer fees, but he succeeded in bringing several internationals from Scotland.

The *Newcastle Journal*, dated 7 May 1915, recalled his pioneering days in the North East, and the huge impact he had on the game there. Tom, after all, had a hand in the eventual success of both Newcastle United and Sunderland AFC:

> Mr. Watson was one of the leading pioneers of professional Association football and for a quarter of a century he played an important part in controlling the fortunes of the Sunderland and Liverpool Clubs in the First Division of the League. A keen, enthusiastic amateur player in his youth, Mr. Watson early assumed the role of an official.
>
> He acted as secretary of both the Newcastle West End and East End Clubs. Whilst associated with the first-named institution, he headed a deputation which resulted in the Newcastle Freemen and the Newcastle Corporation granting permission for football to be played on the site now known as St James' Park, in the occupation of the Newcastle United Football Club.
>
> For the purpose of cultivating the game on the scientific lines practised in Scotland, Mr. Watson introduced several

> smart Scottish professionals into the ranks of the two leading Newcastle clubs. At that period the young Scots readily accepted a £5 note and the offer of a good job in a Tyneside factory. Upon leaving Newcastle, Mr. Watson took over the secretaryship of the Sunderland Club, and under his shrewd management and enterprise the Wearsiders attained great fame as 'The team of all the talents.' He was chiefly responsible for the organisation of the team, including such famous players as Doig, Auld, Gillespie, the Hannah's, Johnny Campbell, Jock Scott, Donald Gow, and Hughie Wilson.

Though a proud native of the North East – he never lost his accent – Tom had become deeply ensconced in the city of Liverpool and, in public life, supporters revered him. He was a president of the Liverpool and District Boxing Association and chairman of the Liverpool Parks and Garden League. In addition, he was involved in many local charities and causes. In September 1902, *Athletic News* had the following to say:

> For five years he represented Division 1, on the Council of the Football Association – a post which he resigned on removing from Sunderland to Liverpool, where he has again made shoals of friends. But, after all, 'a man's career is only the surface of his life.' In the business of a football entrepreneur and schemer he has been eminently successful, but his sterling merit as a man and his magnetic influence over players have gained him the esteem and confidence of his intimates and the loyalty and zealous co-operation of the vast majority of players who have been brought into contract with him. Tom Watson is quite an outstanding figure of his time.

His relationship with his players is exemplified by the words of his great captain Alex Raisbeck, who penned the following words as part of his life story, which was serialised in *Athletic News* on 15 May 1915:

> The late Liverpool manager was more than a friend to me. From the day I became one of his players he took a particular interest in me; he fathered me, to tell the truth. The news of Tom's death came as a great shock to me. I had not even heard that he was ill, and you can easily understand my feelings when the sad news came to hand that pleurisy and pneumonia had cut his life short.
>
> It is difficult for me to realise that I shall never look upon his ruddy countenance again or hear that cheery voice of his, a voice which was known throughout the length and breadth of the British Isles. The Liverpool secretary had friends everywhere. People could not help liking Tom Watson, for he had a way with him of making good and lasting friends. He magnetised by his charming personality, and his unexpected death at the age of 55 [*sic*] will come as a great blow to a great circle of friends associated with football. And none more so than myself.

In his recollections, Alex gives credit to Tom, not just for his prowess at creating a winning team on the pitch, but also playing a major role in Liverpool's success off it. Pointing to Tom's experience in football, and how he had given so many years of his life to the Anfield club, Tom would famously quip to his players that Liverpool were the most attractive team in the league, simply because nobody could ever guess what they were going to do next. Tom could be a stern character, particularly when he felt his players had not given their best, but his anger could quickly turn to humour. He was also known to be so anxious about the results of games that he simply couldn't stand or sit to watch them, for fear of seeing his charges beaten. Instead, he would retire to the rear of the Main Stand, where he would hide away in his 'hut' until the game was over. One particular incident recalled by Raisbeck illustrates the point perfectly. After a game that had seen them play dreadfully against Bury, Tom stormed into the dressing room and declared, 'Well, lads, you have shown shocking form to-day.' To which one of the players, whom Alex didn't name, enquired somewhat meekly as to how the boss could have known, seeing as he had spent the game behind the stand. Of course, Tom immediately saw the humour and was happy to have a laugh at his own expense.

The claim about Tom's inability to watch tense games is supported by the recollection of former Liverpool goalkeeper Ken Campbell, writing about the Bury match in 1921:

> It was an anxious time for the Anfield people. I can remember poor old Tom Watson was in such a state of nerves that he went behind the stand when the match was on. He could not bear to look on. The suspense was terrific.

As Tom grew older, his eyesight began to fail him. The players would often joke that it didn't matter too much if they, as individuals, had a poor game because the manager couldn't tell the difference between them. However, Raisbeck points out that the boss had no trouble pointing out in minute detail what the defects of a particular player were.

There is therefore no doubting that Tom Watson was a respected figure in the game. He was elected to the FA Council and was awarded the Football League's Long Service Medal in 1910. Much later, Watson was honoured by the League Managers Association, who inducted him into their hall of fame.

It must also be remembered that Tom was a family man, and he had a life outside of the game. Sadly, Tom's wife, Kate, passed away in 1917, two years after his death. She left £911 12s and 6d. Their children were Ralph, Mary Ethel, Thomas Oscar and Elizabeth Winifred Watson.

Ralph Watson was a joiner and woodworker. Born on 11 May 1879, he died in Liverpool in 1953. We don't know whether he married, though electoral registers indicate that at one time he lived at 29 Coltart Road. Among the residents at this address were an Edith Watson. He's buried with his mum and dad in Anfield Cemetery.

Mary Ethel Watson was born on 11 May 1885 in Northumberland. She appears to have met an American soldier, Johan Jensen, while he was stationed in England during the First World War. The couple emigrated to Detroit, Michigan, in the United States, where they raised three children: Catherine, Carl and Thomas. She passed away on 31 December 1948, and is buried at Woodlawn Cemetery, Detroit.

Thomas Oscar Watson was born on 5 September 1890 in Sunderland. He died on 24 September 1961. Thomas married Irene, with whom he emigrated to the US in 1920. The couple had two children: Thomas junior and Catherine. Sadly, the marriage didn't last and Thomas senior remarried, to Bessie Baker in 1942.

Finally, Elizabeth Winifred Watson was born on 21 November 1892 in Sunderland. She died on 12 October 1982. She had met her husband, George Wooldridge, a friend of Johan Jensen, while the pair were stationed in England during the First World War. As far as we can tell, the couple had one child, Nanette.

Tom raised a family that went on to explore the world, and some of them settled on foreign shores. He led two football teams to glory in England, and in doing so he greatly influenced the game of football in this country, earning an army of friends and admirers wherever he went. Tom's was a life well lived, and often in the service of others. He cared deeply and passionately about the game and his players. He was a fierce competitor and, although that would often get the better of him, he was renowned as a great sportsman.

It's common for those who are vilified in life to be eulogised in death. We find almost none of this with Tom. We found only one skirmish with a fan in a letters page of a local newspaper, and one barbed quip from a reporter in another, among hundreds of articles reviewed. Of course, that doesn't mean more don't exist, but the evidence is overwhelming that this was quite a remarkable character, revered in life and missed deeply after his passing.

Like the greats who followed in his footsteps, Tom made the people happy. So, as we draw down the curtain, for now at least, on the wonderful life of Tom Watson and the men he led to victory, we say a very fond farewell to 'Owd Tom'. We hope he's resting well. He more than earned his place among the pantheon of football's greatest managers.

# Afterword

## *Conversations on Tom Watson's legacy*

IT'S AUGUST 2025, and the school holidays in the UK are almost over. Kieran and I have just about exhausted our collection of census records, newspaper clippings, books, articles and interviews. We're convinced there's no more surprises lurking within these, waiting to leave us with 'egg on our faces' after the book is published. We're probably wrong, and we'll most likely discover something else later, of course. But, for now, it's time to wrap up the book and submit the manuscript to the publisher, but not before we've properly addressed the problem we identified at the very beginning of this volume.

Tom is the greatest Liverpool manager – maybe the greatest football manager – that most supporters of the game have never heard of. We hope the book has put that right to some extent, but what about his legacy? How does he compare to the great men of our lifetime, and our children's lives? To answer that, we've turned to a group of historians and writers who have devoted their lives to studying and chronicling the life and times of their respective football clubs: Rob Mason, official club historian at Sunderland FC; Stephen Done, author and former museum curator at Liverpool FC; Paul Joannou, author and official historian at Newcastle United FC; Professor Stephen F. Kelly, historian, author and journalist; and Mark Platt, historian, author and current curator at Liverpool FC Museum.

Few people understand the historic connections between Liverpool Football Club and Sunderland FC more than Rob Mason.

In May 2015, he joined Stephen Done, Gerald Jensen (Tom Watson's grandson) and Sunderland's record appearance maker, Jimmy Montgomery, at Anfield Cemetery to commemorate the centenary of Tom Watson's death. To mark the occasion, a headstone was placed on the grave, which includes the badges of both of Tom's football clubs.

Rob points out that Sunderland and Liverpool FC share bonds 'not least through Bob Paisley and Jordan Henderson, as well as the fact that Liverpool were the first and final visitors to Roker Park, Wearside, and the red sides of Merseyside and Wearside have much in common in their footballing history. It was Tom Watson who established the link between the clubs and the love and affection their supporters have for their teams.'

Rob continued:

> Tom Watson is the most successful manager in the history of North East football. Sunderland were the first club to achieve three league titles and Watson led them to all of them. His 'Team of All the Talents' were the first side to score 100 league goals in a season. They did this in just 30 games in 1892/93. They also set a record that to 2025 has never been equalled, that of achieving a 100 per cent home record in the top flight, something they did in 1891/92.
>
> As they became champions for the third time in four seasons in 1895, Sunderland were also proclaimed world champions. This was after beating Hearts 5-3 in Edinburgh in the first-ever meeting of the league champions of England and Scotland, at the time the only countries to be playing football to a high standard.
>
> Tom's team established Sunderland as one of the game's giants from the very early years of the league. The Wearsiders were the first team to join the Football League

> after the dozen founder members. At the beginning of the Second World War no team had been champions more than Sunderland's six times. By this stage they were the only club to have only ever played at the top level, a record they proudly held until a first-ever relegation in 1958. It had been Tom Watson and his side of Scots that had first established Sunderland at the pinnacle of the game.

Stephen Done, who joined Rob and Jimmy at that ceremony in 2015, told us:

> Almost from the moment I became curator of the soon-to-be-built Liverpool FC Museum in Anfield, I was determined that the story told within the museum must take visitors back to the earliest days of the club, reminding us all that just because those who played, managed, coached and supported exist now only in grainy black-and-white photographs and a few minutes of less-than-perfect film, they were every bit as real, as alive and as influential as those still within living memory or now captured on countless hours of video, hi-res photographs, mobile phones and social media. It's perhaps all too easy to overlook a photograph of a 'genial bloke with a moustache' in an old photo – but to do so is a mistake.
>
> Tom Watson, for me, is central to our understanding and appreciation of this mighty club. Without his incredible ability as a man manager, it's doubtful we would be where we are now, as the most successful English football club of all time. For the fledgling Liverpool Association Football Club & Athletic Grounds Company Limited – or whatever other variation of name they were using – to secure the services of Tom Watson was a masterstroke. A move of inspired brilliance arguably unmatched in our incredible history.

> Think of the decision to secure Kenny Dalglish to replace Keegan, or realising that Jürgen Klopp was a motivator on a par with Shankly? Yes, these (and others) were pivotal moments, but back then Watson was simply the best. It was surely crazy to even think he would walk away from Sunderland AFC and the fabulous success he was achieving there, but somehow the club persuaded him.

We asked Stephen how important he thought Watson's achievements more than 120 years ago were. He's convinced that, without Tom, the success the club has enjoyed since may not have been possible. He argued:

> Without those two vital First Division wins and the ability to deftly deal with relegation between, the club could well have spent years reaching the pinnacle of the league. The FA Cup may not have been won in 1914, but to even reach the final in so few years after formation was truly spectacular.

But how did Tom do it? What separated him from others who had tried? Stephen is clear that Watson's character and abilities as a motivator and communicator made the difference:

> Watson was clearly a man who could motivate and should be spoken of in the same breath as Shankly or Klopp in his pomp. He could pick a team to do a job and knew how to handle the earliest footballing superstars and massage egos in a manner the likes of Paisley and Fagan and had cutting-edge opinions about diet and training regimes. He was a master of football management and arguably the most successful football manager in the world at the time – and he was ours!

Stephen believes that today's supporters on the Kop should recognise Watson's brilliance, just as they do many of the club's post-war heroes:

> I hope one day his face will be added to that magnificent line of managers that adorn the huge banner unfurled on the Kop before kick-off. Watson got us up on our perch – twice over. Let's not forget that. I hope Watson will be talked of as the man who first made us great.

Professor Stephen F. Kelly has written about some of Liverpool FC's greatest leaders. His biographies of Bill Shankly and Kenny Dalglish captured the brilliance of the men. However, he's adamant that Tom Watson should join them in the pantheon of Liverpool greats. Indeed, he argues that he should be regarded as one of the greatest managers in football history:

> Tom Watson was the first of football's great managers, not just of Liverpool but in English football. Initially with Newcastle, he went on to join rivals Sunderland taking them into the Football League and subsequently to three league titles with what became known as the 'team of all talents'.
>
> In 1896, Liverpool then a club just four years old, lured him to Merseyside, to take over from John McKenna as their new secretary. Three years later they were runners-up in the First Division and in 1901 claimed their first-ever league title. Although they were relegated in 1904, they were back in the top tier with a vengeance the following season and, a year later in 1906, were champions again.
>
> Watson would also take Liverpool to their first-ever FA Cup Final in 1914, a game they lost to Burnley. A year later he died and to this day still remains Liverpool's longest-

serving manager, a record that will probably never be bettered.

How did Professor Kelly feel that Tom's role evolved at the club, and what impact did that have? As with more modern managers, Kelly points to many similarities with Shankly and other post-war managers, in that Watson's role at the club would become all-encompassing, setting a benchmark for the role of football manager many of us would identify with today. He told us:

> Not only did Watson set Liverpool on the road to their first successes but he was also instrumental in creating the role of manager. Originally, as secretary, Watson had dealt with administrative issues such as fixtures, ticketing and the general running of the club. But in time Watson became more involved with on-field activities as he reshaped and redefined his role to what we today call 'manager'. He was an innovator, a footballing genius and a man with an eye for a good player. In his time at Anfield he signed Scottish international Alex Raisbeck, legendary goalkeepers Sam Hardy and Elisha Scott and prolific goalscorers Sam Raybould and Jack Parkinson. He also signed defender Charlie Wilson, who would go on to coach Liverpool to championship wins in 1922 and 1923.

For Professor Kelly, there's no question where Tom Watson belongs in the annals of Liverpool FC and football history:

> In all, with Sunderland and Liverpool, Watson won five league titles, and was runner-up on three occasions. He was the first manager to win the league title with two different clubs, a feat only equalled by Herbert Chapman,

> Brian Clough and Kenny Dalglish, which surely places him among football's elite. His name will rank among the greats of Liverpool forever.

Before Tom Watson managed Sunderland, and long before he became a celebrated manager of Liverpool, he played a pivotal role in the establishment of association football in Newcastle, the city of his birth. We caught up with Paul Joannou to discuss Tom's legacy in the region. Paul told us:

> Football on Tyneside owes Geordie lad Tom Watson much in developing the game in the distant years of the 1880s and 1890s. Born and raised in the gritty working-class suburbs of Byker and Rosehill on the slopes overlooking the River Tyne, he played a bit in his younger years, then became secretary with the two rival Newcastle clubs that forged the present-day hotbed of football. Both Newcastle West End and Newcastle East End were in their early evolution when Tom became their leader as secretary, and, in all but name, manager.
>
> Having joined West End during the summer of 1886, he transformed their fortunes to become a force in Newcastle, signing the area's first international player, Ralph Aitken from Scotland. He was also the man largely responsible for bringing football back to a rough piece of pasture on the Town Moor, near the city centre at Leazes. He negotiated a new ground for the West Enders, the old site of pioneer club Rangers – now, of course, St James' Park.
>
> Tom was lured across the city in December 1887 to team up with East End at Chillingham Road. He now turned the struggling East Enders around to place them on a course to become Tyneside's best – and eventually to be one of England's finest as Newcastle United.

We asked Paul about Tom's status in the game more broadly:

> He also did much to form the Northern League, which was a major catalyst in the region, then additionally was the Northern Alliance League's first secretary when it was established. Watson did such a good job on Tyneside that he became Sunderland's secretary-boss in the close season of 1889. His magic Geordie touch guided the Wearsiders to a string of trophies before doing the very same on Merseyside. For sure, Tom Watson is one of the game's finest-ever managers.

For Mark Platt, a detailed retelling of Watson's life and achievements is long overdue. Platt points to his achievements in the North East as well as on Merseyside as evidence of the man's greatness:

> Given what he achieved in football, both in the North East and here in Liverpool, it's amazing that it has taken over a century for him to be finally immortalised in print.
>
> A hugely respected and influential figure from the distant past, at Anfield he has never been forgotten but it's fair to say that only those with a passionate and obsessive interest in the club's heritage will be fully aware of just how significant a role he played during those formative years of the late 1890s and early 1900s.
>
> Way back then, it was 'Owd' Tom who first put Liverpool FC firmly on the map. After the trials and tribulations of the 'bitter' split with Everton, Watson arrived with a huge reputation, and it was one he more than lived up to during an unsurpassed 19 years at the helm.

Platt also pinpoints the transformative nature of Watson's reign as significant in setting the club on the path to future glories:

> It was a period in which he completely revolutionised the club. With the innovative training methods he implemented and legendary players he either signed or nurtured, the Reds emerged from the shadow of their then more illustrious near neighbours and became almost perennial challengers for the game's top honours.
>
> The success that then came Liverpool's way has already been well documented on the previous pages of this exhaustively researched and expertly written study of the club's original golden era. The stats alone, however – two league titles and an inaugural FA Cup Final appearance – do scant justice to the impact Watson had on this club. He will forever be best remembered as the man who moulded our first team of champions, but his legacy goes way beyond that pivotal maiden triumph.

So how does Tom Watson's legacy stack up against the more successful – in terms of trophies won – managers who followed him? For Mark, the standards that Watson set paved the way for those future glories:

> In terms of trophies won, others have since exceeded his haul, but the lofty standards set by Watson have been the benchmark for all those who succeeded him at Anfield, both on and off the pitch. Had it not been for his untimely death in 1915, who knows what else he may have gone on to achieve.
>
> We've had more than our fair share of managerial greats at this club, but I have no hesitation in ranking him alongside those in the highest bracket. His story is one that has been begging to be told and thankfully it now has. If nothing else, as a tribute in his memory, he deserves that.

> Tom Watson is a name that should always be among the most prominent whenever the history of Liverpool Football Club is discussed. Hopefully, this book will ensure that once again, after all these years, it is.

Mark's final comments seem like the perfect place to leave this discussion. We will add only a few parting lines of our own, before bidding you farewell.

Tom's story was begging to be told. He deserves to be brought out of the shade and into the light. So much of what he achieved at Liverpool has paved the way for future successes and it's our sincere hope that this book leads to a re-examination of him, and that, as a result, this and future generations of Liverpool supporters will know more of him and his accomplishments.

More than that, though, he should be remembered as one of football's great pioneers. A man who helped guide both Newcastle United and Sunderland FC on their paths to success, and who, as a much respected figure in the Football League, influenced the development of the game in England. He was also, above all, an immensely popular and well-respected man in his time.

Rest in peace 'Owd Tom'. We will remember you.

# Bibliography

Ancestry at www.ancestry.co.uk

AVFC History https://www.avfchistory.co.uk/

Barry, J.M., *The Great Influenza: The Story of the Deadliest Pandemic in History* (Penguin, 1920).

Clemente, C., *19: The Official History of Our League Champions* (Reach Sport, 2020).

Collins, T., *How Football Began: A Global History of How the World's Football Codes Were Born* (Taylor & Francis Distribution, 2020).

Crowley, T., *Scouse: A Social and Cultural History* (Liverpool University Press, 2012).

Days, P., *Sunderland AFC: Club History, Pt. 2: The Talented Team* (World Football, Bleacher Report, 4 June 2018).

English National Football Archive at https://www.enfa.co.uk/

Everton Independent Research Data at www.bluecorrespondent.co.uk

Football Kit Archive at https://www.footballkitarchive.com/

Forces War Records at www.forceswarrecords.com

France, D. and Prentice, D., *Everton Treasures: The David France Collection* (Trinity Mirror Sport Media, 2007).

Goulding, J. and Smith, K., *The Untouchables: Anfield's Band of Brothers* (Pitch Publishing, 2021).

Henchard, J., 'The famous Sunderland v Aston Villa painting that hangs in the lobby of the SoL – a history of Tonight's Championship match-up between Sunderland and Aston Villa serves as a kind reminder of one of the oldest and greatest rivalries in the history of association football – one which was famously captured in art-form by painter Thomas Hemy in the late 19th century' (Roker Report, 2017).

Honigsbaum, M., *The Pandemic Century: A History of Contagion – from Spanish Flu to Covid-19* (Penguin Audio, 1920).

Inglis, S., *Football Grounds of Britain* (Collins Willow, 1996).

Joannou, P. and Hamilton, A., *Newcastle United: The First 100 Years & More* (Polar Print Group Ltd, 2000).

Kelly, S.F., *The Anfield Encyclopaedia: An A-Z of Liverpool FC* (Mainstream Publishing; 5th edition, 2001).

Kelly, S.F., *The Kop: Liverpool's 12th Man* (Virgin Books; UK ed., 2008).

Kennedy, D., *The Man Who Created Merseyside Football: John Houlding, Founding Father of Liverpool and Everton* (Rowman & Littlefield, 2020).

Lees, A., *Liverpool: The Hurricane Port* (Mainstream Publishing, 2011).

LFC History at www.lfchistory.net

London Hearts Supporters Club at www.londonhearts.com

Mason, R., *Sunderland AFC: The Definitive History* (Icon Books, 2024).

Muir, R. and Young, H.E., 'Bygone Liverpool' https://archive.org/details/bygoneliverpool00muiruoft 1913

Museum of the Scottish Shale Oil Industry at www.scottishshale.co.uk

National Football Teams Archive at https://www.national-football-teams.com/

Newcastle United History at https://nufc-history.co.uk/

Platt, M., *The Red Journey: An Oral History of Liverpool Football Club* (De Coubertin Books, 2017).

Platt, M. and Hughes, W., *This is Anfield: The Official Illustrated History of Liverpool FC's Legendary Stadium* (Carlton Books, 2015).

Play Up Liverpool: The History of Liverpool Football Club, their home at Anfield and all the people at https://playupliverpool.com/

Scottish Sport History: devoted to our sporting history at www.scottishsporthistory.com

The British Newspaper Archive at www.britishnewspaperarchive.co.uk

The Everton Collection at www.evertoncollection.org.uk

The National Archive at https://www.nationalarchives.gov.uk/help-with-your-research/research-guides/census-records/

The Thistle Archive: Partick Thistle stats and stories 1876 to date at http://www.thethistlearchive.net/

Thomas, T.J., 'The Origins and Development of Association Football in the Liverpool District c1879–c1915' http://clok.uclan.ac.uk/9733/11/ThomasJohnPreston.pdf 2007

Williams, J., *Red Men: Liverpool Football Club the Biography* (Mainstream Publishing; 1st ed., 2010).

Wilson, A., *The Birth of Liverpool Football Club: Team of All the Macs* (Vertical Editions, 2011).

Wilson, J., 'Sunderland's Victorian all-stars blazed trail for money's rule of football' (*Guardian*, 25 April 2020).